FACTS *and* FASCISM

Books by George Seldes (1890-1995)

You Can't Print That!	1929
Can These Things Be!	1931
World Panorama	1933
The Vatican: Yesterday - Today – Tomorrow	1934
Iron, Blood, and Profits	1934
Sawdust Caesar	1935
Freedom of the Press	1935
Lords of the Press	1938
You Can't Do That	1938
The Catholic Crisis	1940
Witch Hunt	1940
The Facts Are...	1942
Facts and Fascism	1943
1000 Americans: The Real Rulers of the U.S.A.	1947
The People Don't Know	1949
Tell the Truth and Run	1953
The Great Quotations	1961
Never Tire of Protesting	1968
Even the Gods Can't Change History	1976
The Great Thoughts	1985
Witness to a Century	1987
The George Seldes Reader	1994

FACTS *and* FASCISM

by

GEORGE SELDES

Assisted by HELEN SELDES

In Fact, Inc., New York

Facts and Fascism

by George Seldes

Facsimile of the Original 1947 Edition, Reprinted, with kind permission of the Seldes Family, by

Progressive Press.com,
PO Box 126,
Joshua Tree, Calif., 92252

1st reprint edition, July 4, 2009. Printed in the USA.
Length: 288 pages, 86,000 words

ISBN 1-61577-043-7. EAN (ISBN 13) 978-1-61577-043-4

BISAC Classification codes:

POL042030 POLITICAL SCIENCE / Political Ideologies / Fascism & Totalitarianism
HIS036060 HISTORY / United States / 20th Century
SOC050000 SOCIAL SCIENCE / Social Classes
HIS027100 HISTORY / Military / World War II
POL043000 POLITICAL SCIENCE / Political Process / Political Advocacy

Library of Congress Catalog Information for the Original Edition:

LC Control No.: 43015884. LC Classification: E743 .S4 1943.
Dewey Class No.: 973.917. OCLC: 1044851.
Main Title: Facts and fascism, by George Seldes, assisted by Helen Seldes
286 p. illus. (incl. facsims.) 21 cm
Subjects: Fascism; Fascism--United States; Press--United States.
Published: New York, In Fact, inc. [1943]

ProgRESSive

2009

Dedication

THIS BOOK IS DEDICATED TO ALL WHO ARE FIGHTING FASCISM EVERYWHERE.

Facts and Fascism is the definitive account and source book on Fascism in the United States after the First World War and on into the Second. No doubt every subsequent work on this explosive topic owes a great debt to this original research.

By crusading investigative journalist George Seldes, the book is in three parts: 1) The Big Money and Big Profits in Fascism, 2) Native Fascist Forces, and 3) Our Press as a Fascist Force.

The first part reveals the backing of U.S. and British big business behind the rise of Fascism and militarism, with chapters on Germany, Italy, Japan, and Spain, the Nazi cartels and the National Association of Manufacturers. The author was a reporter in Italy in the early 20's as Fascism got its start, and wrote a full-length, critical portrait of Mussolini.

In "Native Fascist Forces," Seldes first tells the story of the botched putsch by J. P. Morgan and the American Legion against FDR in 1934 – surely one of the most hushed-up episodes in US history. Next Seldes dissects the Ford empire's support for Nazism and its repressive, even murderous labor practices, and Nazi apologists like Lindbergh, Father Coughlin and the Reader's Digest.

The third part explores and deplores acts of treason by war-profiteering heavy industry and by the major newspaper chains. He exposes their habit of faking news for their political agenda, going back to the 1850's in support of black slavery, and white servitude – that is, with attacks on labor and social justice. The last chapter discusses profiteering from a different form of slavery, the tobacco addiction. Among the appendices is one on the definition of Fascism, and data on Who Owns America – thirteen plutocratic families.

CONTENTS

PART ONE

THE BIG MONEY AND BIG PROFITS IN FASCISM

PART TWO

NATIVE FASCIST FORCES

PART THREE

OUR PRESS AS A FASCIST FORCE

Part 1

The Big Money and Big Profits in Fascism

CHAPTER I

FASCISM ON THE HOME FRONT

THE TIME will come when people will not believe it was possible to mobilize 10,800,000 Americans to fight Fascism and not tell them the truth about the enemy. And yet, this is exactly what happened in our country in the Global War.

The Office of War Information published millions of words, thousands of pamphlets, posters and other material, most of it very valuable and all of it intended to inspire the people and raise the morale of the soldiers of production and the soldiers of the field; but it is also a fact that to the date of this writing the OWI did not publish a single pamphlet, poster, broadside or paper telling either the civilian population or the men and women in uniform what Fascism really is, what the forces are behind the political and military movements generally known as Fascism, who puts up the money, who make the tremendous profits which Fascism has paid its backers in Germany, Italy, Japan, Spain and other nations.

Certainly when it comes to relating foreign Fascism with native American Fascism there is a conspiracy of silence in which the OWI, the American press, and all the forces of reaction in America are united. Outside of a few books, a few pamphlets, and a few articles in the very small independent weekly press which reaches only a few thousand readers, not one word on this subject has been printed, and not one word has been heard over any of the big commercial radio stations.

Faraway Fascism has been attacked, exposed, and denounced by the same publications (the *Saturday Evening Post* for example) which for years ran articles lauding Mussolini and his notable backers in all lands; and the Hearst newspapers, which published from 1934 to Pearl Harbor dozens of signed propaganda articles by Dr. Goebbels, Goering and other Nazis, now call them names, but no publication which takes money from certain Big Business elements (all of which will be named here) will dare name the native or nearby Fascists. In many instances the publications themselves are part of our own Fascism.

But we must not be fooled into believing that American Fascism consists of a few persons, some crackpots, some mentally perverted, a few criminals such as George W. Christians and Pelley, who are in jail at present, or the 33 indicted for sedition. These are the lunatic fringes of Fascism, they are also the small fry, the unimportant figureheads, just as Hitler was before the Big Money in Germany decided to set him up in business.

The real Fascists of America are never named in the commercial press. It will not even hint at the fact that there are many powerful elements working against a greater democracy, against an America without discrimination based on race, color and creed, an America where never again will one third of the people be without sufficient food, clothing and shelter, where never again will there be 12,000,000 unemployed and many more millions working for semi-starvation wages while the DuPont, Ford, Hearst, Mellon and Rockefeller Empires move into the billions of dollars.

I call these elements Fascist. You may not like names and labels but technically as well as journalistically and morally they are correct. You may substitute Tories, or Economic Royalists, or Vested Interests, or whatever you like for the flag-waving anti-American Americans whose efforts and objectives parallel those of the Liga Industriale which bought out Mussolini in 1920, and the Thyssen-Krupp-Voegeler-Flick Rhineland industry and banking system which subsidized Hitler when Naziism was about to collapse. Their main object was to end the civil liberties of the nation, destroy the labor unions, end the free

OFFICE OF THE VICE PRESIDENT
WASHINGTON

July 1, 1942

Mr. George Seldes
Editor, IN FACT
19 University Place
New York, New York

Dear Mr. Seldes:

I ought to have written you long ago to tell you how much I appreciate all you have done to publicize my Free World speech. I have had a number of enthusiastic letters from people who saw the speech for the first time in your publication.

Thank you so much for sending me copies of the latest issues of "In Fact." I have been very much interested in glancing through them.

Sincerely yours,

H A Wallace

H. A. Wallace

press, and make more money at the expense of a slave nation. Both succeeded. And in America one similar organization has already made the following historical record:

1. Organized big business in a movement against labor.
2. Founded the Liberty League to fight civil liberties.
3. Subsidized anti-labor, Fascist and anti-Semitic organizations (Senator Black's Lobby Investigation).
4. Signed a pact with Nazi agents for political and economic (cartel) penetration of U. S. (Exposed in *In Fact*).
5. Founded a $1,000,000-a-year propaganda outfit to corrupt the press, radio, schools and churches.
6. Stopped the passage of food, drug and other laws aimed to safeguard the consumer, i.e., 132,000,000 Americans.
7. Conspired, with DuPont as leader, in September, 1942, to sabotage the war effort in order to maintain profits.
8. Sabotaged the U. S. defense plan in 1940 by refusing to convert the auto plants and by a sit-down of capital against plant expansion; sabotaged the oil, aluminum and rubber expansion programs. (If any of these facts are not known to you it is because 99% of our press, in the pay of the same elements, suppressed the Tolan, Truman, Bone Committee reports, Thurman Arnold's reports, the TNEC Monopoly reports and other Government documents.)
9. Delayed the winning of the war through the acts of $-a-year men looking out for present profits and future monopoly rather than the quick defeat of Fascism. (Documented in the labor press for two years; and again at the 1942 C.I.O. Convention.)

Naturally enough the President of the United States and other high officials cannot name the men, organizations, pressure lobbyists, and national associations which have made this and similar records; they can only refer to "noisy traitors," Quislings, defeatists, the "Cliveden Set" or to the Tories and Economic Royalists. And you may be certain that our press will never name the defeatists because the same elements which made the above 9-point record are the main advertisers and biggest subsidizers of the newspapers and magazines. In many instances even the general charges by the President himself have been suppressed. In Germany, in Italy until the seizure of government by the Fascists, the majority of newspapers were brave enough to be anti-Fascist, whereas in America strangely enough a large part of the press (Hearst, Scripps-Howard, McCormick-Patterson) has for years been pro-Fascist and almost all big papers live on the money of the biggest Tory and reactionary corporations and reflect their viewpoint now.

On the anti-Fascist side, unfortunately, there is not one publication which can boast of more than one or two hundred thousand circulation, whereas the reactionary press has its *New York News* with 2,000,000 daily, its *Saturday Evening Post* with 3,000,000 weekly and its *Reader's Digest* with 9,000,000 monthly, which means up to 50,000,000 readers.

It is a shameful and tragic situation that in America, with 132,000,000 persons of whom 50,000,000 read anti-labor and anti-liberal propaganda in *Reader's Digest,* only a few hundred thousand buy and read intelligent, honest, unbribed, uncorrupted publications, issued in the public interest.

CHAPTER II

PROFITS IN FASCISM: GERMANY

IT SEEMS to this writer that the most important thing in the world today next to destroying Fascism on the field of battle, is to fight Fascism which has not yet taken up the gun.

This other Fascism will become more active—and drape itself in the national flag everywhere—when military Fascism has been defeated. So far as America is concerned, its first notable Fascist leader, Huey Long, a very smart demagogue, once said, "Sure we'll have Fascism here, but it will come as an anti-Fascist movement."

To know what Fascism really is and why we must fight it and destroy it here in America, we must first of all know what it is we are fighting, what the Fascist regimes really are and do, who puts up the money and backs Fascism in every country (including the United States at this very moment), and who owns the nations under such regimes, and why the natives of all Fascist countries must be driven into harder work, less money, reduced standard of living, poverty and desperation so that the men and corporations who found, subsidize and own Fascism can grow unbelievably rich.

This is what has happened in Germany, Italy, Japan and other countries; it is true to a great extent in Spain, Finland, Hungary, Rumania, the Polish so-called Republic, and although not one standard newspaper or magazine has ever breathed a word about it, the same Fascist movement—the march of the men of wealth and power, not the crackpot doings of the two or three dozen who have been indicted for sedition—is taking place in America.

These matters are all related, both as systems of government and as business enterprises. It is the purpose of Part I of this book to show who really owns the Fascist International, who profits from it, and just how far the United States has gone along the Fascist line.

The true story of Hitler-Germany is the real clue to the situation everywhere. In 1923, after his monkeyshines in the Munich Beer Hall Putsch, Hitler received his first big money from Fritz Thyssen. January 30, 1933, Hitler came into power after a deal with Hindenburg and the big Prussian landlords (Junkers). Since then, and in all of vast occupied Europe, Hitler has been paying off the men who invested in Fascism as a purely money-making enterprise. A personal dispute put Thyssen out, but his brother and the thousand biggest industrialists and bankers of Germany have as a result of financing Hitler become millionaires; the I. G. Farbenindustrie and other cartel organizations have become billionaires.

Big money entrenched itself completely after the departure of Fritz Thyssen, with his rather quaint ideas of placing limits on corruption in business, with his repugnance to the murder of Jews as a national policy, and other rather old-fashioned ethical concepts of monopoly and exploitation which he inherited from his father and which did not encompass robbery and bloodshed as means of commercial aggression. The cartels moved forward with the troops.

There were, of course, exposés of Hitler as a tool of Germany's Big Money, written before he became dictator, but inasmuch as publication occurred in small non-commercial weeklies which few people read, or in the radical press, which is always accused of misrepresentation (by the commercial press which is always lying) the fact remains that few people knew what really was going on. This conspiracy of silence became even more intense when the big American and other banking houses floated their great loans for Hitler—and other fascist dictators in many lands.

As early as 1931 Gerhard Hirschfeld published in a Catholic

literary weekly a tiny part of the evidence that Hitler was the political arm of the biggest branch of German capitalism. Recalling that Hitler vowed that the Krupps, the Thyssens and the Kirdorffs, the Mannesmanns, the Borsigs and the Siemens (who are the Garys, Schwabs and Mellons of Germany)—would be stripped of wealth and power, Hirschfeld pointed out that "it is from the ranks of heavy industry, however, that Hitler is drawing much of the money which is making German Fascism something to be reckoned with. Hitler received considerable support from the heavy industries of Bavaria where he started the Fascist movement. The Borsig works and the Eisenheuttenleute (Association of iron forgers and founders) are important pillars of the Fascist structure. . . . From the machine industry of Wuerttemberg and from many other branches of the iron and steel industries, marks flow into the bulging coffers. In addition, money comes from abroad. Swiss friends sent him 330,000 francs just before last year's elections. Baron von Bissing, the university professor, collected many thousands of florins in the Netherlands . . . German-American friends expressed their sympathy in dollar bills . . . even directors of the French-controlled Skoda-Works (of Czechoslovakia), famous in the manufacture of armaments, may be found among Hitler's supporters."

It requires neither integrity nor courage today to say that Hitler was made the Fuehrer of Germany by the biggest industrialists of his country. (It does require integrity and courage even today to relate the German men and forces to those in America, to point out the equivalents, and that is why no commercial newspaper or magazine has ever done so.) But as early as Summer, 1933, in the *Week-End Review,* a light which shows up Fascism as nothing but a military-political-economic movement to grab all the money and resources of the world was already focused on Germany by the man who wrote under the name of "Ernst Henri."

He denies, first of all, the myth that Naziism is a "rebellion of the middle classes." The middle classes, it is true, were most united and outspoken for Hitler, they did in fact send in their contributions, but when "these sons of butchers and publicans, of postoffice officials and insurance agents, of doctors and lawyers" imagined they were fighting for their own interests, when "they swarmed out of the Storm Troops barracks and struck down defenseless workers, Jews, Socialists and Communists" they would not have been able to do it, had they not been mobilized by other sources. "Hitler, the idol of this mass, and himself only a petty bourgeois—a petty bourgeois posing as a Napoleon—in reality followed the dictates of a higher power."

The secret, continues Henri, "must be sought in the hidden history of Germany's industrial oligarchy, in the post-war politics of coal and steel. . . . Not Hitler, but Thyssen, the great magnate of the Ruhr, is the prime mover of German Fascism."

Thyssen's main undertaking was the German Steel Trust, the equivalent of U. S. Steel. Vereinigte Stahlwerke Aktien Gesellschaft, incidentally, was heavily financed by American banking houses—Episcopalian, Catholic and Jewish—throughout the pre-Hitler and Hitler regimes. The Steel Trust was the basis of German economy, and when it found itself in a desperate situation, during the Bruening regime which preceded Hitler, the foundations of Germany were threatened. It was then that the state came to the trust's aid by buying nearly half the shares of Gelsenkirchener Bergwerke, holding company, nominally worth 125,000,000 marks, at a fantastic price, estimated at double the market. Immediately thereafter the political parties of the nation began fighting for control of this weapon.

The Bruening regime, Catholic, favored the Otto Wolff-Deutsche Bank group which was affiliated with powerful Catholic groups. The Thyssen-Flick-Voegeler group was opposed, although Thyssen himself was a Catholic. Otto Wolff is a leading Catholic, but one of his partners, Ottmar Strauss, is a Jewish liberal. Another affiliate of Wolff's was General Schleicher. The rivalry in Germany was something like that between the Morgan and Rockefeller interests in America, except that the

Wolff group was known as liberal and the Thyssen group included Flick and Voegeler, political heirs of Hugo Stinnes who had been, Henri says, "perhaps the first National Socialist in Germany."

Stinnes, Hugenberg, Thyssen and other multi-millionaire owners of Germany had never hidden their participation in political movements nor their subsidization of all reactionary anti-labor political parties. These men put their money into the parties of the right wing and were powerful enough at all times to prevent the Social-Democratic Party, which took over the nation (with the aid of the victorious Allies) in 1918 from doing anything radical to aid the majority of the people—even if the Social-Democrats had sincerely attempted to do so. The historic facts speak for themselves. Germany under Ebert and all the liberal coalitions which preceded the reactionary regimes, which naturally culminated in the advent of big business Fascism, never did more than make gestures towards the working class and permitted joblessness and poverty to increase while the Stinneses and Hugenbergs and Thyssens grew in wealth and power.

Thyssen became interested in Hitler in the year of the Beer Hall Putsch, when Hitler was regarded as a revolver-firing clown who would end up in an insane asylum rather than the chancellor's chair. But Thyssen saw possibilities. In 1927 Thyssen took his partner in the Steel Trust, Voegeler, to Rome, they interviewed Mussolini, and when they returned it was noticeable that the Nazi Party suddenly grew rich and began its march to power.

In 1927 Thyssen joined the Nazi Party officially and began that cooperation with Hitler which led to the latter's overthrow of the Republic in 1933.

"Hitler," writes Henri, "never took an important step without first consulting Thyssen and his friends. Thyssen systematically financed all the election funds of the National Socialist Party. It was he who, by a majority decision and against the most pointed opposition on the part of Otto Wolff and Kloeckner, persuaded the two political centers of German Ruhr capital, the Bergbauverein Essen and the Nordwestgruppe der Eisen-und Stahlindustrie, to agree that every coal and steel concern had, by way of a particular obligatory tax, to deliver a certain sum into the election cash of the National Socialists. In order to raise this money, the price of coal was raised in Germany.

"For the presidential elections of 1932 alone, Thyssen provided the Nazis within a few days with more than 3,000,000 marks. Without this help the fantastic measures resorted to by Hitler in the years 1930-1933 would never have been possible. Without Thyssen's money Hitler would never have achieved such a success, and the party would probably have broken up at the time of the Papen elections at the end of 1932, when it lost 2,000,000 votes and the Strasser group announced its secession. In January, 1933, Schleicher was on the point of hitting the Hitler movement on the head and putting it under his own command. But, just as before Thyssen had raised Hitler by his financial machinery, so now he rescued him by his political machinery.

"To bring off this coup Thyssen employed two of his political friends and agents: Hugenberg (who is one of the directors of the Thyssen Steel Trust group) and Von Papen. In the middle of January a secret meeting between Hitler and Papen was held at Cologne in the house of Baron von Schroeder, partner of the banking House of J. H. Stein, which is closely related with Flick and Thyssen. Although, thanks to an indiscretion, the news of this meeting got into the papers, a few days later, the conspiracy against Schleicher was ready. The allied group, Thyssen-Hitler-Von Papen-Hugenberg, which was backed by the entire German reactionary force, succeeded in drawing to its side the son of President von Hindenburg, Major Oskar von Hindenburg, who had so far stood by his old regimental friend, Schleicher. In this way the sudden fall of Schleicher and the sensational nomination of Hitler came about. Thyssen had won, and Hitler set the scene for his St. Bartholomew's day.

"What followed was a continual triumph of the capitalistic interests of the Thyssen group. The National Socialist Government of Germany today carries out Thyssen's policy on all matters, as though the entire nation were but a part of the Steel Trust. Every step taken by the new Government corresponds exactly to the private interests of this clique; Stinnes's days have returned.

"Thyssen had six main objectives: (1) to secure the Steel Trust for his own group; (2) to save the great coal and steel syndicates, the basis of the entire capitalist system of monopolies in Germany; (3) to eliminate the Catholic and Jewish rival groups and to capture the whole industrial machine for the extreme reactionary wing of heavy industry; (4) to crush the workers and abolish the trade unions, so as to strengthen German competition in the world's markets by means of further wage reductions, etc.; (5) to increase the chances of inflation, in order to devaluate the debts of heavy industry (a repetition of the astute transaction invented by Stinnes in 1923); and finally (6) to initiate a pronouncedly imperialist tendency in foreign politics in order to satisfy the powerful drive for expansion in Ruhr capital. All these items of his programs, without exception, have been, are, or will now be executed by the Hitler government." (The reader must remember that this prediction was written in early 1933, within a few months of Hitler's triumph.)

How did Hitler repay Thyssen? There were general and specific ways. Thyssen was made sub-dictator of Germany (Reichs Minister of Economics), in charge of all industry. The labor problem for Thyssen and all employers of Germany was solved when Hitler abolished the unions, confiscated the union treasuries, reduced labor to a form of serfdom. Specifically, Hitler poured hundreds of millions of dollars into Thyssen's pocketbook by the manipulation of Gelsenkirchener. The new capitalization was 660,000,000 marks instead of 125,000,000. The state, which had owned more than half of Gelsenkirchener, came out holding less than 20% of the new corporation, and Thyssen, who had feared the collapse of his empire, came out king of coal and steel again, and therefore the most powerful industrialist in the land.

Within a few weeks after taking power Hitler used his anti-Semitism for commercial purposes as an aid to his main financial backer, Thyssen. Oscar Wassermann, of the Catholic-Jewish Deutsche Bank, had been chief rival of the Thyssen bankers. Hitler retired him on "grounds of health." Thyssen's one opponent within the Steel Trust, Kloeckner, a Catholic like Thyssen, was forced to resign from the Hitler Reichstag. A charge of corruption was filed against Otto Wolff, who led the financial battle against Thyssen. Goering appointed Thyssen chief representative of private capital in his new Prussian State Council. And, finally, the Fighting League of the Trading Middle Class, the little business men who put up their small money and who went into the streets killing and robbing industrial working men and Jews, was ordered dissolved by Hitler early in 1933 because it might menace the upper class.

It is with especial interest that one reads Henri's conclusion and prediction a full decade after he made it. He said in 1933: "The trade unions have been destroyed. Thyssen can dictate wages through the new 'corporations' and thus reduce still further the prices of export goods in the face of English and American competition. Armaments are being prepared; Thyssen provides the steel. Thyssen needs the Danube markets, where he owns the Alpine Montan-Gesellschaft, the greatest steel producers in Austria. But the primal objective of this new system in Germany has not yet been attained. Thyssen wants war, and it looks as though Hitler may yet provide him with one."

The historic facts are that armaments were being prepared, although the British and French closed their eyes to this fact and believed the promise that they would be used only against Russia; the Nazi army did march into Austria and did unite the Alpine works with their own, and it is also true that Hitler did provide a war, although it was Thyssen's brother, Baron von Thyssen, and Thyssen's partner and successor as head of the Vereinigte Stahlwerke, Voegeler, who reaped the profit, and not Thyssen himself. Naziism paid all its original backers (except one man) and all its present owners colossal profits.

The relation between money and elections was more clearly illustrated in the German elections in the decade of 1923-1933 than in any American elections—although a volume could be written to prove that the Republican or Democratic Party which wins every four years is the party (with only a very few exceptions) which has the larger number of millions to spend.

"Seven months before he (Hitler) got there (the chancellor's seat) he polled his legitimate maximum of 13,745,781 votes, just over one third of those recorded. Four months later, in the last constitutional Reichstag election, he lost over 2,000,000 votes. That was in November, 1932. The huge Nazi Party was rapidly declining; it had been overblown with millions of mere malcontents, victims of the slump, lured in by desperation rather than Hitler's glib tongue and splendid showmanship. Yet, after the landslide of the November elections, the Party was broke to the wide and in what looked like hopeless dissolution. Hitler moodily (not for the first time nor for the last) threatened suicide. A few weeks later he was in power."

The foregoing statement is from the Fabian Society of Great Britain. It states the situation truthfully. How then explain what followed?

"How had the miracle happened? Goebbels grandly called it 'The National Socialist Revolution'; it was nothing of the kind. It was just a bargain with Big Business and the Junkers. Strong in money, power and influence, but with hardly any popular backing, these vested interests (with arch-intriguer Von Papen as their political representative) were worried by the Schleicher government's threat to expose the worst of their graft; they were even more worried by the possibility of a swing to the Left through a coalition of Schleicher and the Trade Unions. That's why the Papen group, having cold-shouldered the slipping Nazi Party for some time, were now keen on an alliance capable of adding a mass movement to their own financial and industrial power. That's how Hitler got his much-needed cash for his Party and his own appointment as Chancellor in a new Coalition Government."

Hitler's entire history is one of spending big money to build up a party, big money to get millions of votes, and when his backers' money failed to put him in office, he made the conclusive deal with them, finally selling out the great majority who voted for him in the belief he would keep his 26 promises, most of them directed against Big Business, the Junkers and the other enemies of the people.

Hitler's fascist party was never a majority party. In many countries where several political parties exist—and even in the United States at those times when three major parties are in the field—the chancellor or president elected to office represents only a minority of the electorate. Nevertheless, it is true that Hitler did succeed in fairly honest times before he was able to use bloodshed and terrorism for his "Ja" elections, in making his the largest of a score of parties.

Why was he able to do this?

There are of course many reasons, notably the disillusion of the nation, national egotism, the natural desire to be a great nation, the psychological moment for a dictator of any party, right or left, economic breakdown, the need of a change, and so forth. But important, if not most important, was the platform of the Nazi party which promised the people what they were hungering for.

It must not be forgotten that the word Nazi stands for national socialist German workers party, and that Hitler, while secretly in the pay of the industrialists who wanted the unions disbanded and labor turned into serfdom, was openly boasting that his was a socialist party—socialism without Karl Marx—and a nationalist-socialist party whatever that may mean. But it did mean a great deal to millions. The followers of Marxian socialism in Germany, split into several parties, would if united constitute the greatest force in the nation, and socialism and labor were almost synonymous in Germany. Hitler knew this. He capitalized on it. He stole the word.

Hitler was able to get thirteen million followers before 1933 by a pseudo-socialistic reform program and by great promises of aid to the common people. In the 26 points of the Nazi platform, adopted in 1920 and never repudiated, Hitler promised the miserable people of Germany:

1. The abolition of all unearned incomes.

2. The end of interest slavery. This was aimed against all bankers, not only Jewish bankers.

3. Nationalization of all joint-stock companies. This meant

the end of all private industry, not only the monopolies but all big business.

4. Participation of the workers in the profits of all corporations—the mill, mine, factory, industrial worker was to become a part owner of industry.

5. Establishment of a sound middle class. Naziism, like Italian Fascism, made a great appeal to the big middle class, the small business man, the millions caught between the millstones of Big Business and labor. The big department stores, for example, were to be smashed. This promise delighted every small shopkeeper in Germany. Bernard Shaw once said that Britain was a nation of shopkeepers. This was just as true for Germany—and German shopkeepers were more alive politically. They were for Hitler's Naziism to a man—and they supplied a large number of his murderous S.S. and S.A. troops.

6. Death penalty for usurers and profiteers.

7. Distinction between "raffendes" and "schaffendes" capital—between predatory and creative capital. This was the Gregor Strasser thesis: that there were two kinds of money, usury and profiteering money on one hand, and creative money on the other, and that the former had to be eliminated. Naturally all money-owners who invested in the Nazi Party were listed as creative capitalists, whereas the Jews (some of whom incidentally invested in Hitler) and all who opposed Hitler were listed as exploiters.

The vast middle class, always caught between the aspirations of the still more vast working class and the cruel greed of the small but most powerful ruling class, has throughout history made the mistake of allying itself with the latter. In America we have the same thing: all the real fascist movements are subsidized by Big Money, but powerful organizations, such as the National Small Business Men's Association, follow the program of the NAM in the hope they will benefit financially when the Ruling Families benefit.

In all instances, however, history shows us that when the latter take over a country with a fascist army they may give the middle class privileges, benefits, a chance to earn larger profits for a while, but in the end monopoly triumphs, and the Big Money drives the Little Money into bankruptcy.

This is one of the many important facts which Albert Norden presented in his most impressive pamphlet *The Thugs of Europe,* a documentary exposé of the profits in Naziism taken entirely from Nazi sources. My thanks are due to Mr. Norden —a German writer who escaped to America and who went to work in a war plant recently—for permission to quote some of the evidence. Norden takes up the matter of Naziism and its promises to the middle class:

"If the Third Reich were for the common man, the middle-class would not have been sacrificed to the Moloch of Big Business. If the Third Reich were for the common man, the banks and industries and resources of the sub-soil would belong to the people and not be the private affair of a few score old and newly rich. . . . As it is now, it is the rich man's Reich. That is why there is such a widespread underground anti-Nazi movement among the German people.

"This war is being waged by the Third Reich, the heart of the Axis, as a 'struggle of German Socialism against the plutocracies.' Goebbels has duped millions of young Germans with this slogan. Not only that: Nazi propaganda outside Germany and particularly in North and South America has succeeded in recruiting trusted followers with this slogan. . . .

"The Nazi theory of a struggle of the Have-nots against the so-called 'sated' nations is as true as the myth that Goebbels is an Aryan and Goering a Socialist! The following facts, taken from official German statistics, prove that in the Third Reich there is a boundless dictatorship of the plutocrats; that a small group of magnates in the banking, industrial and chemical world hae taken hold of the entire economic apparatus at the expense of the broad sections of medium and small manufacturers, artisans, storekeepers and workers, and are making unprecedented profits.

"In his program Hitler promised the middle class preference in all government jobs, abolition of interest on loans, breaking of the power of the trusts and cartels, and dividing up the department stores. Each of these points could only have been carried out at the expense of finance-capital to which Hitler had made definite commitments which, in turn, spell ruin for the middle class and workers. . . . The Kampfbund des Gewerblichen Mittlestandes, a Nazi organization . . . had been schooled to destroy Marxism. Everywhere they had killed Socialists and Communists, demolished workers' headquarters and trade union offices. Now that Hitler had triumphed they wanted to reap the fruits. But the Nazi leaders offered them cheap laurels instead—laurels which pleased neither their senses nor their pocketbooks. . . .

"Never yet in modern history has the middle class, relying solely on itself and without an alliance with other social strata, successfully played an independent role or triumphed in the social struggle. . . . The Nazi leaders did not hesitate one moment in their decision when the big industrialists and bankers began to complain. One after another, Hitler, Goering and Hess in May, June and July, 1933—issued sharp warnings against 'attacks on business'; and Hess ordered all activities against department stores to cease. . . . Already by August, 1933, the high hopes which millions of little people had pinned on Hitler had been rudely shattered. . . . Leaders of the struggle of the middle class against the trusts . . . were sent to concentration camps. Before the month had ended the Fighting League of the Middle Class was no more. . . . The massacre of the entire leadership of the Storm Troopers on the pretext of homosexuality closed the short chapter of independent action by the middle class with a smashing political victory by Big Capital. . . . The department store of the Jewish owner Tietz was handed over to a consortium consisting of the three largest banks, the Deutsche Bank, the Dresdener Bank and the Commerz-und Privatbank. . . . The large department store Karstadt . . . of its eight directors four are big bankers, one a large exporter and a sixth an influential figure in the Deutsche Bank. . . .

"The more Jews were dragged off and murdered in concentration camps, the richer Germany's magnates became. They let the S.S. and S.A. mobs riot and trample all human laws under their hobnail boots—meanwhile the Dresdener Bank acquired the Berlin bank of Bleichroeder (Jewish bank, patronized by the former Kaiser) and Arnhold Bros. (Jewish bank, one of the best banks in Germany, patronized by U. S. Embassy and newspapers); the Deutsche Bank seized the Mendelssohn Bank. In the Berliner Handelsgesellschaft, an important private bank, Herbert Goering, a relative of Marshal Hermann Goering, replaced the Jewish partner Fuerstenberg. The Warburg Bank in Hamburg was taken over by the Deutsche Bank and the Dresdener Bank in conjunction with the Montan Combine of Haniel and the Siemens Trust. The latter also took out of Jewish hands the Cassierer Cable Works. . . . The armaments kings of the Ruhr did not shrink from profiting from the pogroms. As a result of Hitler's persecution of the Jews, the Mannesmann concern received the metal company of Wolff, Netter & Jacobi, and the Hahnschen Works; while the big industrialist Friedrich Flick (one of the dozen men who put up most of the money to establish Naziism), today one of the 20 richest men in the Third Reich, seized the metal company of Rawak and Gruenfeld. This list could be expanded at will. It illustrates the prosperous business which the solidly established German trusts acquired as a result of the infamous crimes against the Jews. Together with the top Nazi leaders these German financial magnates were the main beneficiaries of the sadistic persecution of the Jews. . . .

"Moreover, the turnover tax on big business was reduced to one-half per cent on all commodities, while for little business it was raised to 2 per cent. The decree establishing price ceilings was eliminated so that Big Business under Hitler was able to raise prices on numerous occasions. Thus in two years immediately preceding the outbreak of the present war, tens of thousands of small businessmen were able to get prices which just barely covered their own costs, and sometimes were even lower. That is why small businesses were liquidated on a mass scale in Germany. . . . The government of the Third Reich, a long time before the outbreak of the war, had passed the death-sentence on over one million members of the middle class, and carried it out, thus profiting the wealthiest sections of German finance-capital. . . . The result is inevitably the same: a blood-letting without parallel and impoverishment all along the line. Hitler's regime of a 'people's community' and elimination of the class struggle has hastened, as no previous regime has done, the crystallization of classes in German society, dealing terrible blows to the middle class and favoring the upper ten thousand in striking fashion. In ten years of the Nazi regime the lower middle class in Germany has been more ruined and declassed than in the preceding 50 years.

"In 1932 a tremendous scandal exploded in Germany. It concerned the so-called Osthilfe, government subsidies destined for the needy farmers. . . . Among the beneficiaries were the House of Hohenzollern and the President of the Republic, Field Marshal von Hindenburg, whose East Prussian property of Neudeck was involved in tax frauds. Hitler promised to suppress the entire scandal if he became Chancellor of the Reich. The interests of the aristocracy and of the munitions-kings, whose war-mongering appetites were whetted by the appointment of Hitler, coincided. So Hindenburg covered over his scandal of corruption with his disgraceful appointment of Hitler as chancellor.

"Today the princes and their followers among the nobility are still the largest landowners in Germany. Three thousand aristocrats own 2,630,000 hectares (1 hectare equals 2.47 acres) of agriculturally tilled land. On the other hand 3,000,000 families of small farmers —60% of all those occupied in agriculture—own together only 1,-500,000 hectares. 0.15% of the landowners each possessing 5,000 hectares own altogether 10,100,000 hectares or almost 40% of the entire land under cultivation. . . . 412 Junkers owned as much land as 1,000,000 peasants (Darre admitted this).

"The Reichstag deputies in their S.S., S.A. and army uniforms raised their arms and shouted Heil for several minutes as Hitler told them, after the outbreak of war in September, 1939: 'No one will make money out of this war.' One lie more or less makes no difference to Hitler. The fact is, the profits of the upper 10,000 in Germany have reached astronomical proportions in this war. To detect these profits, however, one must know how to read between the lines of company reports. . . . German industry wrote off 'between a half and one billion marks' above the normal amount for reserves, etc., during the period just before the outbreak of the war. This is a clear case of concealing profits. . . .

"Exactly 24 hours before Hitler's armies attacked the Soviet Union the Nazi newspapers published a decree that was intended to prove the Socialist character of the Third Reich and to incite German soldiers to fight the 'bolshevik-plutocratic world conspiracy.' This decree called for a compulsory payment to the State of dividends that exceeded 6%. As if by magic the stock companies immediately began to increase their capital. They did not have to lay claim to their bank credits, but simply converted their hidden profits, their secret and open reserves, into additional capital. Thus the dividends decreased in percentage but remained the same in actual profit. By May, 1942, 883 stock companies had already increased their capital from 4,900,000,000 to 7,800,000,000 marks by making use of their concealed profits. . . . Baron von Thyssen-Bornemisza, Fritz Thyssen's older brother . . . increased the capital of one of his companies, the Duesseldorfer Press und Walzwerk to 3 times its former amount. Thus, when he pays 5% dividends now they correspond in cold cash to 15%. . . ."

Another pamphlet which exposes the profits in Naziism is *The Economics of Barbarism* by J. Kuczynski and M. Witt, who, after showing how by violence and by illegal means disguised as legal the Germans have seized the wealth of all occupied Europe, arrive at the conclusion that "The European continent in the hands of German monopoly means the end of the United States as a great economic power. It is the first step towards the enslavement of the Americas."

The Nazi plan, after taking over all of Europe, has been to use monopoly capital to reduce imports permanently and to increase the volume of cheap exports rapidly. German monopoly would exclude American goods from all markets except within the two Americas at first, then enter the South and Central American markets as a formidable competitor and eventually, with the aid of Japan, to exclude the United States and England from both the Asiatic and British Empire markets. All this of course based on a victory of the Fascist International.

The three principles of fascist economic strategy, according to these authors, are:

1. To achieve the economic subjugation of a conquered nation it is essential to control the heavy industries. The first principle of Nazi economic strategy: keep intact, build up, and above all else, take into their own hands the heavy industries.

2. Fascist economy centers on war production. Since it has no interest in the welfare of the masses of people and prefers to depress wages of workers and farmers and lower their standard of living, goods for popular consumption are of secondary importance. Since all the big industrialists are linked with Fascism, it is a policy to give the consumer goods manufacturers

a monopoly for all of Europe. There is therefore a tendency towards decentralization in the heavy industries, with centralization in Germany of consumer goods industry. The Nazi principle is: kill consumption goods industries outside Germany.

3. The third principle is to increase the numbers of millions dependent upon agriculture with a corresponding increase in the holdings of the great landed proprietors. This pays back the Junkers who financed Hitler, provides materials for the chemical industry and profits the same industry in the sale of artificial fertilizers, and furthers the policy of complete self-independence or autarchy.

These principles of barbarism, conclude the authors, would, if realized, "put back the technical and economic structure of certain parts of Europe a hundred years or more, while overdeveloping economy in other parts of the continent."

The pamphlet, written before America was attacked by Japan, warns our country that Fascism is an epidemic disease, and that we cannot escape.

So far as this writer knows, the only publication of any kind —book, pamphlet, newspaper story, radio address, etc.—which shows the relationship between Big Business in America and the international fascist system, is to be found in the works of Prof. Robert A. Brady. The serious student of Fascism must read both books listed below.

The relationship of the big money system to the Fascist Party itself is more clearly shown in what happened in Italy than anywhere else. Let us look beyond the Alps.

Fritz Thyssen, *I Paid Hitler,* Farrar & Rinehart, 1941.

Week-End Review, London, August 5 and 12, 1933.

Fabian Society, London, *Tract Series No.* 254, p. 5.

Albert Norden, *The Thugs of Europe,* German American League for Culture, 45 Astor Place, New York City.

J. Kuczynski and M. Witt, *The Economics of Barbarism,* International Publishers, New York.

Robert A. Brady, *The Spirit and Structure of German Fascism,* Viking Press, 1937; *Business as a System of Power,* Columbia University Press, 1943.

The Theory of Capitalist Development, by Paul M. Sweezey, Oxford University Press, 1943.

CHAPTER III

BIG BUSINESS BOSSED MUSSOLINI

THE FIRST modern fascist regime is the Italian. (Fascism itself is as old as history, and although Mussolini is a colossal liar, he told the truth for once when he defined Fascism as Reaction.)

Who put up the money for Mussolini?

Why did they invest in Fascism?

How were they repaid, and who footed the bill?

The original Fascist Party of Italy, likewise the Nazi Party which was formed almost at the same time, was subsidized by a handful of the richest industrialists and landowners who wanted to preserve their wealth and power and prevent the majority of people from living a better life. (The American Legion was organized for the same reason: to preserve the privileges of the few and fool the millions who believed better things would come after victory.)

Here is the complete list of main subsidizers of Mussolini's Fascism—(compiled from fascist, neutral and anti-fascist sources, including Prezzolini, Salvemini, Bolitho and Prof. Robert A. Brady)—and their American equivalents:

1. Lega Industriale of Turin. The American equivalent is the Associated Industries of Cleveland (also A. I. of Florida, Mass., Missouri, New York and Utah). Anti-labor organizations, corrupters of the free press, employers of spies, racketeers and murderers as strikebreakers, users of poison gas, all exposed by the La Follette Committee.

2. Confederazione Generale dell'Industria. Nearest equiva-

lent is the National Association of Manufacturers, which has some 8,000 members but which is run by a small group of men, including the DuPonts, who have subsidized the worst native fascist outfits in America. The NAM works "in secrecy and by deceit," according to the final La Follette report, employs prostitute college professors, prostitute preachers, and prostitute journalists. (Mussolini is the most famous prostitute journalist of our time; he sold out to the French government for 50,000 francs a month. Documentation in *Sawdust Caesar.*)

3. Associazione fra Industriali Metallurgici Mecannici ed Affini. Similar to the Iron & Steel Institute, operated by our steel barons, including Weir and Girdler, one of whom employed the columnist George E. Sokolsky, the other the idol of Westbrook Pegler.

4. Fiat Automobile Works. Similar to General Motors, largest stockholder of which is DuPonts which is also the largest subsidizer of most native fascist organizations.

5. Societa Ansaldo (shipbuilders); Fiume Oil Corp; Venezia Giulia steel furnaces, Upper-Italy Hydroelectric Works, and other big outfits. (Equivalents in NAM leadership.)

6. Ente Nazionale per le Industrie Turistiche and Grandi Alberghi associations. No equivalents in the U. S., these being the tourist bureau and the hotelkeepers' association, both more interested in having the trains run on time than the trainmen eating on time—or at all.

7. Landowners Association, chairmanned by Senator Tittoni. U. S. equivalent: Associated Farmers. The Italian outfit consists of feudal landlords, the superwealthy of the nation and is the cause of poverty and starvation among the farming population of Italy. The U. S. outfit includes the packers and canners who control the Farm Bloc in Congress, constitute the Farm Lobby, and are in reality manufacturers of food and the enemies of the homestead farmer.

8. Banca Commerciale of Milan, Banca Italiana di Sconto, and other leading banks, the equivalent of the Chase, National City, Guaranty Trust and other banks which have spread dol-

lar imperialism in Mexico, Cuba, and the rest of Latin America.

As early as 1923 the fascist Prezzolini wrote:

"During the days of the coup d'état Mussolini's hotel was literally besieged by the most notorious speculators of northern Italy. The Confederazione Generale dell'Industria published a communiqué in which it claimed to have played an active part in the solution of the crisis . . . the Perrone brothers, formerly heads of the Ansaldo Company and of the Banca Italiana di Sconto, who had dropped out of sight after the panic of 1921, have come to life again."

Italia reported (November 1, 1931) that the subsidizers of Fascism included the brothers Perrone, Pogliani, Borletti, Odero and Mazzotti of Fondi Rustici and the Isotta auto works. Borletti, a textile manufacturer and owner of the Rinascente department store, also subsidized d'Annunzio in the Fiume adventure. Concludes *Italia*: "In 1931 among the richest men in Italy were the Fascists who had had the good sense to put considerable money in foreign issues or send them abroad, notably C. Volpi, Arnaldo Mussolini, M. Ciano, Balbo and Beneduce."

Bolitho reported (*Manchester Guardian* and *New York World* in the early 1920's) that when De Vecchi burned the liberal newspaper *Avanti* in Rome "this for the first time gave the Fascists general press notice and attracted the attention of great capitalist bodies, the Lega Industriale . . . Associazione fra Industriali . . . Confederazione Generale dell'Industria. . . . This latter body openly, the rest credibly, have continued to be the biggest subscribers to Fascist funds. . . . Those shrewd fellows of the Confederazione dell'Industria, the factory owners' organization of Milan, whose generosity is visible though discreet, at every stage of Fascism's progress, through Benni and Gino Olivetti managed to induce Mussolini and the (Fascist) Grand Council to accept 25,000,000 lire for the purpose of the Party, in its conquest of the South."

Mussolini was subsidized by the Italian equivalent of our

NAM and similar Big Money outfits shortly after the seizure of the factories in 1920.

In March, 1919, fascist agitators caused the workers to seize the Franchi-Gregorini plant. Mussolini called this a "creative strike," because the workers intended to run the plant for their own benefit. One of Mussolini's colleagues wrote: "At Dalmine he was the Lenin of Italy." At this time Mussolini was trying to get back into the labor movement.

When the factories of Milan and Turin were occupied by the workers Mussolini held a conference with Bruno Buozzi, who then held a place equivalent to that of Sam Gompers in our American Federation of Labor. He proposed using the factory occupation as the beginning of a military movement to seize Rome and establish a dictatorship of the proletariat. Buozzi indignantly kicked Mussolini out—labor believed in the democratic political processes, and the main proof was that not an act of violence marked the factory seizures, although the press of the world for a month ran daily lies of bloodshed and terrorism.

Within a few days Mussolini had sold the same idea to the owners of the occupied factories—only this time the same Blackshirts were to be used to create a dictatorship of Big Business, rather than of workers. Signor Agnelli, head of Fiat, admitted to Buozzi that Mussolini actually had dealt with Olivetti, of the Confederazione dell'Industria, while dealing with Buozzi. (This document in Chapter VIII of *Sawdust Caesar.*)

Olivetti and company put up the money. Mussolini took Rome. And in payment to the subsidizers his first important act was the abolition of all labor unions—the equivalent of our A. F. of L., C. I. O. and Railroad Brotherhoods.

From the day he became dictator Mussolini began paying back the men who paid him in 1920. He abolished the tax on inheritance, for example, because it was supposed to end big fortunes, and that of course meant loss of money for the rich, who had in a body gone over to Fascism after 1922. But Mussolini did not have the courage to abolish the political democratic system all at once, and he had many opposition parties which criticized and attacked him. His chief opponent was the Socialist deputy Matteotti.

The reason Matteotti had to die was because he committed the one unforgivable crime in a Fascist nation: he exposed the profits in Fascism.

There is no program, no policy, no ideology and certainly no philosophy back of Fascism, as there is back of almost every other form of government. It is nothing but a spoils system. We too in America have a spoils system, which is talked about every four years when a President is elected, and sometimes when a governor is elected, but this refers largely to a few jobs, a little graft, a considerable payoff for the boys in the back room of politics. It is also true that we in America have ruling families, men and corporations who put up most of the money for elections, and do not do so because one candidate has baby blue eyes and the other is beetlebrowed. It is done for money, and the investors in politics are repaid. But Fascism is a system whereby a handful of ruling families get the entire nation.

It was Matteotti who discovered in 1924 that Mussolini, who had "marched" to Rome in a Pullman sleeper in 1922, was beginning to pay back the secret forces which had paid the money to put Fascism in power.

On May 27th, a few days before he was kidnapped and assassinated by Mussolini's gangsters and family friends, Matteotti denounced in the Italian parliament a law which would have given a monopoly in oil to the Sinclair firm—the same corporation run by Harry Sinclair which was involved in the filthy muck of the Teapot Dome Scandal, and incidentally the same Harry Sinclair who told Dorothy Thompson that he and his associates put up most of the money to buy the Presidency of the United States every four years.

On June 10, 1924, when the entire front pages of the American press were given over to the Loeb-Leopold case in Chicago, Matteotti was killed by Mussolini's own orders, and not a line appeared in most newspapers. On the 16th Arnaldo, brother of the Duce, printed a warning in his *Popolo d'Italia* against public clamor for an investigation of the murder, saying such a request was in reality a demand that Mussolini abdicate. But the *London Daily Herald* told the truth. Matteotti, having challenged the Sinclair oil deal, had prepared a documentary exposé proving that Balbo, Grandi, Arnaldo Mussolini himself and the biggest men in the Fascist government had been engaged in a tremendous graft and corruption deal in relation to the oil monopoly.

For all this the Undersecretary of Home Affairs, Finzi, was made the scapegoat; the evidence was plain that he was among the grafters, and as he was also one of the big financial profiteers of a Fascist law legalizing gambling, he resigned in an uproar. In apology the Roman press said that "thousands of jailbirds have joined the Fascist Party since the March on Rome," and that Finzi was not a good party member.

Finzi was a small shot. Matteotti was using the Sinclair oil graft scandal to hit at the big shots, and the Fascists were throwing Finzi to the mob to save the real profiteers of the system. Matteotti had prepared a documentation which showed that the big bankers, the great industrial baronies such as Ansaldo, the great landowners and the war profiteers who had made billions while Italy hungered, were to be given the wealth of Italy. Here is a small part of Matteotti's documentation:

Ansaldo: A decree-law of June 14, 1923, supplied national funds for refloating this private corporation whose owners had been chiefly responsible for the bankruptcy of the Banca di Sconto. The Fascist regime, with 72,000,000 lire (against 78,000,000 lire worth of shares given the creditors), became almost half owner; it also took a mortgage for 41,500,000 lire.

Fascism subsidized the Ansaldo shipbuilding company at 900 lire a ton.

It gave Ansaldo 230 locomotives for repair, without accepting competitive bids.

Fiume Mineral Oil Refining Company. On April 29, 1923, the Fascist State purchased 18,000 shares of this corporation for

8,300,443 lire. It made itself party to the success of this private firm. Among the new directors the State put on the governing board were three of the "Fascists of the first hour," Dino Grandi, Massimo Rocca and Iginio Magrini.

Banking Houses: The Banca di Roma was in the same straits as the Sconto. When the latter failed it appealed to Mussolini as a friend and subsidizer of the Fascist movement, and Musso the Duce repaid the directors by bypassing the old law requiring them to make good the bank's losses. One of the men who profited most was a certain Senator Marconi, member of the board of the Sconto, who suddenly joined the Fascist Party in October, 1923. In November, Matteotti showed, he was relieved of the financial burden of putting up his fortune to repay the poor devils who had trusted the Sconto and lost all their money. This is, of course, the same Marconi who claimed he had invented the radio—a claim disputed by several. That Marconi made a fortune in wireless is beyond dispute.

War Profiteers: Every nation had a war profiteering scandal after 1918. Mussolini, in his demagogic orations in which he promised everything to everybody, said that he would take back every cent the profiteers made. At the very time he was saying this, Mussolini, as Matteotti later revealed, was accepting big money from the very same profiteers for organizing his Blackshirts and outfitting them with castor oil, clubs and revolvers.

The various regimes before October, 1922, had begun the investigation of the war profiteering frauds and several suits resulted in large sums being regained. Mussolini had denounced these suits as slow, the sums returned as small: he promised quick suits and complete confiscation of all the property of the war profiteers. On November 19, 1922, less than a month after he took office, Mussolini with a sweep of his pen wrote Decree No. 1487 which abolished the Committee of Enquiry into War Profiteering, and the crooks who paid for his election were relieved of all worry.

Railroads: The Societa Italiana per le F. S. del Mediterraneo, a private railway line, was granted treasury bonds up to 100,-

000,000 lire by Decree 1386 of June 17, 1923. A concession for the construction of 800 kilometers of Sicilian railroads was granted two important Fascist industrialists, Nicolini and Romano; the cost of the work was to be about a billion lire, and no government returns, rights, or privileges were asked. It was purely a big payoff to early subsidizers of Fascism.

Peasant Lands: On this subject an entire book could be written. The whole history of early Fascism centers upon this problem. As early as November, 1918, and internationally in the days of the peace conference of Versailles, the promises of "land for the returned soldiers" were being made by leading statesmen of the world, and notably by Giolitti, Orlando, Sonnino and other Italians. But in most lands there was no public domain, and little land available at a small price. There was, on the other hand, a feudal system—it still exists in fascist countries such as Poland, Hungary, Rumania, etc.—where a few land barons were even more powerful nationally than the industrial barons of the mills, mines and factories.

From Armistice Day to the "March" on Rome there had been a slight agrarian reform in Italy and considerable seizure of land by impoverished and dispossessed peasants. Mussolini in his (fake) radical days had urged the returned soldiers and the landless farmers to seize the estates of the wealthy. At this time a new movement arose, the Populari, or Catholic Popular Party, led by the priest Don Luigi Sturzo, which had as its chief aim the restoration of land to the farmers. However, whenever some of his restless and impatient followers seized some land, Don Sturzo would get together some money and make a settlement with the owner, because he was a strict legalitarian.

A study of the history of early Fascism shows that it concentrated its violence and its oratory against the Catholic Party, not against the Left. It was not until Mussolini hired an American press agent in 1925 to help float the Morgan $100,-000,000 loan and the Dillon, Read & Co. loans to the municipalities, that the myth of "fighting Bolshevism" was invented to please Wall Street. There was a tiny, ineffective Communist Party in Italy, and a large and powerful Socialist Party with which Mussolini could do (and did) business. But Mussolini could not appease the Popolari of Don Sturzo, and he could not do anything to stop the agrarian reform movement. As Bolitho wrote in 1925: "The enemy was not, however, the Communists, but the Catholic peasants of Don Luigi Sturzo's People's Party which was preaching seizure of land."

The landowners (and the industrial owners) were Mussolini's chief backers. No one knew of the subsidies he had received from the great estates. Immediately on becoming dictator Mussolini granted his first important interview to the press of the world. He said:

> "I love the working classes. The supremest ambition and the dearest hope of my life has been, and is still, to see them better treated and enjoying conditions of life worthy of the citizens of a great nation. . . . I do not believe in the class war, but in cooperation between classes. The Fascist government will devote all its efforts to the creation of an agrarian democracy based on the principle of small ownership. The great estates must be handed over to peasant communities; the great capitalists of agriculture must submit to a process of harmonization of their rights with those of the peasants."

This interview was printed in America on November 15, 1922, but on January 11, 1923, less than two months later, Mussolini issued a decree-law which dispossessed all the small peasants who since the war had settled on the seized lands of the "latifundia" of the great landowners. Needless to say, there has been no agrarian reform, no division of estates into small holdings, no "harmonization" of "the great capitalists of agriculture." The landowners were paid off with a return of all land which had been given the landless and by the employment of the Blackshirt Militia which prevented any further attempts to divide the land.

Mussolini's one stroke in issuing this decree-law restored more profits to more Fascists than probably any act in the totalitarian history of that land.

Although Mussolini himself had not laid up a cent—or a million dollars—as has Hitler, he has made it possible for all "Fascists of the first hour," be they bankers or burglars, to make all the money possible out of his success.

Dumini, the actual murderer of Matteotti, was given vast sums of money by Mussolini and the Fascist Party. Cesare Rossi, one of the founders of the party, was granted the right to sell concessions to foreigners. It was Rossi whom Matteotti was to expose as dealing with the Sinclair Oil Company for the oil monopoly. The graft was to be shared between him and Filippelli and Marinelli, also implicated in the assassination, and because the others tried to make him the scapegoat Rossi wrote confessions which were later published.

In its July, 1934, issue, a song of praise for Fascism, *Fortune* magazine (owned by Henry Luce, a Morgan partner, and other powerful and wealthy Americans) told of the great corporations and how they progressed under Mussolini. Montecatini, for example, was listed as having assets of $77,000,000; it consumes 10% of the nation's electricity, it is managed by Guido Donegani, with funds from the Banca Commerciale Italiana. Donegani is "a fascist from the very beginning." Montecatini owns 51% of Acna chemical company, and I. G. Farben, the Hitler cartel, the other 49%.

Signor Giovanni Agnelli, manager of Fiat, is "one of the financial backers of the march on Rome, he stands high in Fascist councils and has been a senator since Anno I of Fascismo. He owns *La Stampa,* the leading Turin newspaper. . . ."

Riccardo Gualino of Snia Viscosa, occupies the same place in Fascism-for-money history as the bankers and industrialists who backed Hitler and whom Hitler purged. But *Fortune* in 1934 reported: "Along with Agnelli of Fiat and several other big capitalists, Gualino helped finance the march on Rome and in the early years of Fascism flourished mightily." He went to jail later along with other Fascist notables who resorted to common swindling in addition to the legal Fascist way of draining the nation of its wealth.

Martini & Rossi, the vermouth and cocktail lords, is run by Count Napoleon Rossi di Montelara, a member of the Fascist party.

Fratelli Alberto and Pietro Pirelli own a $10,000,000 company which in 1933 made a net profit of $1,500,000 thanks to Mussolini's help. The Pirellis control 39 joint stock companies with a capital of 7,818,000,000 lire. Agnelli controls 32 such corporations with a capital of 1,890,000,000 lire. Senator Ettore Conti, president of the Banca Commerciale—the bank once headed by Giuseppi Toeplitz, one of the many fascist Jews who supported Mussolini, and who was treasurer and cashier for Fascism—controls 18 firms with a capital of 3,474,000,000 lire.

"The significant facts to hang on to," concluded *Fortune,* "are these: if you were an early Fascist, or contributed generously to the March on Rome, you are likely to enjoy the business benefits that accrue to a high position within the Fascist Party."

Curiously enough *Fortune* (and Luce's other publications, *Time* and *Life*), which had a long record (before Pearl Harbor) of applauding Fascismo, will not even now print any news which would in any way indicate that there is at least a slight resemblance between the former object of their affection, and the constant love of their lives, the American Big Business equivalent of the Fascist industrial system.

Ever since Pearl Harbor courage is not required to speak out against faraway Fascism. The Scripps-Howard papers, which are under the reactionary rule of a man who never got over the fact he was permitted to kowtow to the Emperor of Japan, the Hearst papers, which had a deal with the Nazi press and which published signed propaganda articles of Goering, Goebbels and Co., Patterson's *New York Daily News,* which said "Let's Appease Japan" because Japan was a good customer, and which favored betraying China because China did not put as much money into American pockets as the Hirohito regime,

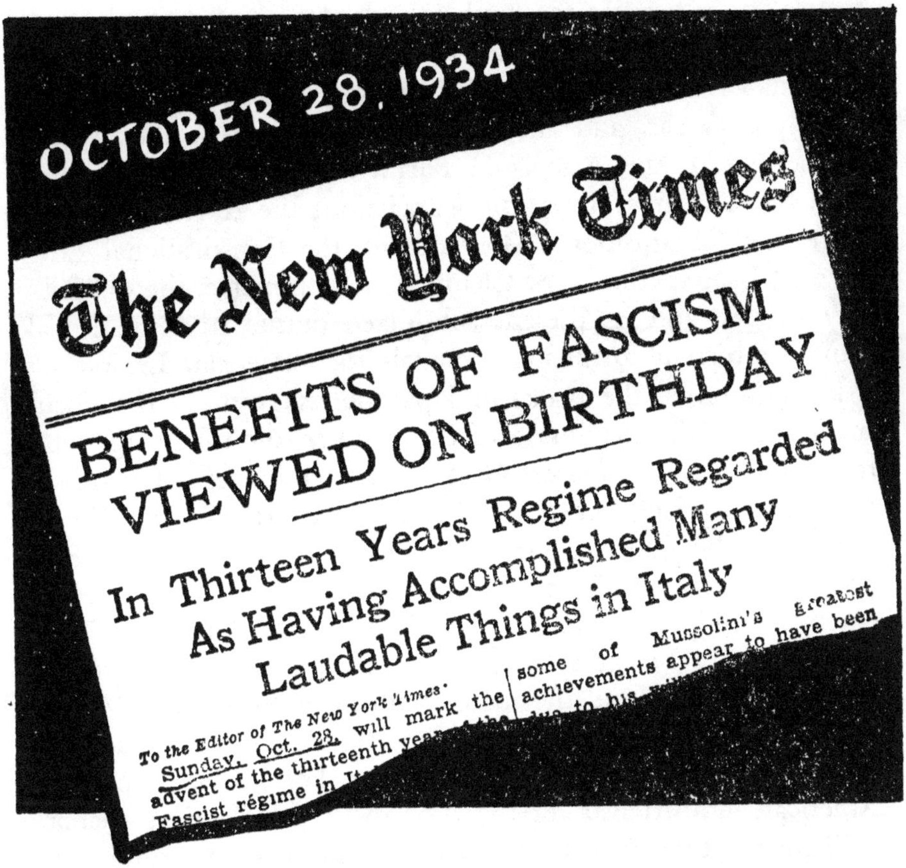

OCTOBER 28, 1934
The New York Times
BENEFITS OF FASCISM VIEWED ON BIRTHDAY
In Thirteen Years Regime Regarded As Having Accomplished Many Laudable Things in Italy
To the Editor of The New York Times:
Sunday, Oct. 28, will mark the
advent of the thirteenth
Fascist régime in
some of Mussolini's greatest
achievements appear to have been

America's most influential newspaper, the New York Times, was friendly to Mussolini, employed Italian Fascists as correspondents, played up the news from Franco's side, turned against the New Deal, attacked the Wagner Act, and still represents Reaction.

have used flaring headlines against the three brands of Fascism which rule the three chief enemy countries. But there are surely not a half dozen newspapers—perhaps not even three—which have ever had the courage to show the relationship between foreign and domestic Fascism.

You will have to read the free and independent press, which is largely the press of small unbribed weeklies, and a few pamphlets and book to get the truth. The truth is not in the commercial press because the truth is a dagger pointed at its heart, which is its pocketbook. Native American Fascism is largely the policy of the employers of gangsters, stoolpigeons, labor spies, poison gas, and anti-labor propaganda; it is the fascism of the NAM, the Associated Farmers and Associated Industries, the Christian American Association; the KKK, the Committee for Constitutional Government, the Constitutional Educational League, the U. S. Chamber of Commerce, the old Liberty League and its present subsidized outfits, and the Royal Family which unfortunately controls the American Legion.

In addition to the books and pamphlets given in the documentation at the conclusion of this chapter, the following statement made by Professor Gaetano Salvemini of Harvard is noteworthy. Professor Salvemini told Reporter Joseph Philip Lyford of the undergraduate daily that "a new brand of Fascism" threatens America, "the Fascism of corporate business enterprise in this country." He believed that "almost 100% of American Big Business" is in sympathy with the "philosophy" of government behind the totalitarianism of Hitler and Mussolini; the bond of sympathy between Big Business and the Fascist Axis, said the professor of history, lies in the respect of American industrialists for the Axis methods of coercing labor.

There are two means which the industrialist can employ to crush labor, Professor Salvemini explained; one way is to hire strikebreakers to "crack the workers' skulls," the other way is to pass a law outlawing strikes. "Mussolini has used both methods in Italy," Professor Salvemini asserted; "in America Big Business has only been able to use the first." But business is definitely sympathetic to anti-strike legislation, he added, and compared the organization of the Ford plant at River Rouge to the organization of the Fascist auto industry, and the strikebreaking methods used by Ford there to those which had been used by Italian industry to crush the workers on the eve of Mussolini's rise to power.

Salvemini's statement, based on Italian Fascism, paralleled the statement which Ambassador Dodd made on returning to

America from Germany. Both these men noted the relationship between foreign Fascism and American business monopolies and the handful of super-industrialists who rule most countries for their own profit.

BIBLIOGRAPHY

William Bolitho, *Italy Under Mussolini; New York World* dispatches, 1925.

Giacomo Matteotti, *The Fascists Exposed,* London, 1924.

Gaetano Salvemini, *The Fascist Dictatorship.*

Harvard *Crimson,* April 22, 1940.

George Seldes, *Sawdust Caesar,* Harpers, 1935.

CHAPTER IV

THE FIVE WHO OWN JAPAN

EVERY Japanese gun, bullet, torpedo, ship and airplane that has killed or wounded an American soldier, sailor, airman or marine has meant actual cash money in the pocket of Emperor Hirohito.

When the "merchants of death," the armaments manufacturers who had a financial interest in waging previous wars, and who still do in fascist dictatorships, were exposed in 1934, it was found that Mitsui and Mitsubishi were the Japanese members of the cartel, and that the reigning family was a large stockholder in both.

Hirohito owns 3,800,000 acres of land with all the buildings on them, many being tenements from which he makes a rent; the total value when the yen was still 50c was estimated at 637,-234,000 yen. The son of the Sun Goddess has also invested 300,000,000 yen in the Bank of Japan, the South Manchuria Railroad, the Yokohama Specie Bank, Nippon Yusen Kaisha (the shipping line of the Mitsubishi firm), the Imperial Hotel of Tokyo, and Mitsui and Mitsubishi enterprises.

In the wave of disillusion which swept over the world after the Treaty of Versailles and proved that the old march of the imperialists would be resumed and that all international idealism (Woodrow Wilson's for example) would be destroyed, many secrets were uncovered and one of the most sensational was that concerning the international of blood—the cartels of the merchants of death, the armaments makers, who made a profit on the guns, the shells and the bullets. The manufacturing corporations in many instances were found linked to governments and to have arranged, even in wartime, for the continuance of their dividends and distribution of their profits.

There were several hundred members of the cartels, but only fifty were powerful and of these the handful which influenced world events and formed the Harvey United Steel Co. cartel, the Nobel Dynamite Trust, the various rifle, gunpowder and similar cartels were: Krupp in Germany, Vickers-Armstrong in Britain, Schneider Creusot in France, Skoda in Austria-Hungary, Terni-Ansaldo in Italy, Mitsui in Japan and the Bethlehem Steel Company and DuPont Empire in the United States. Charles M. Schwab's Bethlehem held 4,301 shares in the Harvey cartel. Albert Vickers was chairman.

It should be noted here that just as American Big Business was found at the time of the first World War to be linked to Japanese Big Business through the Harvey cartel, Nobel international trust and other agencies, so just before the outbreak of the Global War it was discovered that the international of money was even stronger than ever. One of the links was the I. G. Farbenindustrie, which Hitler and Goering controlled and which involved Standard Oil, Standard Drug, General Motors, General Electric and other of our greater corporations.

Just as American Big Business was linked to Japan through the Harvey combine (steel), the Nobel Dynamite Trust (munitions) and the other munitions cartels before the last war, so before the Global War there were the usual international cartels in which both the U. S. and Japan shared with Germany, Italy and other nations.

In addition, according to the San Francisco journalist John Pittman, "among the owners of Japanese business are International General Electric, which operates plants through its subsidiary, Tokyo Shibaura; Westinghouse Electric International, associated with Mitsubishi Electric Manufacturing Co.; Tide Water Associated Oil, handled by Mitsubishi; Libby-Owens-Ford, represented by the Nippon Plate Glass Co.; Standard Oil, with a known direct investment of $5,000,000, exclusive of frozen credits and oil in storage; Ford, and General Motors, with approximately $10,000,000 sunk in Japan proper; Eastman Kodak, and Singer Sewing Machine, with big organizations in the Japanese Empire; United Engineering & Foundry Co., holding a large stake in Shibaura-United Engineering Co.

"Besides these shares in the industry of Japan proper, American capital is heavily invested in Manchukuo and other exploitation companies of a Japanese origin scattered throughout the Far East."

In Japan one of Mitsui's partly owned corporations is the Nippon Steel Works, but this firm was controlled by Vickers. Their French connection was through the Franco-Japanese Bank, founded with the aid of Schneider Creusot, whose 1933 report stated that "our bank has acquired important participation in various activities of the Mitsui group, a group destined to have a fine future."

Baron Hachirumon Mitsui was reported at the time as controlling 65% of the industry of Japan, with the Japanese royal family owning a large interest in the Mitsui Consortium. Mitsui, referred to in the Japanese press as King of Armament-makers, Emperor of Steel, Caesar of Petroleum, and Demigod of the Banking System, owned or controlled most of the mines, factories, steamships, newspapers and commercial enterprises of the first order, not only in Japan but in Korea, China, Indo-China, Manchuria, the Philippines and Hawaii.

The conquest of Manchuria was popularly said to have been instigated by Mitsui, and there is no doubt that this firm was the largest beneficiary from the coal and steel Japan seized. This firm also gained most from the first Sino-Japanese war. It was also credited with dictating Japan's peace terms at the end of the Russo-Japanese war, using the Tokyo Foreign Office as one of its many handy instruments. It may be remembered that one of the points Japan would not cede was the occupation by its troops of North Sakhalin, and they remained there until the oil deposits were leased to Japan. Russia was forced to agree. The lease was then given by Japan to one of the owners of the government and nation, the Mitsui Consortium.

The so-called "Asia for the Asiatics" doctrine, which means simply "Asia for Japan," found Baron Hachirumon Mitsui its chief exponent. This is a Monroe Doctrine which marches with banners and is followed by an army of salesmen and exploiters. Hachirumon's fascist imperialism burned even more ardently in his successor, Baron Takakimi Mitsui.

"Japan's financial oligarchy," wrote Anthony Jenkinson for the Institute of Pacific Relations, "is composed of great family trusts known as Zaibatsu. Its leading members are the Houses of Mitsui, Mitsubishi, Sumitomo and Yasuda. Between them they own the greater part of industry, trade, banking, and shipping. By 1937 they controlled more than one third of the total deposits in private banks, 70% of the deposits in all trust companies, and one third of total foreign trade. By controlling the banks, they controlled the smaller credit institutions throughout the country."

The income tax returns of 1938-39 showed that Japan consists of a vast majority of farm workers and farmers and industrial workers who earn less than the equivalent of $10 a week. There is almost no middle class, only 1,500,000 or about one family in 40, which earns less than $2,500 a year, but on the other hand there is a small rich and powerful ruling class consisting of 3,233 persons with incomes of $50,000 or more a year. The top flight consists of 7 persons who paid an income tax on more than $2,000,000 each. (*New York Times,* April 2, 1939.)

On July 30, 1941, income tax authorities announced that during the year 1940-41 there were 24 millionaires who paid more than 1,000,000 yen each in income taxes, the total for the two dozen being 57,000,000 yen. Baron Takakimi Mitsui was listed as the richest man in the country (although actually he is not richer than the emperor); he had an income of 7,500,000 yen and paid 4,450,000. Kichizaemon Sumitomo, earning 5,800,000 annually, was next, and after him Baron Kikoyata Iwasaki, head of the Mitsubishi interests, who makes 3,800,000 yen a year.

In all countries where the regime in power prohibits the full development of the nation's industries—or the manufacturers and raw materials producers themselves limit production (the economy of scarcity), as in the United States—there must be poverty. In Japan, thanks to the fact that four industrial families and the royal family have colossal wealth—Mitsui is said to be richer than Ford—the majority of the people, farmers and workers, are poor. Moreover, the International Labor Office of the League of Nations reported in 1938 that one quarter of the entire population did "not earn enough to maintain health and efficiency." Official Japanese statistics as of May, 1941, show the average wage for men at 82 yen ($19.25 at current rate of exchange) and 31 yen ($7.30) for women.

The trade unions were abolished in 1940 when the royal-military dictatorship began following the Fascist Axis line in action as well as form. "Workers," writes Jenkinson, "were ordered to become members of the League for Service to the State through industry," which approximates the Mussolini labor corporations and the Nazi Hitler's forced labor. The Minister of Welfare in announcing the abolition of the trade unions made this statement: "Our primary aim is to drive communist ideas and dangerous social thoughts from the minds of the people by ordering the dissolution of the established labor unions, which have a tendency to sharpen class consciousness among workers, which hamper the development of industry, and disturb the peace and order of the country." November 23, 1940, the Japanese Patriotic Industrial Society, or Sampo, absorbed the League, and claimed it had 4,500,000 members. It was declared to be a wing of the Imperial Rule Assistance Association.

This Imperial Rule Assistance Association (IRAA) is an outright fascist body. Up to July 6, 1940, there had been many parties in Japan, which gave the nation the semblance of a constitutional monarchy in accordance with its Constitution, granted by the Emperor in 1889 and modeled on that of Bismarck's Prussia. Like Prussia it created a Diet consisting of a House of Peers and a House of Representatives actually elected by popular vote. Leading parties were the Seiyukai and Minseito, both controlled by the big industrialists, the Zaibatsu (very much as our Republican and Democratic Parties are frequently, but not always, controlled by the National Association of Manufacturers). In 1936, however, the Minseito Party came out against Fascism and won a victory and the Social Mass and Proletarian Parties elected 23 working men to the Diet.

But on July 6, 1940, the Social Mass Party was ordered dissolved, and within a few weeks all other parties dissolved "voluntarily." An attempt to form a Laboring People's Party was suppressed.

This left the IRAA in control, a one-party system without an official dictator, but Japan is actually a fascist dictatorship ruled by the Emperor, the Army and Navy, and the Zaibatsu.

No one can tell where the political rule and industrial ownership of these three elements (Royal Family, Big Business, Military) begin and end; they intermingle and draw their money profits from the same seizure and exploitation of foreign lands, exploitation of the impoverished majority not only of Japan but Korea, Manchuria and China.

Japan has been described as an ancient feudal, modern capitalistic, fascist dictatorship. Wilfrid Fleisher dubbed it a "collective dictatorship."

Fascism, as any study of Hitler-Germany shows, has been built up as a system of super-colossal robber barons, thanks largely to the international cartels, of which I. G. Farbenindustrie was the largest.

Nationally, all forms of Fascism have flourished thanks to the aid the state has given them in maintaining monopolies or trusts. In every instance where business men subsidized a reactionary party—whether it was the Fiat works in Italy paying Mussolini or a landed estate owner bribing a Rumanian premier—the party and the most powerful few of the subsidizers have always engaged in forming national monopolies when they took over the rule of the country.

Professor Brady is the only economist who has related the "peak associations" or Spitzenverbaende as they were known in Germany—that is, the biggest trade associations, such as the NAM and the U. S. Chamber of Commerce—with the subsidization of fascist movements, and shown how business, whether or not it is officially on the throne, has in all countries become a political power—in fact, the ruling power behind the thrones of fascism.

In Japan, the "peak associations" are dominated by the Zaibatsu, or four ruling families, who are comparatively more powerful and richer than the thirteen ruling families of America.

"Almost all economic organizations in Japan" stated the *Monthly Circular* issued by Mitsubishi Economic Research Bureau of December, 1937, "have developed after the World War. Excepting chambers of commerce and industry, they have no legal basis, but as governmental control of the national economy becomes stricter, the part played by these organizations is necessarily of greater importance. The most representative organizations, the members of which include all branches of the national economy, are the Japan Chamber of Commerce and Industry, Nippon Kogyo Club, Nippon Keizei Renmeikwai, and Zensanren." The Chamber of Commerce is quasi-governmental. It belongs to the International Chamber of Commerce, and is dominated by the Zaibatsu. The Kogyo Club "exclusively represents the interests of large industries which developed during the World War," and is compared to the Union League Club by Dr. Brady.

Nippon Keizei Renmeikwai, the Japan Economic Association, is comparable to the Federation of British Industries of London (which is the equivalent of the NAM) and the U. S. Chamber of Commerce. Zensanren (Zenkoku Sangyo Dantai Rengokai) is the National Federation of Industrialists which is described in the *Monthly Circular* already quoted as having for its main objective "protecting employers' interests against attack from the labor movement." Says *Trans-Pacific*: "It is that the Federation was organized to present a united front of capitalists against the labor class."

In 1937 the government brought all the leading employers and business confederations together in the Japanese League of Economic Organizations, which Brady describes as a sort of private National Defense Council for business enterprise. He concludes: "It would be hard to imagine a much higher degree of policy-determining power than is indicated by the combination of the Zaibatsu and its concentric cartel and federational machinery. The hierarchy of business control seems well-nigh complete." The government of Japan and the business interests of Japan are bound together "from center to circumference." "What is being accomplished is the gradual rounding out of a highly coordinated fascist-type of totalitarian economy."

Professor Brady points out the fact that it was because the old system of feudalism prevailed longer in Japan than elsewhere that "the new Japanese totalitarianism has been easier to achieve than in any other major industrial-capitalistic country." The "feudal and patriarchal-minded hierarchies of business" and the political and military bureaucracies were identified and centralized. Government and business are more intermarried in Japan than anywhere else, much more so than in the ruling family of Goering-Hitler and company. But all in all the fascist pattern is pretty much the same in all countries where wealth and power have taken over the military-economic-political rule. Professor Brady writes that in Japan the elements "are not greatly dissimilar to those noted for other totalitarian systems of the general fascist type." He lists:

"1. The Zaibatsu, the monopolistically-oriented enterprises centered around them, and the extensive network of trade associations, chambers of commerce, cartels, and similar bodies of which they are the acknowledged leaders, constitute an elaborate, semi-legal, hierarchy of graduated economic power. . . .

"2. The hierarchy works very closely with the civil and administrative bureaucracy of the state. . . . This constitutes the Japanese version of National Socialism. . . .

"3. The military is becoming increasingly part and parcel of the same control pyramid. . . .

"4. And finally, the psychopathic, ideological, propaganda cement which holds the Kokutai (Corporate State) amalgam together in the fused power of Shinto (the main religion) and Bushido (Precepts of Knighthood)."

DOCUMENTATION AND REFERENCES:

Anthony Jenkinson, *Know Your Enemy: Japan,* American Council, Institute of Pacific Relations.

Robert A. Brady, *Business as a System of Power.*

Carl Randau and Leane Zugsmith, *The Setting Sun of Japan,* Random House, 1942.

CHAPTER V

WHO PAID FOR FRANCO'S WAR?

FASCISM in Spain was bought and paid for by numerous elements who would profit by the destruction of the democratic Republican Loyalist government. There were generals who wanted glory and others who wanted the easy graft money some of their predecessors had made. There was the established Church, and more especially the powerful Society of Jesus, which had suffered loss of property when King Alfonso was thrown out. There was the aristocracy, and there were other elements as there are in all fascist regimes, but more important than all these forces combined was the force of Money.

The Big Money conspired with General Sanjurjo and the Nazi government in early 1936 to establish a fascist regime which would not only protect profits but insure bigger profits at the expense of the majority and end the heavy fear that the masses preferred the benefits which even a weak republic could obtain for them.

Prominent among the owners of Spain and Fascism are:

1. The Duke of Alba. Of him it has been said that he could cross Spain from the French border at Irun to the outskirts of Gibraltar and never take his feet off his own land. True or not, it is a fact that he is one of the holders of vast lands, in a nation where thousands starve to death and millions pray for two or three acres.

2. Juan March. This multimillionaire crook is typical of one element of all fascist regimes. In Italy Mussolini had his murderers and assorted gangsters whom he gave big graft jobs and

made into millionaires as a reward for their aiding him before 1922. Hitler's assassins are known. March has a penitentiary record as a common smuggler, and also a record as the holder of the state monopoly in tobacco. He is said to have put more millions into the Franco movement than any other man.

3. Rio Tinto. This is one of the biggest mining ventures in the world. Big British and Spanish capital is invested in it, and it is a truism that all big capital prefers a fascist regime, which it can own completely, to a democracy where elections change things—and the tax rate. The British probably have the controlling interest in Rio Tinto. When Claude Bowers, American Ambassador to Spain, suggested to the British Ambassador that if Franco won Britain would have Hitler at Gibraltar and perhaps lose the control of the Mediterranean, "the lifeline of empire," the British Ambassador answered that "private interests at home are stronger than national interests." He meant that Rio Tinto and other Spanish mine, electricity, railroad and other stockholders in Britain preferred Fascism and even Hitler in Spain to the safety of Britain itself.

In all agrarian countries—notably Poland, Hungary, Spain, Roumania—the big landowners are almost without exception fascists. The Duke of Alba, who put millions into the Franco investment, was joined by all the Spanish holders of estates who, with the Church, had owned the best and largest areas of fertile Spain.

There had been no large seizure of land under the Republic, but all the liberal parties were pledged to agrarian reform. Big pieces of land had been bought from the great landlords and parceled out—in three or four acres and perhaps ten—to several thousand landless. The Republic did accomplish something, but although it was not anything very big, it was enough to scare the multimillionaire estate owners. They therefore joined the conspiracy with Franco so that they could keep the land. It was as simple as all that.

Of course the people of Spain—the vast majority, the farmers and workers—wanted land and a decent living. Franco therefore did the usual fascist thing: he made big promises.

The Republic had divided several hundred thousand acres among the impoverished. Franco repeated the Republic's promises. Here, for example, is the rabidly fascist Coughlinite paper, *The Tablet* of Brooklyn, which (believe it or not) is also the official organ of the largest diocese in the world. Said the *Tablet* in 1937:

"GENERAL FRANCO STARTS LAND MOVEMENT

"Cordoba, May 26.—General Queipo de Llano, in Ecija, a small town in Andalucia, has formally settled 100 peasants on small parcels of land, the first of a series of such experiments by General Franco to interest the peasant in a small holding of his own. . . . Franco has stated that all workers on outlying farms and haciendas must be given facilities to hear Mass every week."

It is indeed an amazing item. In 1936, about election time, when the Fascists were beaten and thrown out of office, peasants in many parts of Spain thought the great day had arrived, and they helped themselves to land. In many districts there was violence as the Republic ejected the men who had seized the soil. The Republic promised the land-hungry peasants would get land—later—and legally. Now the American fascists report Franco making an "experiment . . . to interest the peasant in a small holding of his own." What corrupt irony!

In its issue of March 19, 1938, the native fascist *Tablet* reported that Franco (blessed by the Church and called a "child of God" although he had pinned the bleeding heart of Christ on the tunics of the bloodthirsty Moors, some 150,000 of whom had been imported to do most of the fighting) had given a total of 17,000 acres of land to the peasantry of Spain.

This appears to be something more than it is. Republican Spain from 1931 to 1936 had failed to satisfy the needs of the peasants—thanks to sabotage by the wealthy—and had succeeded in distributing only 13,000,000 hectares of land, which is some 30,000,000 acres. Thirty million was not enough, because the impoverished peasantry numbered many millions, and that figure would have allowed too few acres per family. However, it was something.

In the Twenty-Six Points of the Phalanx, the ruling Fascist Party of today—all other parties have been abolished and Spain is totalitarian—the nation was to be turned into "one gigantic syndicate of producers," so that there would be plenty for all, instead of superabundance for only the rich, as had been the case under both monarchy and fascist dictatorship; the banks were to be nationalized, land was to be irrigated, and those large estates which were found to be neglected were to be broken up.

What does the balance sheet today show of the Franco "experiment" of 100 parcels of land, the distribution of a glorious total of 17,000 acres in 1938, and the promise that at least neglected estates would be broken up? The writer-journalist Thomas J. Hamilton presents the latest and final report:

"The landed aristocrats of Spain . . . had little real cause for complaint against the Franco regime which addressed itself to the work of undoing any damage to their interests that they had suffered from the Republic. This was not large. The grandees had been frightened by talk of breaking up the great estates, but they had managed to sabotage the Republic's first Agrarian Reform Law and the second was just getting into operation when the Civil War began. Only a few hundred thousand acres had actually been taken over, either in accordance with law or as a result of the movement among the peasants in the Spring of 1936 to seize the land without waiting for the slow operations of the government.

"The test of any Spanish regime was its attitude toward this fundamental question, and it may be supposed that some of the grandees had anxious moments when Franco adopted the Phalanx program with its demand for land reform. Carlists and moderate royalists together, however, proved more than strong enough to prevent the regime from harming the interests of the landowners. All land which had been occupied by the peasants, legally or otherwise, was returned to the owners, and soon there was no longer even any mention of breaking up the great estates. . . .

"In general, the old nobility, fighting very much the same type of fight that it had under the Republic, managed to keep the Phalanx from hitting its pocketbook."

Mussolini's prediction, made years before the Global War broke out in September, 1939, that the entire world was lining up in two camps, Fascism and Democracy, and that it was "Either We or They," showed itself a matter of fact in the so-called civil war in Spain. It was actually a rebellion of the military leadership—which committed wholesale treason by betraying the government to which it had taken an oath of allegiance—armed and paid for by the vested interests. The "We" consisted of Fascists from all parts of the world, hundreds of thousands of soldiers from Germany, Italy and Portugal, all fascist lands, whereas the "They" of Democracy consisted of some 30,000 men of the International Brigade, not one a conscript soldier as were all on Franco's side, but every man a volunteer, a man of intelligence, a first fighter against Fascism. (Of the foreigners on the Loyalist side about 700 were Russians, mostly aviators and technicians, and not one infantry soldier. The press of America, Britain and other countries as usual lied about Russian aid and perpetuated the myth that the Loyalists were Communists.)

On Franco's march to Madrid he took not only the labor union leaders but a large percentage of the industrial workers of each town he captured, lined them up, and shot them down with machine guns. In Madrid the Fifth Column of Fascism killed as many of the working class as it could.

From Madrid early in 1937 this journalist wrote to the *New York Post* that Fascism had made it a class war in Spain; that Fascism was determined to kill off all leaders of the working class so it could enslave the workers, whereas the Loyalists had as their objective the redistribution of land and wealth.

The most enlightening proof of a class war was given in Madrid on the 7th and 8th of November, 1936, when the capital was given up as lost, when the censors in the Telefonica let the newspapermen send out the most pessimistic reports, and the

Loyalist militiamen sat around waiting for Franco to arrive and murder them.

On the 8th there was considerable shooting in the streets. It was Franco's Fifth Column—the hidden pro-fascist column which the fascist international has created in every country, and which still flourishes in the United States, and has its supporters in Congress. The Loyalists estimated the snipers at twenty or thirty thousand. Now, when Franco appeared about to enter the city, they boldly appeared in windows and on roofs and around street corners, and began their guerrilla warfare.

How did the Spanish Fascists know which Spaniards to murder?

Obviously every man in Loyalist uniform was a possible victim. But the Loyalists never had enough money to put all of their men in uniform, and tens of thousands fought the war in the blue overalls of their shops and factories.

The Fifth Column, hidden Fascists, were the people who had subsidized Franco. To them every working man was an anti-Fascist and therefore marked for death. And since the Loyalists in wartime did not wear white shirts, or white collars, or fine suits of clothes, or felt hats, or even neckties, the Fascists of the Fifth Column, fighting their guerrilla war in the streets of Madrid on November 8, 1936, spared every well-dressed wealthy-looking man as a possible ally, and murdered the men of the working class. Men in overalls were always shot by the Fascists.

An interesting footnote on the Spanish situation was published in the fascist press early in 1940. Said *Voice of Spain*:

"Apologists for the Nationalist Movement have gone to some trouble to point out that the Church in Spain is poor, and has been for some time. They have emphasized that nobody has yet produced concrete evidence of the holdings which the Church was known to have in commercial undertakings, that is to say, that nobody has been able to produce the share certificates and exhibit them publicly. We should like to have been able to do so for the information of the doubters, but now we do the next best thing. On page 172 will be found a facsimile from a page of *A B C* (Madrid Franco paper) of January 7, 1940, showing a list of Church shares which were confiscated by the Republican Government, and now claimed back by the Church. What we publish refers only to shares in the Telefonica. . . . Do our readers consider that this evidence is good enough or, if not, what more do they want in the way of evidence?

"The fabulous wealth of the Church before July 19, 1936, is very well known, especially that held by the Company of Jesus, which is estimated at 6,000 million pesetas. The man with 'power of attorney' in all these holdings was Ruiz Senen, who was on the board of 40 important companies as agent of the Jesuits, and whose tentacles stretched out into all sorts of industrial undertakings."

The Telefonica of course is the American-owned I. T. & T. building and national telephone system. The advertisement reproduced lists the Metropolitan of Valencia owning hundreds of shares; the Casa Diocesana of the Archbishop of Lerida, 14 shares preferred stock; the rector of the College of San Jose of Valencia, of the Society of Jesus, the College of Maria the Immaculate, and several other Church organizations.

On January 24, 1940, *A B C* published a similar advertisement restoring preferred and common stocks and bonds to investors of the Compania Trasatlantica, the steamship line. Among the holders listed were: Rev. Pedro Pujol, the Archbishop of Madrid-Alcala, 50 shares numbered 91,101 to 91,150, the vicar general of the Congregation of Hermanas Descalzas de la Tercera Orden de la B. V. M. del Carmen of Tarragona, 9 shares.

On January 27, 1940, General Franco signed a decree formally restoring "the vast property holdings of the Society of Jesus which had been confiscated by the Republic in 1932," at the time the Jesuits were expelled. How vast this property is few persons know, as much of it was held in the names of individuals. M. Angel Margaud in "L'Espagne au XXe Siecle" quoted Aguilera as writing that "one can evaluate about one third of the national wealth, the goods, movable and immovable, owned by the Congregations. The North Railroad, the Transatlantic Co., the orange groves of Andalusia, the mines of the Basque provinces, and in the Rif, many factories in Barcelona, are under their open or occult direction. . . ."

The Republic of 1931 had separated Church and State. The Church supported the Fascist side in 1936. In 1940 the Fascists restored all the confiscated wealth, including stocks and bonds, to the Church. Fascism paid off in this instance.

The final lesson from Spain, however, should not be lost by the thousands of American business men, big and little, who from 1922 on have been saying kind things about Mussolini and others who made trains run on time and seemed to insure bigger profits by outlawing unions, and the rights of the working people.

In Germany a million business men were ruined by Hitler, and only the upper thousand, the wealthiest and most powerful, profited by Nazi rule. As in Italy, so in Germany, the fascist regime had to rob not only the poor and reimpose serfdom on millions, but it also had to rob its own supporters to maintain a new bureaucracy, and a new army on whose bayonets the bureaucracy tried to build a permanent government. Fascism has to exploit either a foreign people or its own people; it has to have money, and if it must pay off the top subsidizers this means it has to destroy its millions of smaller helpers.

Hitler and Mussolini robbed and impoverished their own party members in order to feed the super-monopolists. In Spain the situation is similar. Hamilton writes:

"Spain was traditionally the land of special privilege. Franco's success in restoring these privileges therefore produced a singularly vicious combination: the rich stayed rich, if they did not get richer, and the poor were even hungrier than they had been in the worst days of the civil war. . . . Suffering was increased immeasurably by the restoration of the old privileges; despite the steadily increasing misery of the poor, the wealthy managed to obtain virtually everything they needed. And a new class of parvenus, who had made their money by the special 'favours' obtained from the

A B C. DOMINGO 7 DE ENERO DE 19

Compañía Telefónica Nacional de España

A los efectos de la declaración de nulidad de los títulos primitivos y expedición de duplicados, prevenidas ambas en la ley de la Jefatura del Estado del día 1.° de junio de 1939, se recuerdan al público por segunda vez las denuncias siguientes, anunciadas por primera vez en el "Boletín Oficial del Estado", número 332 de fecha 28 de noviembre último, y se hace constar que finalizan los tres meses para formalizar la oposición el día 28 de febrero de 1940 y pasada esta fecha se procederá a solicitar del Juzgado la autorización para anular los títulos desaparecidos y expedir los correspondientes duplicados.

SEGUNDA RELACION

SEGUNDA INSERCION RECTIFICADA

Denunciante: Ilustre Cabildo Metropolitano de Valencia. Acciones preferentes números 17 781/62, 37 313/909, 47 738/42, 49 033/33, 59 346/47, 67 984/90, 69 951/53, 72 068/70, 91 885/59, 98 260, 101.096/100, 113 201, 117 423, 132 731, 34, 136 165, 144 725, 111 543 al 44, 161 118/27, 161 437/38, 171,723/24, 178 104, 185 619/23, 135 675, 191 501/505, 193 373, 194 933, 214 626, 217 641, 227 003, 228 016/17, 244 197/98, 270 909, 273 777/93, 282 251/303, 282 500 al 504, 288 955/56, 291 357/59, 298 539/40, 299 683, 299 686, 298.690, 304 253/55, 332 235/36, 332 440, 361 459/60, 367 861/63, 368 242, 371,430, 373 503, 388 333/34, 393 063/78, 404 205, 425.216 al 18, 437 169/70, 456 913/14, 503 893, 518 636, 551 781, 566 100 al 17, 563 512 y 593 665/66. Denunciante: Caja Diocesana del Obispado de Lérida. Acciones preferentes números 2.135/37, 247.533/43, 376.923/35, 522.078.

Denunciante: D. Francisco Clavero Fenollosa, Obligaciones 5 ½ % números 89 251/57 y 169.953/61. Denunciante: D. Eusebio Ferrer Laporta, como rector del Colegio de Padres Escolapios de Barbastro. Acciones preferentes números 693 932/35. Denunciante. D. Antonio de León [illegible] como rector del Colegio de San José de Valencia [illegible] ... ñía de Jesús. Acciones preferentes números 4[illegible] ... Denunciante: D. Eladio España Navarro, como [illegible] ... Corpus Christi, de Valencia del Cid. Acciones ... ros 50 982/83, 429.613/14, 512 324/27 ... 161 778, 177 8[illegible] ... 262 57[illegible] ... 371 705/[illegible] ... ciante ... de ...

Denunciante. Revda. Comunidad de Carmelitas Descalzas, de Mataró. Acciones preferentes números 52 463/64 y 273 597/98. Denunciante: Revda. Comunidad y Colegio de Misioneros Hijos del Inmaculado Corazón de María de Barbastro. Acciones preferentes números 46 700/3, 4 779/81, 28 606 y 741 391. Denunciante. Revda. Comunidad de Madres Carmelitas Descalzas, de Vich. Acciones preferentes números 417 953/56. Denunciante: Señor arcipreste y presidente de la Comunidad de Presbíteros de Igualada, acciones preferentes números 132 173, 197 496, 203 173, 213 283 y 372 573. Denunciante: Revda. Comunidad de Presbíteros de San Jaime Apóstol, de Barcelona. Acciones preferentes números 53 063/63, 136 031, 175 135/36, 207 197/98, 297 733/34, 509 398, 362,833/35 y 278 631. Denunciante: Doña Ana Estarriol Punset. Acciones preferentes números 17 252, 30 077, 33 230, 34 128 y 373 560/61. Denunciante: Revda. Comunidad de Religiosas de San J[illegible] ... léh, de Barcelona. Obligaciones 5 ½ % números ...

Denunciante: Casa de Beneficencia ... rentes números 755 817/19 ...

Madrid, 29 de dic[illegible] ...

A B C. MIERCOLES 24 DE ENERO DE 1940.

Compañía Trasatlántica

BARCELONA

A los efectos de la ley de 1.° de junio del pasado año, se hace público que, por parte de los señores que a continuación se expresan, ha sido comunicada a esta Compañía la desposesión de los títulos siguientes de Obligaciones de la misma, de las emisiones que se dirán:

Obligaciones al 6 por 100, emisión 1.° de julio de 1920

Reverendo Pedro Pernal Pujol, una obligación, número 40.687.

Ilustrísimo Sr. Obispo de Madrid-Alcalá, 50 Obligaciones, números 91.101 a 91.150.

Reverenda M. Vicaria General de la Congregación de Hermanas Descalzas de la Tercera Orden de la B. V. M. del Carmen, de Tarragona, nueve Obligaciones, números 30.521/23, 30.545/50, 76.397/99 y 81.155.

Obligaciones al 6 por 100, emisión 1.° de junio de 1922

Don José Luis Arnalot, presbítero, cuatro Obligaciones, números 10.391, 94.750/51 y 94.796.

Lo que se hace público para conocimiento de todos aquellos a quienes pueda interesar, con advertencia de que si, en el término de tres meses, desde la inserción de este anuncio en el "Boletín Oficial del Estado", no hubiera sido notificada a esta Compañía la existencia de oposición, procederá a solicitar del Juzgado autorización para la anulación de los expresados títulos y expedición de los oportunos duplicados.

Barcelona, 2 de enero de 1940.—Por la Compañía Trasatlántica, el Subadministrador, Juan Ferrer y Puig.

In "Voice of Spain," No. 43, page 172, we published a facsimile from "ABC" of 7th January, 1940, showing the Church's holdings of shares in the Compañía Telefónica, and above we give a facsimile showing ecclesiastical shares in the Compañía Trasatlántica. ("ABC" 24/1/40). Jan 24. 40

Big Business and the Landlords profited by the restoration of Fascism in Spain; so did the Church. Here is the proof: the ownership by the church in stocks of commercial enterprises.

government officials in charge of operating the faltering economic machine, spent their profits with an abandon which was one failing that could not be charged against the old families.

"The Franco regime had, in fact, loaded still more privileged classes upon a suffering country. . . ."

British fascists most deeply involved in the Spanish war were the stockholders and directors of the Rio Tinto, the numerous light, power and street car companies of Madrid, Barcelona and other big cities.

In 1937 Franco sent the Duke of Alba to London to arrange for the financing of the fascist rebellion. Alba is also the British Duke of Berwick, a direct descendant of King James II. The founder of the Duchy of Berwick was an illegitimate son of the Duke of York (afterwards James II) and Arabella Churchill.

"The Duke began his mission with a well directed appeal to the Englishman's pocketbook," Frank R. Keeley cabled the *New York Herald Tribune* (January 9, 1938). "He declared in an interview: '. . . If there were no higher consideration, surely your markets and your invested capital in Spain should prompt you at least to be just to the Nationalist cause. . . . We offer commercial freedom. . . . You know that in the Republican zone great British concerns like, for example, Barcelona Traction, have been seized. . . . Ask the Rio Tinto people, ask your sherry trade. . . .' The Duke pointed out that England had a direct interest in Spain's mineral wealth."

Sir Oliver Lyttleton, member of the British Cabinet, chairman of the Board of Trade, was a director of Metallgesellschaft, of Frankfurt, Germany, which with Rio Tinto, Ltd., owns European Pyrites Co., Ltd. Other Rio Tinto directors are P. A. Cooper, director of the Bank of England and of CHADE, whose controlling stock was held by Von Gwinner of the Deutsches Bank of Berlin; F. D. Docker, vice-president of the Federation of British Industries—equivalent to our NAM and Chamber of Commerce; Sir Edward Wildbore Smith, director of the Suez.

In his speech at Burgos on April 19, 1939, Franco announced a Nationalist Syndicalist state which would restore the status quo ante 1931—the time the Republic was overthrown. The *New York Times* headline was: "Franco Reassures Owners of Capital."

DOCUMENTATION AND REFERENCES:

Thomas J. Hamilton, *Appeasement's Child,* Knopf, 1943.
Voice of Spain (Edited by Charles Duff), January 27, 1940.

CHAPTER VI

THE NAZI CARTEL PLOT IN AMERICA

ONLY THE little seditionists and traitors have been rounded up by the F. B. I. The real Nazi Fifth Column in America remains immune. And yet there is evidence that those in both countries who place profits above patriotism—and Fascism is based entirely upon profits although all its propaganda speaks of patriotism—have conspired to make America part of the Nazi Big Business system.

Thurman Arnold, as assistant district attorney of the United States, his assistant, Norman Littell, and several Congressional investigations, have produced incontrovertible evidence that some of our biggest monopolies entered into secret agreements with the Nazi cartels and divided the world among them. Most notorious of all was Alcoa, the Mellon-Davis-Duke monopoly which is largely responsible for the fact America did not have the aluminum with which to build airplanes before and after Pearl Harbor, while Germany had an unlimited supply. Of the Aluminum Corporation sabotage and that of other leading companies the press said very little, but several books have now been written out of the official record.

The document which follows, and which was first published by *In Fact* on July 13, 1942, goes much further than the mere cartel conspiracies of Big Business of both countries, because it has political clauses and points to a bigger conspiracy of money and politicians such as helped betray Norway and France and other lands to the Nazi machine. The most powerful fortress in America is the production monopolies, but its betrayal would involve, as it did in France, the participation of some of the most powerful figures of the political as well as the industrial world. The real Fifth Column is built on more than economic penetration, and much more than a few pro-Nazi preachers, red network manipulators, publishers of cheap and lying anti-Semitic pamphlets, and crackpots of all sorts. In Spain, where the term Fifth Column originated, it was not reported generally that the pro-Franco traitors within Madrid, who hid on roofs and murdered people in the streets, were—except for hired gunmen—members of the upper ruling class, the aristocrats, the landowners, and the members of the big business ruling families, and all the dead and wounded were working men.

Our press, which had nothing but praise for Mussolini for almost a generation, and which has always protected Fascism, Naziism and reaction in general by redbaiting every person and movement which is anti-Fascist, anti-Nazi and anti-reactionary, later made a grand noise over the traitors, seditionists and propagandists such as Coughlin, Fritz Kuhn and Pelley, who were the outstanding loudmouths at the time of Pearl Harbor. These small-fry fascisti and the Rev. Gerald Winrod and numerous others spread the same lies which they received from Hitler's World-Service (Welt-Dienst) of Erfurt; all these noisy propagandists and traitors, repeating Hitler's propaganda, did succeed in raising a huge smokescreen over America. Behind this artificial redbaiting, anti-Semitic, anti-New Deal fog of confusion and falsehood, however, there was a real Fifth Column of greater importance, the great owners and rulers of America who planned world domination through political and military Fascism, just as surely as Hitler did in Germany, and like groups and like leaders did in other countries. There is no reason to believe that the United States was the one exception to the spread of Fascism.

Nine men, two representing Hitler and several leading American industrialists, members of the Congress of the United States, and representatives of large business and political organizations met at the Hotel S........... in Boston, on November 23,

1937—at a time Hitler was trying out his Condor Legion, his divebombers, his new tanks and his Panzerdivisionen and his Blitzkrieg tactics on the poor and practically unarmed people of Spain—to formulate a working agreement by which American forces would join Nazi forces in the monopolistic control of the world's business and the political and military domination of the whole world.

The document which follows is a memorandum written at the conclusion of the meeting. The secretary who collected the notes from five of the persons present, each of whom contributed a part, was not versed in social, economic and political matters, but was impressed somehow with the importance of the event, and although her notes were taken away from her, she did succeed in retaining a carbon copy of the document. It had a long journey, went to Scotland, was copied by persons who realized its value, and brought back to the United States, where I was able to obtain it for the readers of *In Fact*. Here it is in its entirety:

Text of the Nazi-U. S. Cartel Memorandum

"The purpose of this draft is not to commit anyone who attended our formal conference. On the contrary, the memorandum should only retain and preserve the main topics of our conversation which, if desired, could be reported to proper organizations or individuals having the competence and privilege to draw practical conclusions or take appropriate steps.

"1. One of our German guests emphasized in his statement that he has no authority to give any official viewpoint. Nevertheless, his personal impression is after years-long service in connection with consular representations here that radical changes took place in America's foreign policy with regard to Germany. 'Our country,' he said, 'was accustomed to regard the United States as a source of friendly influence. Its contributions have alleviated Germany's burden under the peace treaty. President Hoover's step leading up to the complete elimination of the financial debt resulting from the Versailles treaty was considered always as characteristic manifestation of the American attitude towards the German people.

" 'The Roosevelt Administration has introduced important changes which tend to alter the German opinion concerning the American attitude. A certain agitation was allowed to interfere with German-American relations. Instead of cooperating in the opening of tremendous potential markets, Germany and America were forced to join hostile diplomatic camps. The potential markets China and Russia cannot be organized with(out) the active collaboration of American capital, however. World recovery is thus delayed.

" 'Germany is therefore willing to undertake everything humanly possible, in order to approach directly the financial and industrial leaders of the United States. The creation of a Japanese monopoly in the Far East is not desirable. Nor is for that matter a Chinese victory. The new Presidential elections must bring the United States on the side of the powers fighting for the reorganization of the world markets.

" 'To support those trends in the American public opinion, which definitely favor such a change, is the paramount task of the German foreign policy. This support does not only include the swinging of the German-American vote to a presidential candidate definitely sympathetic to the aforementioned aims, but also all possible cooperation with truly national forces. This, of course, cannot be construed as interference into American internal affairs, since the concrete form as well as the extent of that support must be determined by the political groups concerned.'

"2. Our second German guest, who was just recently appointed to a diplomatic post in this country, supplemented the above statements with the following points:

"Germany has been grossly misrepresented before the American public by Jewish propaganda. 'In order to clarify the picture,' he said, 'it is necessary to recall that Germany of the Republican period has thrown a remarkable confusion into the minds of the Germans. The state has been identified with some popular welfare institution. Creative capital was overburdened by the effects of a Utopian "social welfare" legislation. Unemployed insurance, sick, old-age, and death benefits, social security and war pensions meant terrible handicaps already. Trade union wages and hours have lifted productive costs above world standards.'

"What is the paramount achievement of National Socialism? 'The spirit of New Germany was conducive to a kind of national solidarity. Exaggerated demands and "social service" were reduced and production costs realistically brought into harmony with the requirements of competition on the world markets. This is what we have done. Not more and not less. It is true that many objections had to be overcome. The conception featuring the State as a supreme welfare agency had to be eradicated and a policy of increased production pursued instead. We had to silence therefore all centers from where class struggle was being fomented and imprison dangerous Utopians and sentimental philanthropists. It is true that Jewish propaganda was able to capitalize on some stern measures and slander New Germany before the world opinion. This is undoubtedly a detrimental fact. But we have gotten more by the rebirth of national solidarity and the cooperation of all for the same purpose.

" 'Without wishing to arouse any semblance of interfering with domestic questions in the United States, I cannot help mentioning that today's America presents a very close picture of Social-Democratic Germany. Unrealistic "welfare legislation" sponsored by the Administration, chaotic class struggles and wage demands absolutely out of any proportion, strong Jewish influence in the political, cultural and public life of the country are disquieting phenomena. We Germans, at any rate, are disquieted. We carry on a good work for world recovery and we know what potential danger an increasing red influence in the United States would mean for the whole world.

" 'Another disquieting characteristic of the situation is the lack of unity and clear-sighted leadership in the scattered national camp. You cannot start a strong concerted drive of all forces and agencies for the revival of American nationalism as long as this situation prevails.

" 'It is time to think seriously of the centralization of all forces of American nationalism and traditionalism. We Germans are seeking the cooperation of all American nationalists. Above all we believe in cooperating with the economic leaders of the country, whatever the suitable form of the cooperation may be. There is little comprehension on behalf of the United States Government, but in our belief there must be comprehension for our viewpoint on behalf of business.

" 'We would advance the idea of such informal conferences between responsible business and political leaders in order to consider questions of national and international importance affecting economic and, yes, political recovery.'

"The following opinions were expressed by the American participants of the conference:

"(a) The substance of the German suggestion amounts to changing the spirit of our nation as expressed by recent elections. That is possible but by no means easy. The people must become aware of the disastrous economic effects of the policies of the present Administration first. In the wake of the reorientation of the public opinion a vigorous drive must start in the press and radio. Technically it remains a question as to whether this drive may center around the Republican National Committee.

"(b) Farsighted business men will welcome conferences of this kind. A tremendous inspiration might come out of them. There is no reason why we should not learn of emergencies similar to those prevailing in our own country and the methods by which farsighted governments were trying to overcome them. It is also clear that manufacturers, who usually contributed to the campaigns of all candidates, must realize that their support must be reserved to one, in whose selection they must take an active hand.

"We must just as well recognize that the business leaders of this country must get together in the present emergency. By now they must have realized that they cannot expect much from Washington. We will have to resort to concrete planning.

"We can all agree that it is desirable to convince our business leaders that it is a good investment to embark on subsidizing our patriotic citizens' organizations and secure their fusion for the common purpose.

"Unified leadership with one conspicuous leader will be a sound policy. We will be grateful for any service our German friends may give us in this respect.

"(c) American foreign policy must be chiefly guarded against the danger of the sovietization of the Far East. More than ever we must supervise by Congress what the State Department does. Rapprochement with Germany, while unpopular, is a necessity, if we consider the strong pro-Soviet agitation going on and finding patronage in the United States. It is of the greatest importance that leading and influential figures in our business life and the policy-making bodies of both political parties should be appraised of this first conversation and prevailed upon to discuss the possibilities of a non-partisan cooperation on the subject."

Three Americans, Two Nazis Wrote Memo

The importance of the foregoing memorandum, the first of a proposed series of notes upon which a political-commercial pact between the Nazi regime and pro-fascist Americans could be arranged, was recognized at the time. Shortly afterwards a so-called "little Dies" committee, one of several flourishing in many states in imitation of and sincerest flattery to the big native Fascist Martin, was invited to make an investigation into the origins of the plot. But the informant was told by a Boston member of the Massachusetts redbaiting organization that this was not the stuff it was after, this memorandum, in fact, was "all right." In other words, plots by Nazis and their American friends were passed over or approved in Boston in just the same manner Nazi activities throughout the United States were passed up by Martin Dies, the fair-haired boy of the Goebbels broadcasting stations.

Each of the five parts, listed as 1 and 2, and a, b, and c, was written by a participant in the 1937 meeting. No. 1 is the work of Baron von Tippleskirch, No. 2 that of Baron von Killinger, "a" was written by a member of the U. S. Senate who was at this meeting, "b" by a representative of General Motors, and "c" by the representative of the DuPont interests.

In 1939, shortly before Germany invaded Poland and started the Global War from which the Nazis and their Quislings and Fifth Columns in all lands but Russia hoped to emerge rulers of the world, a diplomatic representative visited the seven Americans each of whom owned a copy of the foregoing memorandum. The importance of the document lies largely in the prominence and importance of the nine men who attended the conference and the forces and corporations they represented. Of these nine, their governments, and their corporations and other interests, I have information on five. These are:

Baron von Tippleskirch, Nazi consul general in Boston.

Manfred Freiherr von Killinger, then newly appointed consul general in San Francisco. Killinger was one of the eight men who participated in the murder of the Catholic statesman Erzberger in Republican Germany. The fact that he was found persona grata by our State Department, where Mr. Hull has a dozen pro-Fascist assistants functioning even today, is interesting. Killinger arrived just before Japan began her invasion of China, and conferred also with Japanese agents.

General Motors Representative. General Motors was completely involved in Nazi affairs. Until Pearl Harbor it was the owner of the Adam Opel A. G., worth more than $100,000,000. It had paid $30,000,000 for 80% of the stock. It had made 30% of Germany's peacetime passenger cars. After Hitler came into power, it began manufacturing the trucks and panzer division equipment with which Hitler waged war. In 10 years it had made a profit estimated at $36,000,000. But, since Hitler banned the export of capital, and American stockholders were thereby denied these dividends, General Motors invested at least $20,000,000 in other industries, all owned or controlled by Goering and other Nazi officials, and thus General Motors was completely affiliated with Nazi success or failure. (Source for statistics: *Poor's Manual.*)

Alfred P. Sloan, president of General Motors and director of DuPonts, was charged by the U. S. Treasury (June 29, 1937), just five months before the date of our memorandum, with cheating the government out of $1,921,587 in three years through establishing personal holding companies to dodge taxes.

DuPont Representative. The four most important facts about the DuPont Empire are:

a. that it controls General Motors, owning $197,000,000 of General Motors stock;

b. that it financed the Liberty League, Sentinels, Crusaders and one dozen native American fascist outfits;

c. that it knowingly and secretly and in violation of the U. S. and other laws, aided Hitler to arm for this war;

d. that the DuPonts betrayed military secrets to Hitler.

One great cartel of the merchants of death is called Dynamit-Aktien-Gesellschaft (DAG). Exhibit 456 in the Nye-Vandenberg munitions investigation shows that DuPonts not only own stock but a voting right and a voice in the management of the cartel. Exhibit 456 also shows DuPont has a financial interest in I. G. Farbenindustrie, the Nazi cartel which ties up with the Aluminum monopoly, Standard Oil, synthetic rubber, Sterling and other drug concerns.

The DuPont contract with DAG, British Imperial Chemicals and Nazi interests, as published by the munitions committee, says in part: "Each party agrees . . . upon making or obtaining any patented invention or discovery or acquiring any secret invention, to disclose in writing to the other party immediately, or in any event within six months thereafter, full particulars." It may be noted that according to Thurman Arnold the Nazified I. G. Farben obtained Standard Oil synthetic rubber patents, that Standard Oil did not receive all German patents, and that Standard Oil refused to make the German patents known to the U. S. Government even after Germany attacked.

The DuPonts knew that according to the Thyssen plan German Fascism was nothing more than a system by which the biggest German industries got control of the nation, smashing small business, seizing political rule. Wendell R. Swint, director of DuPont foreign relations, testified the DuPonts knew of the "scheme whereby industry would contribute to the (Nazi) Party Organization funds, and in fact industry is called upon to pay one-half percent of the annual wage or salary roll to the Nazi organization." (Munitions Hearing, Vol. XII.)

The relationship of the DuPonts to Nazi Germany—the story of how they armed Hitler with the help of Mr. Hoover—as exposed by the munitions investigation, gives valuable support to the foregoing.

On December 4, 1938, the Associated Press, Moscow bureau, sent out a list issued by the official Tass government press bureau of a "fascist clique" in the United States, which list follows with explanatory facts about each person:

"War Industry Magnate" DuPont. The official statement said the DuPonts had "great capital investments in fascist Germany."

William S. Knudsen, president of General Motors. Knudsen told a *New York Times* reporter (October 6, 1933) on arriving from Europe that Hitler's Germany was "the miracle of the 20th Century." Nevertheless paragraph "c" in our memorandum was not written by Knudsen, but by another G.M. official of equal prominence.

Colonel Lindbergh. In addition to collaborating with the British Cliveden Set, Lindbergh had written an article for the reactionary *Reader's Digest* stating Hitler's Aryan myth and other fascist doctrines.

Former President Herbert Hoover. (See Bibliography).

Ambassador to Britain Joseph P. Kennedy. Kennedy's secret report to Roosevelt on the war favored Britain going Fascist.

Henry Ford. (See Chapter IX.)

Bruce Barton. One of America's leading advertising men, head of an agency controlling $40,000,000, Barton has a tremendous influence on America's corrupt commercial press. Barton is a native Fascist. He praised "the sense of national obligation which Mussolini has recreated in the soul of Italy." He wrote: "Must we abolish the Senate and have a dictatorship to do it? I sometimes think it would be almost worth the cost." (*American Magazine,* June, 1930. Barton objected to ideas he had written being used against him when he ran for the Senate. He said they were years old. But when he wrote an endorsement of Mussolini, the Duce had already murdered thousands of persons, destroyed the labor unions, outlawed civil liberties.)

Senator Arthur H. Vandenberg. As part of the Nye-Vandenberg Munitions inquiry, Senator Vandenberg went after the DuPonts and exposed their relations with Hitler. This was not a hardship for Vandenberg. He has always been Ford's friend, and Ford was the rival of General Motors, which the DuPonts controlled. By Mussolini's definition of Fascism as Reaction, Vandenberg qualifies as one of America's leading Fascists. In his Congressional record are votes against the Wagner Act (the Magna Carta of American labor), the Wages and Hours Act, TVA, AAA. In opposing the Black-Connery Wages and Hours Bill, three months before the date of the foregoing memorandum, Vandenberg said it would make for a "centralized, authoritarian state with its tyranny of oppressive, government-blessed monopolies." In 1936 Vandenberg had urged a coalition of reactionary Republicans and reactionary Democrats to block the New Deal.

On November 27, 1937, Captain Fritz Wiedemann, Hitler's personal adjutant, en route to the U. S., was exposed in Paris as heading a Nazi political mission whose purpose was to seek the support of leading American reactionaries and pro-Fascists to further Hitler's aggressive aim in Europe.

Mme. Genevieve Tabouis, militant editor of *L'Oeuvre,* one of the 2% of the French press which was not bribed, wrote in her paper that day that it was the object of the Nazi mission to make contact with Senator Vandenberg of Michigan.

The United Press cabled a similar statement from Paris that day, adding that it was based on information from a reliable source in Berlin.

The *New York Herald Tribune,* which receives United Press service, suppressed the item concerning Vandenberg.

Mme. Tabouis stated that Germany was seeking assurances from the United States and Britain in order "to leave her hands free in the East, particularly concerning expansion in Central Europe towards Russia." (Note: Mme. Tabouis, also called "Cassandra," was proved absolutely right when Germany attacked Russia in June, 1941.) Mme. Tabouis continued:

> "The aim of the mission is to try to convince the American people that Germany wants peace but desires facilities in Central Europe. It also wants to show that Germany's great aim is opposition to Communism throughout the world. This mission will enter into close relations with Senator Vandenberg. . . ."

DOCUMENTATION AND REFERENCES:

Guenther Reimann, *Patents for Hitler,* Vanguard, 1942.

Joseph Borking and Charles A. Welsh, *Germany's Master Plan,* Duell, Sloan & Pearce, 1943.

Munitions Industry, 73rd Congress, Part 9 (Hoover and the Du-Ponts, pp. 2138ff; 2150; 2169-70; 2242.)

CHAPTER VII

NAM: THE MEN WHO FINANCE AMERICAN FASCISM

THE TWO corporations which were part of the Nazi cartel plot in the United States are two of the main vertebrae of the backbone of American Fascism. Lammot DuPont and Alfred P. Sloan, Jr., of the DuPont Empire and General Motors respectively, have been exposed by Congressional committees as subsidizers of fascist organizations and movements. Both corporations and both men are also among the top flight rulers of the National Association of Manufacturers.

Before producing a small fraction of the documentation—it would require volumes to present a real indictment—showing that the NAM is the center of American Fascism, and that its leaders are the Thyssens, Flicks and Voegelers of America, this statement must be made about the organization.

The NAM is something like a nation, like a people—say the Finns, or the Germans. Our country passed through a great emotional phase which favored the Finns, and is naturally emotionally set against the Germans, nevertheless—thanks largely to the press—the American people as a whole refused to accept the fact that Finland has been in fascist hands for a long period of its independent history, and also refuses to accept the view that there are millions of good and innocent Germans. The facts are that both Finland and Germany are in the hands of fascist rulers, that a large proportion of the population in each country accepts Fascism, and that it is necessary in the war against Fascism to destroy not only the leadership but as large a part as possible of its armed might in the field. But it is the leadership which is totally vicious, and it is an unfortunate fact which apparently cannot be changed by the innocent, no matter how many of them there are, that rulers and ruled have a united destiny.

It may therefore be true that the majority of the estimated 8,000 members of the NAM are as innocent as the Finnish man-in-the-street, or the German farmer or industrial worker, of the crimes of Fascism, but it is truer yet that the inner group which rules the NAM is just as vicious a clique as the one Thyssen organized to put Hitler into power.

There are actually three groups in the NAM, as the National Maritime Union's organ, *The Pilot,* once pointed out:

"The large majority of NAM members are reasonably assured that a United Nations victory is in their own and the country's best interests. A smaller group moves along with the feelings strongest at the time and yields one way or the other if pressured. A still smaller but very much more powerful group is in the saddle now and its program is remarkable for a nation at war.

"The group swinging the NAM whip is headed by Frederick C. Crawford, who has no beef with the Axis. He has the perfect background for a model version of a homegrown Fascist. During the middle thirties he was active as a director in Associated Industries, a Cleveland strikebreaking agency which tried to doctor up its records when the La Follette Committee went to work on it. The F. B. I. proved that this fink outfit paid out to a labor spy agency . . . which means he okayed the hiring of goons, spies, thugs, and stoolies, and financed the use of tear gas, sawed-off shotguns and blackjacks, etc.

"Mussolini got splashed with Crawford's praise after a trip to Europe in 1939. About Hitler he said: 'What difference does it make if the dictatorship of Germany is consuming one-fourth of production for military grandeur, or whether the bureaucracy of the New Deal is consuming one-fourth of production to maintain itself? . . .'

"Crawford's fighting a war . . . but it's a war against President

Roosevelt, against the American people, and against the coming defeat of Hitler."

Crawford, DuPont, Sloan and a handful of others boss the NAM. Several years ago, when it had only half its present membership, the La Follette Committee reported that "about 207 companies, or approximately 5% of the NAM, are in a position to formulate the policies." Actually a dozen or so native Fascists control the most powerful private organization in the history of America, but they control it as absolutely as Hitler, Mussolini, Hirohito and other Fascists controlled their own nations (until their downfall); they are just as responsible for its political and social activities, and the entire NAM is just as guilty (or innocent) as the mass of people is in each fascist nation. (In this connection it may be pointed out that whereas a German cannot very well quit Germany in wartime, although there are Germans who have done better than that by becoming guerrilla fighters, it is easy for an American business man or corporation to quit the fascist NAM on the spur of the moment, and General Mills, for one example, did do so when one of its presidents, a Mr. Witherow, said we were not fighting the war to put TVA's on the Danube.)

From the foregoing and following facts the reader may decide for himself whether the NAM, which represents the best part of American industry, and whose annual meetings are said to represent $60,000,000,000, is to be blamed as a whole, or whether a distinction is to be made between its Fuehrer (plural) and its following. But there can be no question about certain things, and the first and most important of all is that the NAM, which had been merely one of many trade associations from 1895 on, became a national force when it became the spearhead of the anti-labor movement at its convention in New Orleans in April, 1903.

The history of this campaign of the biggest industries of America to prevent the majority of the American people from forming any sort of organization which would improve working conditions and raise the standard of living of the nation, is punctuated by three Congressional investigations which show up the NAM for exactly what it is: the counterpart of the fascist organizations of the fascist nations of Europe and Asia.

1. The Garrett Committee disclosed the existence of the NAM lobby in Washington, its "secretive" and "reprehensible" activities, its "questionable and disreputable" means of defeating Congressmen who refused to obey it, and its general criminal character in using money in a corrupt manner to fight the labor unions.

2. The La Follette Investigations into the violations of the rights of free speech and the criminal actions used against labor established the fact that certain corporations—almost without exception leading members of the NAM—employed poison gas and machine guns in their plants, also spies, thugs, stool pigeons and murderers and other racketeers; also that the NAM corrupted public opinion in America by using the largest network of propaganda.

3. The O'Mahoney Monopoly Investigation showed in one of its reports that 200 industrial and 50 financial families own, control and rule America and that of the industrial families 13 are the most powerful. Ford is not a member of the NAM; the others are also its heaviest subsidizers. Another report shows that the NAM uses its money and power for its own profits, and against the general welfare of the people of the United States.

NAM Guilty of Bribery

The Garrett Committee's work is better known as the Mulhall investigation, thanks to the fact that "Colonel" Martin M. Mulhall, who was one of the chief secret lobbyists of the NAM, consented to expose that organization and did so in a series of articles which began running in the *New York World* June 29, 1913.

Mulhall's charges dealt chiefly with the NAM's corruption of members of Congress. The reader should note that Mulhall had been employed in 1903, the year the NAM became the chief labor-busting outfit in the country, and the year it decided to become a power in politics in Washington. It is still that power. What Mulhall proved is that it was not content to get anti-labor legislation through Congress as it is today by putting up the money to elect members, but that it passed out cold cash in a criminal manner.

Speaker Champ Clark could not turn deaf ears or blind eyes to the national scandal, although few wanted the *World's* charges aired. A committee headed by Majority Leader Finis J. Garrett of Tennessee finally began a 4-month inquiry and published 60 volumes of findings condemning the NAM as a crooked outfit.

In other words, the 10 years during which the NAM employed Mulhall, James A. Emery and other lobbyists, were also the 10 years it devoted its time to fighting labor, and coincidentally the 10 years in which it committed criminal acts for which private individuals would have gone to the penitentiary.

Said William J. McDonald, Michigan Progressive, of the Mulhall exposé of the bribery of Congressmen by the NAM:

> "The naive effrontery shown upon the witness stand by officers of the NAM in assuming that the committee would accept at face value the bald denials and ridiculous evasion and perversion of the meaning of actions all too plainly corrupt and sinister . . . cannot be permitted to pass without mention. Their plainly shown attitude was that the American Congress was considered by them as their legislative department and was viewed with the same arrogant manner in which they viewed their other employees, and that those legislators who dare to oppose them would be disciplined in the same manner in which they were accustomed to discipline recalcitrant employees."

Of the NAM lobby Representative McDonald, who was the backbone of the Garrett investigation of Mulhall and Emery, NAM lobbyists, said:

> "They did, by the expenditure of exorbitant sums of money, aid

and attempt to aid in the election of those who they believed would readily serve their interests, and by the same means sought to and did accomplish the defeat of others whom they opposed. In carrying out these multifarious activities, they did not hesitate as to means, but made use of any method of corruption found to be effectual . . . they instituted a new and complete system of commercialized treachery."

Caught and exposed as bribers and corrupters of the American Congress—and incidentally of the American Way of Life about which it brags—the NAM decided at that time to reorganize and to concentrate on another way in which to corrupt the American people to its way of doing business. It decided to corrupt public opinion. In doing so it planned on using every available method but concentrating chiefly on corrupting the American press. It was highly successful. It is still the greatest force controlling the American press today.

Hired Gunmen and Hired Editors

The real picture of American Fascism emerges from the numerous volumes of reports of the Committee on Education and Labor, better known as the La Follette investigation.

There is only one major difference between the Fascism practiced by the NAM and the Fascism practiced by its modern leaders, Hitler and Mussolini: the latter established by force what the former either wholly or partly succeeded in establishing by other means.

Hitler confiscated the treasuries of the labor unions and later established the so-called Labor Front which put the workmen of Germany in a state between serfdom and slavery, while Mussolini organized his so-called corporations in which labor and capital were supposed to have equal rights, whereas in truth capital runs Italy and the living standards of labor have been reduced to their worst point in modern history. The NAM could not destroy labor by official decrees, but it fought labor with its hired gunmen, thugs, racketeers, gangsters and murderers; it did employ poison gas in strikes, and machine guns; it did shoot and kill; and it did poison the minds of the majority of the American people by carrying on a campaign against labor and especially against labor unions, in 1,995 of the 2,000 daily newspapers of the country. The NAM needs no lessons in the way to corrupt a people by propaganda; it was in this business long before Dr. Goebbels came to power.

In the hearings of one day—March 2, 1938, to be exact—the following points were made for which documentary evidence was later entered into the record:

1. That the NAM is directed, controlled and financed by only 207 firms, each giving it more than $2,000; that the leading firms are General Motors, DuPont, Chrysler, Weir's National Steel and the Pennsylvania Railroad.

2. That the leading contributors to the NAM and the leading directors are also the leading contributors to a number of purely fascist, anti-Semitic and reactionary organizations such as the American Liberty League, the Crusaders, the Sentinels of the Republic, National Economy League, Farmers' Independence League and Johnstown Citizens Committee, the last named a vigilante outfit later exposed as secretly started by the Mavor with $50,000 received from Bethlehem Steel.

3. That these 207 firms purchased 60% of all the tear gas used in the United States; they also used the majority of spies in industry, the majority of strikebreakers, the majority of criminals. The NAM is associated with the Metal Trades Association, the Associated Industries of Cleveland (and other large cities) and other similar organizations which have taken the leading part in industrial espionage and the use of violence in labor troubles.

4. That the NAM ran the largest propaganda network in America; that it worked this propaganda campaign in secrecy, and that it employed deceit as a method—these are actual quotations from a summary published later. This point is especially important because right now the NAM is engaging in a larger campaign than ever in its history to poison the minds of the American people so that it will accept "free enterprise" rather than any plan for social justice and social security.

The foregoing charges were made by Robert Wohlforth, secretary of the La Follette Committee, which immediately began grilling witnesses it had called, notably W. B. Weisenberger, a vice-president, Noel Sargent, the secretary, J. A. Emery, chief counsel, and John C. Gall, attorney. The day was notable for the fact that these NAM officials made certain statements which were immediately proven absolute falsehoods after Senators La Follette and Thomas produced documentary evidence from the NAM files (which had been seized) proving the mendacity of the defenders of this native-fascist outfit.

In establishing the fact that the NAM was founded primarily to fight labor, and that it was still doing so, Senator La Follette introduced a statement published in 1904 in an NAM magazine called *American Industries*. In objecting to the only large union of its time—1904—this publication said:

"We are not opposed to good unionism if such exists anywhere. The American Federation brand of unionism, however, is un-American, illegal and indecent."

(On the same subject, the usual NAM statement that it was not against unions but insisted on unions that were "properly conducted," the leading humorist of the time, Finley Peter Dunn, wrote:

("Shure," said Mr. Dooley, "if properly conducted. An' there we are; an' how would they have thim conducted? No strikes, no rules, no contracts, no scales, hardly iny wages an' dam few members.")

Most Un-American Force in America

The O'Mahoney Monopoly Investigation did not disclose anything as sensational regarding the NAM as its bribery of Congressmen or its use of gangsters and poison gas, but its scores of volumes of evidence furnish a complete and unanswerable indictment of the entire American Big Business system. (The two most valuable volumes for the lay reader are Monograph 29 which deals with the 200 ruling industrial families, and Monograph 26 which reveals the NAM as the most powerful lobby and most sinister force in America; they are sold by the Superintendent of Documents, Washington, D. C., at $2 and 25c respectively.)

When the O'Mahoney committee released its Monograph 26 the newspapers of the nation, always happy to suppress anything that is critical of the hand that feeds it—that is, Big Business, through the medium of advertising—obliged by refraining from mentioning the matter at all, or, like the *New York Times,* published a report that lobbying had been condemned but omitted the name of the NAM.

The *Times,* which did publish a column story, and therefore did publish much more than other papers, nevertheless omitted most of the following quotations—which will give the reader a taste of the tremendously important material Monograph 26 contains. (The figures in parentheses refer to the page numbers):

"The American people are confronted with the problem of who shall control the government" (1). The monograph then discusses the big pressure group, notably the American Legion lobby, farmers, peace groups, but concludes that the National Association of Manufacturers, the Chamber of Commerce, and their agents, the lawyers' associations, the newspaper publishers' associations, rule the country.

"From the beginning, business has been intent upon wielding economic power and, where necessary, political control for its own purposes. . . . Even today, when the purposeful use of government power for the general welfare is more widely accepted than at any time in our history, government does not begin to approach the fusion of power and will characteristic of business" (1). Everyone is fighting for power, for control, in Washington, but "by far the largest and most important of these groups is to be found in 'business' . . . as dominated by the 200 largest non-financial and the 50 largest financial corporations, and the employer and trade associations into which it and its satellites are organized" (3). The 200 non-financial corporations in 1935 controlled $60,000,000,000 of physical assets. The

DEATH TO
ORGANIZED LABOR
DEATH TO
LABOR LAWS
S'DEATH!
$$$$$$
FREE
ENTERPRISE
FREE
PROFITS
NAM
BOOOOOOOOO
LOUDER AND FUNNIER
ROTTEN
THE PATIENT PUBLIC

march of America toward public betterment "has been hindered, obstructed and at times apparently completely stopped by pressure groups" (5).

"Business . . . has fought . . . government ownership. (5) Through the press, public opinion and pressure groups it is possible to influence the political process. . . . Both press and radio are, after all, 'big business' and even when they possess the highest integrity, they are the prisoners of their own beliefs."

Business, continues the report, operates on the principle that $60,000,000,000 can't be wrong.

"In this connection the business orientation of the newspaper press is a valuable asset. In the nature of things public opinion is usually well disposed toward business. . . . Newspapers have it in their power materially to influence public opinion on particular issues. . . . With others, editorializing is practiced as a matter of course. And even where editors and publishers are men of the highest integrity, they are owners and managers of big business enterprises, and their papers inevitably reflect, at least to some extent, their economic interest. When organized business deliberately propagandizes the country, using newspaper advertising as one medium, the press is a direct means of channeling business views into the public mind. . . . Lawyers have remade constitutional guarantees in the image of business. . . . The law, the newspaper press, and the advertising professions have all helped business by spreading this changed conception of the Jeffersonian idea" (10).

In other words, Business, using lawyers, the press and advertising, has undermined Jeffersonian democracy.

The report names the business pressure lobbies, notably the National Association of Manufacturers, U. S. Chamber of Commerce, Edison Electric Institute (successor to N.E.L.A.), Association of Life Insurance Presidents, American Iron and Steel Institute, American Petroleum Institute, American Bankers Association, American Investment Bankers Association, American Bar Association, and adds: "Through the American Newspaper Publishers Association [Lords of the Press] the country's daily newspapers join their strength for business and against government." This is a most damning indictment. It did not appear in the *Times*. But the indictment against the corporations and the press goes even further.

"Public policy in the field of industrial relations has been formulated by Congress over the bitter opposition of organized industry, an opposition which is still continuing in a determined effort to change that policy. The economic power of business and the 'educational' persuasiveness of its newspaper, advertising, and legal allies enabled it between the years 1933 and 1937 to frustrate the initial efforts of the Federal Government to regulate labor relations. (81) The NAM and the C. of C. are as one in their opposition to the N.L.R.A. . . . The American Bar Association . . . indicated its fundamental community of interest with business. The American Newspaper Publishers Association shares a similar community of interest (p. 82)." This was also suppressed in the *Times*.

"National Association of Manufacturers' President Lund [Listerine Lund] in a press release on September 7, 1933, urged 'the strongest possible employer opposition to union organization' (97). Business has managed to maintain most of its control of industrial relations despite the efforts of labor and government to lessen it. . . . The staying power of corporate business, its resources and ability to give aid and assistance in the fields of law, of the newspaper press, and of advertising, have proved powerful weapons in this struggle, and the intensity of the battle on the labor relations field since 1933 has indicated their effectiveness."

Pages 171 and 172 of the report show how Big Business betrayed the nation for profits in the European War, and how in 1940 "business displayed much of the same attitude. . . . Profits, taxes, loans, and so forth appeared more important to business than getting guns, tanks, and airplane motors into production."

"Speaking bluntly the government and the public are 'over a barrel' when it comes to dealing with business in time of war or other crisis. Business refuses to work except on terms which it dictates. . . . In effect this is blackmail."

And what is the final conclusion?

"Democracy in America is on the defensive. In the preceding pages it has been shown that pressure groups as now operating usually fail to promote the general welfare."

Since the NAM has been named as the most powerful of the pressure groups, and the publishers' association one of its two agents, the minor one being the bar association, it is merely putting two and two together to arrive at the statement that Big Business is the main enemy of the general welfare of the American people, and the press the main weapon of this enemy.

NAM's New Propaganda Agency: N. I. I. C.

The main objective of the NAM today is the corruption of public opinion. Of course, the organization calls it "enlightenment" or the spreading of the doctrine of "free enterprise," but it is nevertheless propaganda, and since it is aimed to insure the private profits of the few, as against the general welfare of the many, it is propaganda that corrupts.

The La Follette investigation showed that, after it was caught bribing Congressmen to pass anti-labor laws, the NAM changed its tactic to cooperating with the editors and publishers of all the newspapers of the country, all but one of them being dependent upon advertising and all but three or four of them having a record of journalistic prostitution.

Here is a short summary of the findings of the La Follette Committee on the NAM propaganda campaign:

1. *Daily newspapers.* Realizing that public thought is shaped to a large degree by the newspapers, NAM Public Information program regularly covered the newspaper field to industry's advantage.

a. *Bulletin to newspaper editors.* Publishers and editorial writers were furnished with propaganda entitled *Voice of American Industry.*

b. *Daily comic feature.* "Uncle Abner Says" is big business, anti-labor, propaganda placed in papers by NAM but the public is not told that fact.

c. *News stories.* NAM sent spot news releases to local papers, Associated Press, United Press, International News Service, news syndicates.

2. *Weekly newspapers.* More than 5,000 weeklies propagandized regularly.

3. *Advertising.*

a. Full page ads in newspapers favoring industry.

b. Outdoor ads. "The American Way," etc.

4. *Radio.* Good will for industry was propagandized in many ways:

a. NAM program, "The American Family Robinson."

b. Foreign language transcriptions.

c. Propaganda furnished news commentators.

5. *Motion Pictures.* One of the many NAM propaganda projects was called "Men and Machines" with narration by Lowell Thomas.

6. *Secretly bought columnists.* Example: George E. Sokolsky, put on $1,000 a month payroll while writing column syndicated by the *New York Herald Tribune.*

7. *Bought college professors.* "You and your nation's affairs," or "Six Star Service." The La Follette Report said contributors to this service included Gus W. Dyer, professor of economics, Vanderbilt University; Eliot Jones, professor of transportation, Stanford University; Walter Spahr, secretary, Economists National Committee on Monetary Policy; Clarence W. Fackler, assistant professor of economics, New York University.

Articles of the following writers appeared only in the first few weeks; Neil Carothers, director, College of Business Administration, Lehigh University; James S. Thomas, president, Clarkson College of Technology; T. N. Carver, professor emeritus, Harvard.

Contributions from the following were added: Harley L. Lutz, professor of public finance, Princeton; Erik McK. Erickson, associate professor of history, University of Southern California; J. E. LeRossignol, dean, college of business administration, University of Nebraska.

Whereas the National Electric Light Association (N.E.L.A.) spent about $25,000,000 each year (sometimes as high as $29,000,000) to turn public opinion against municipal and public ownership of light and power plants, the NAM lobby got free ads because it was able to blackmail the newspapers, radio, movies and billboard corporations with threats that its membership would withdraw commercial advertising already placed.

The La Follette report tells in detail how labor was smeared, how everything for the general benefit of the American people was labeled "radical," "red," "unsound" and how men and organizations opposed to the corrupt Big Business program of the NAM were smeared as "propagandists," "impatient reformers" and "disturbers." The NAM did not hesitate, says the report, to present an "uncritical and false picture." The aim of the NAM was the same as that of the old N.E.L.A.: to pervert the public mind so that it accepted the big corporation program although that program was and is a program for the benefit of 250 ruling families and the enemy of 52,000,000 wage earners. This is happening today.

The new propaganda agency of the NAM is called the National Industrial Information Committee (N.I.I.C.). In 1942, when I discovered its campaign to raise $1,000,000 for a fund to fight labor, it denied that it had any relation with the NAM although it was part of the latter's office, had the same phone, and was operated by the same agents. In 1943, however, it sent a letter to its sustainers saying that it was still affiliated, but was becoming more and more a separate organization. These technicalities are of no importance. What is important is that the worst Fascists of the reactionary clique which bosses the NAM are the very men who are behind this new propaganda movement.

The N.I.I.C. claims it has 350 of the leading industrialists in its ranks. It was prompted to begin a big campaign in 1942 because the various Congressional committees, notably the Truman and O'Mahoney, and numerous official reports, notably those of Toland and Thurman Arnold, had exposed American

Big Business as linked to Nazi Germany in the cartels, as actually doing business with Hitler and planning to do so in case of war, and to resume doing business should a war involve the two countries. Corporations—Standard Oil for one—had been branded traitors in Senate hearings, and the news could not be suppressed that it was due to the monopoly arrangements with I. G. Farbenindustrie that America had a shortage of aluminum for making airplanes, no synthetic rubber at all, a lack of tungsten, carboloy and other vital materials, no substitute for quinine (atabrine), etc. The very same corporations and men who had been exposed by Monograph 29 as ruling America—notably Mellon—were shown to be the men of the Nazi cartels. And on top of this scandal the labor press was proving that Big Business was refusing to convert to war, that Big Money was on a sit-down strike, and that, in short, the men of wealth and power were the traitors while the men in the fields, factories and workshops were working to win the war.

It is true that the *New York World-Telegram* and the 18 other papers controlled by Roy Howard of the Scripps-Howard press, and the 19 papers controlled by America's No. 1 Nazi, William Randolph Hearst, did their best to whitewash Aluminum Corporation, Standard Oil, General Motors and General Electric and all the other members of the Nazi trusts. But it is also true that the scandal was so big that enough of it became generally known to cover (not smear) Big Business with the truthful *muck* of Fascism. Before and after Pearl Harbor America's foremost enemy in the war against Fascism was the ruling clique of the NAM.

Said the N.I.I.C. appeal which asked every business to pay a sum to its propaganda fund in proportion to its income:

"Why war increases your need of the N.I.I.C.: Because winning the war must mean also restoring a method of living that is traditionally and characteristically American. This the American people must be told and retold. . . . Because full public confidence in management's motives is an essential raw material to the fabric of maximum arms production and victory. This confidence must be built and held. Because private enterprise must be built firmly into the people's ideals for the postwar world."

This statement also invites anti-labor, anti-progressive corporations to help keep America ignorant of the great liberal and democratic movement throughout the world which is based on the belief that all democratic peoples after overthrowing the main enemy of democracy, Fascism, can remake the world for the benefit of the millions of men who were at the front, instead of the special interests represented by the N.I.I.C.

Native Fascists of N.I.I.C.

A glance at the list of officers and executive committee of the N.I.I.C. reveals that whereas many NAM leaders, who are also America's biggest industrialists, now working on a victory program are not on the N.I.I.C. list, the most notorious anti-liberals and labor-fighters are running the new propaganda outfit. Here are some of the N.I.I.C. executives:

J. H. Rand, Jr., President of Remington Rand. Originator of the Mohawk Valley Formula, the most notorious strikebreaking technique in our history, exposed by La Follette Committee. It was Rand who instructed all manufacturers to use the newspapers for propagating big anti-labor lies during strikes, and to start the "back-to-work" movements.

Walter D. Fuller, president of Curtis Publishing Company, ex-president of the NAM and still director. Fuller is largely responsible for the pro-fascist attitude of his *Saturday Evening Post,* which in the 1920's began a series of articles praising Mussolini and which more recently published two native-Nazi articles, "The Case Against the Jew" and "Will Labor Lose the War?" In his listing of 6 American fascist men and organizations, Attorney General (now Justice) Jackson denounced the *Saturday Evening Post* as un-American, anti-democratic. (Source: *Law Society Journal,* Boston, November, 1940.)

H. W. Prentis, Jr., ex-president NAM, president of Armstrong Cork Co., pro-Franco, pro-Fascist. Listed as un-American, anti-democratic by Mr. Justice Jackson for attacking American democratic institutions at the time he was president of the NAM. Mr. Justice Jackson quoted Prentis saying: "Hope for the future of our republic does not lie in more and more democracy."

J. Howard Pew, president of the Sun Oil Company (Sunoco), and chairman of the N.I.I.C. Exposed by Senator Gillette as main subsidizer of Republican Party in Pennsylvania. The Pew family owns $75,628,000 of Sunoco stock. According to A. H. Sulzberger, publisher and half owner of the *New York Times,* Pew arranged the 1936 Sunoco advertising only for papers favoring Landon. He withdrew a big ad contract from the *New York Times.* In 1940 the *Times* went Republican. The *C.I.O. News* (Jan. 27, 1941) accused the Pew family of anti-labor tactics in the Sun Shipbuilding strike when the Pews called out the fire department to fight strikers. During the Liberty League investigation it was disclosed that the Pews subsidized the Sentinels, Crusaders, and other native fascist subsidiaries of the League and the fascist Associated Farmers of California. When the U. S. Government needed auxiliary ships for the Navy, J. Howard and Joseph N. Pew, who had given $90,000 to the Willkie campaign, got the same sum for their 12-year-old yacht Egeria. (At the same time the U. S. got several yachts for nothing—Major Bowes, S. P. Loomis, W. P. Murphy, Joseph Seaman and Robert S. Herick—but paid $180,000 for H. E. Manville's, $275,000 for W. B. Thompson's—Source: Pearson & Allen, January 20, 1941.)

When Senator Black's lobby investigation committee seized the records of the Sentinels of the Republic, it found letters of its executives, W. Cleveland Runyon and Alexander Lincoln, president, saying, "The New Deal is Communist," "the Jewish threat is a real one" and "the old-line Americans of $1200 a year want a Hitler." Backers of Sentinels: Pitcairn Family, $91,000; J. Howard Pew, Sunoco, $6,000.

Jasper E. Crane, vice-president DuPonts, and Lammot du Pont.

Charles R. Hook, president of the American Rolling Mills, and ex-president of the NAM. Hook is also one of the backers of the Committee to Uphold Constitutional Government, a strike-breaking, anti-labor native fascist outfit in which chain publisher Gannett is a leading figure and former German agent Rumely an organizer. On January 8, 1942, the National Labor Relations Board ordered Hook to disestablish his company union, accused Hook of violating the Wagner Act by vilifying, ridiculing and denouncing unions, the C.I.O., and labor organizers; espionage of union meetings, pilfering labor records; threatening workers; enticing workers to resign from unions; sponsoring organizations of employees devoted to combating unions. During the trial Hook's speeches before the NAM were read in which he pleaded for peace, unity, friendship with the unions.

Colby M. Chester, and William B. Warner, respectively heads of General Foods and *McCall's* magazine, both former heads of NAM, now vice-chairman and member of the executive committee of the N.I.I.C., were president and vice-president respectively of the NAM when the La Follette investigation found it guilty of employing an army of spies, attacking the Wagner Act, and being the "fountainhead of attacks on labor."

NAM Against Victory

On September 17, 1942, the resolutions committee of the National Association of Manufacturers met in a secret session at the Hotel Pennsylvania, New York, to prepare a program for the December NAM convention. What took place in that closed meeting amounts to a conspiracy against the government, against the people, and against winning the war. The objectives of the NAM, overriding all other considerations, are: more profits, now and after the war, the destruction of the labor movement, and the wiping out of all New Deal progress.

The delegates heard its research expert, Dr. Claude Robinson, report that the public, when asked which group was most guilty of war profiteering, was answering: big business, 49%; government officials, 40%; labor leaders 11%. To the question as to what was the main concern of the people today, the answers were predominantly: "The winning of the war; next important, unemployment in the postwar period." The NAM delegates, after considerable discussion, then took their stand—directly opposed to that of the people as reported to them: Thirty-five delegates voted for dealing with war and postwar problems on an equal basis, fifteen for emphasizing "winning the war" while dealing with postwar issues, and only three for "winning the war" as the only problem for 1943.

Here are some of the things said at their closed meeting of the NAM resolutions committee:

When James D. Cunningham, president of Republic Flow Meters Co., urged the NAM 1943 program to stick to one issue, winning the war, because "if we don't win the war, there won't be a postwar," Lammot du Pont, chairman of the board of E. I. du Pont de Nemours & Co., Liberty Leaguer, supporter of native fascist organizations, replied:

> "Deal with the government and the rest of the squawkers the way you deal with a buyer in a seller's market! If the buyer wants to buy, he has to meet your price. Nineteen hundred and twenty-nine to 1942 was the buyer's market—we had to sell on their terms. When the war is over, it will be a buyer's market again. But this is a seller's market. They want what we've got. Good. Make them pay the right price for it. The price isn't unfair or unreasonable. And if they don't like the price, why don't they think it over?"
>
> "The way to view the issue is this: Are there common denominators for winning the war and the peace? If there are, then, we should deal with both in 1943. What are they? We will win the war (a) by reducing taxes on corporations, high income brackets, and increasing taxes on lower incomes; (b) by removing the unions from any power to tell industry how to produce, how to deal with their employees, or anything else; (c) by destroying any and all government agencies that stand in the way of free enterprise."

DuPont's voice was the dominating one at the sessions. The chairman of the committee was Crawford of Thompson Products.

Others who took a leading part were Rand, who was once

the chairman of Charles E. Coughlin's Committee for the Nation and Luther B. Stein, southern bourbon and official of the Belknap Hardware Co. Certain important financial and industrial organizations were not represented. These include J. P. Morgan, Rockefeller, Chrysler, General Electric and Westinghouse interests. Several others, who were represented, opposed the program dictated in the main by DuPont and Crawford.

Other notable utterances by delegates not yet publicly named:

"If we are to come out of this war with a Marxist brand of National Socialism, then I say negotiate peace now and bring Adolf over here to run the show. He knows how. He's efficient. He can do a better job than any of us can and a damned sight better job than Roosevelt, who is nothing but a left-wing bungling amateur."

"We've got Roosevelt on the run. We licked production and the Axis is licking him. The finger points where it belongs. We'll keep him on the run. Let's spend some real money this year, what the hell!—it'll only cost us 20 per cent, the rest would go in taxes anyway."

A big business delegate told of being asked by F.D.R. to join an unofficial economic committee of five to work out postwar plans, involving visits abroad. "I kidded Washington along until I found out all I wanted to know and then begged off because of other activities," he laughed.

A lot of other things were said, all heading up to the great conspiracy being engineered now by the NAM, which it intends to carry on to the next election. This includes:

A fight against management-labor committees (credited by government officials with a prominent part in getting war production going); driving women out of industry after the war; freeing Wall Street speculation from all restrictions; a propaganda program in high schools and colleges; wiping out of all social agencies set up under the New Deal. Together with this program goes the clear threat to sabotage war production, and to seize on every development to undermine the President's prestige, unless the NAM's demands for taxes that make the poor pay for the war are met.

The facts of the NAM's secret meeting, of which the foregoing is a partial and necessarily inadequate summary, have not appeared in the commercial press, although they are known to all the news agencies and to every newspaper editor in the country.

As forecast by this secret meeting, the NAM convened and elected Frederick C. Crawford president for 1943. This is the man who keeps a picture of President Roosevelt hanging upside down in his office next to a picture of Mrs. Roosevelt with a pipe in her mouth. He also keeps a loaded shotgun and tells people he'll use it if any legislation is passed which he does not like. This is the same Crawford who told his colleagues of the NAM:

> "We are fighting for our freedom. Freedom from renegotiation of contracts. Freedom from Pansy Perkins. Freedom from Prostituting Attorney Arnold. Freedom from the Alice-in-Wonderland War Labor Board. Freedom from that . . . . (unprintable) gentleman on the hill."

As *The Pilot* said, "Crawford's fighting a war, but it's a war against the American people and against the coming defeat of Hitler."

Crawford has violated the Wagner Act and has been forced by several N.L.R.B. decisions to stop using spies, stop employing a company union, stop interfering with unionization. But the government did not make him hire union men at 8c more per hour than non-union men, and therefore there were many machines in his Cleveland plant, which make valves for airplanes, which stood idle.

Workmen pasted stickers on them. These read: "This machine works for Hitler."

So do many of the biggest men in the National Association of Manufacturers.

DOCUMENTATION AND REFERENCES:

Lobby Investigation Report (Senator Black).

Garrett Committee Report.

Committee on Education and Labor (La Follette Committee) 76th Congress, Senate Report No. 6, Part 6 (Especially pp. 159, 162-3).

Investigation of Concentration of Economic Power, T.N.E.C., Monograph 26.

Part 2

Native Fascist Forces

CHAPTER I

THE AMERICAN LEGION

THE American Legion is one of the largest and most powerful organizations in this country. The men who control it and have been in the saddle since its inception have made it one of the leading reactionary forces in America. The Legion is composed of a vast majority of men who are the victims of a plan financed by our ruling families. There is probably no greater example of mass misguidance in American history since World War I and the present Global War than the history of the million men of the Legion and its handful of misleaders.

An important movement is now under way to take the American Legion out of the control of the bankers, corporations, corporation lawyers, big business men and native Fascists who have controlled it ever since it was started. That it can be one of the greatest forces for progress or reaction depends on the rank and file membership, and what they do in the next year or two.

If any reader is unaware of the fact that the Legion was organized by special moneyed interests, and that it has been in fascist hands a large part of its existence, the fault is with the daily newspapers which have suppressed the facts. The facts are:

1. In order to keep American soldiers from getting what was promised them in the World War, namely, a "Land Fit for Heroes," and to check what was termed "radical" thought for a better world, certain officers, aided by a big fund raised by corporations, founded the Legion.

2. Almost all Legion commanders have been corporation men.

3. More than one Legion commander has come out for Fascism.

4. The Legion has been the greatest unofficial force attempting to smash the labor movement; it was the greatest strikebreaking force in America until recently.

5. The Legion announced its policy of 100% Americanism; it denounced all other Isms, but never in its entire history did it publish one word against Fascism.

6. Year after year, from its beginning, the Legion was listed as the No. 1 enemy of civil liberties in the annual report of the American Civil Liberties Union, which published documentary evidence to prove this charge.

7. The Legion was found to be an undemocratic force and its control by a handful of politicians and corporation lawyers was also found to be undemocratic.

8. When one liberal post of the Legion published a pamphlet favoring genuine democratic Americanism, the Legion moved to suppress it.

9. Only 1,000,000 of the 4,000,000 men entitled to belong have ever been members. Legion statistics show it to be composed of the wealthier elements, and few workingmen.

10. In 1943 while Commander Roane Waring, aided by the Hearst press, smeared labor, a movement was started among union men in the Legion for knocking out native fascist control.

Anyone who looks into the origin of the American Legion will find that it was organized by the agents of big business and profits for the purpose of destroying the great American idealism of the Army in France. We really believed in making the world safe for democracy. All of us who were in the Army of Occupation believed that Wilson would win through and that Lloyd George and the others would live up to the wartime promises, which were:

"A New World."—Lloyd George (Note: Similar to Wallace's Century of the Common Man of today).

"A New Deal for Everybody."—Lloyd George (Similar to F.D.R.'s New Deal a generation later).

"Industrial Democracy."—Wilson (Most of Congress today is trying to smash the few gains labor has made, rather than enlarge industrial democracy).

"A Land Fit for Heroes."—Promised by prime ministers, kings and presidents on the winning side.

"End of the Conflict Between Capital and Labor; Workingmen's Cooperation in Industry."—Promised by Giolitti to the workmen of Italy and by Charles M. Schwab of Bethlehem Steel, spokesman for U. S. industry.

Professor William Gellermann, in his book *The American Legion as Education,* gives all the evidence which he and other researchers have gathered on the reasons the Legion was started by such men as Col. Bill Donovan, Theodore Roosevelt, Jr., Major (now Congressman) Ham Fish, and Captain Ogden Mills, the multi-millionaire who later became Secretary of the Treasury. This is his summary:

"The American Legion was in no sense a 'spontaneous expression . . . of Americans who helped crush autocracy.' On the contrary, it is evident that it was intended to circumvent any spontaneous organization on the part of ex-service men. . . . The morale of the American Army after the armistice was unsatisfactory. . . . Those responsible for the initiation of the American Legion have been satisfied with the results. . . . It not only met the threat of Bolshevism at the end of the World War but has been a satisfactory antidote to 'radicalism' throughout the entire postwar period and promises to be so for a number of years yet to come.

"It required a quarter of a million dollars to finance the American Legion during its organization period. This money was borrowed . . . but it seemed expedient to make it appear that the money came exclusively from Legion members. No one has yet satisfactorily explained the letter on Swift & Co. stationery. . . ."

"SWIFT AND COMPANY
"Chicago

"December 26, 1919

"(Addressed to numerous packing interests in Chicago).

"At a meeting held on December 23, 1919, presided over by Mr. Thomas E. Wilson, there were present representatives of the different stockyard interests and it was voted that they contribute $10,000 toward a campaign for funds for the American Legion.

"A national drive is being made for the Legion and the amount asked from Illinois is $100,000, Mr. James B. Forgan, chairman of the First National Bank being treasurer of the fund for Illinois.

"The Illinois enrollment in the Legion, in comparison with other states, is very much less than it should be. We are all interested in the Legion, the results it will obtain, and the ultimate effect in helping to offset radicalism.

"It is very important that we assist this worthy work, and at the meeting I was asked by the chairman to write to the different stockyard interests for their contribution.

"In prorating the amounts it was suggested that we use an arbitrary percentage as a basis and the amount you are asked to contribute is $100.00.

"Will you please make check for this amount payable to Mr. Thomas E. Wilson, chairman?

"Kindly send me copy of your letter to Mr. Wilson.

"Very truly yours,

"Nathan B. Higbie."

Radicalism—the idealistic desire of all our soldiers for a better world, a new deal, a land fit for heroes, a greater democracy—was the enemy of the founders of the American Legion, just as today it is the enemy of the Dies Committee and just as it is the enemy of fascist forces the world over. They always pin the red flag on it, call it vile names, denounce it in the corrupt commercial newspapers, and organize all the forces of wealth and power against the desire of the majority of the people for higher wages, a better standard of living, a truer democracy.

Gellermann's book concludes: "The American Legion is a potential force in the direction of Fascism in the U. S. . . . In the

American Legion program of suppression [of free speech, labor rights, minorities, books, public assembly, strikes, etc., all detailed previously] we see Fascism in its incipient states. The American Legion is irritated by those movements in American society which seem to threaten the status quo."

The Legion's Fascist Record

One of the first commanders of the Legion was Alvin Owsley, of Texas, and the 36th Division. He was elected at the San Francisco convention which went on record by sending an invitation to Mussolini to make the principal address. Learning of the pro-fascist tendency of the Legion and its new commander, the N.E.A. Service (Cleveland syndicate operated by the Scripps-Howard press) had one of its star men, Edward Thierry, interview Commander Owsley. This copyright interview was released December 9, 1922, and was published throughout the country on that and the following days. Here is the main part:

> " 'If ever needed, the American Legion stands ready to protect our country's institutions and ideals as the Fascisti dealt with the destructionists who menaced Italy!'
>
> "Colonel Alvin Owsley, commander of the American Legion, made this statement in an exclusive interview with N.E.A. service today.
>
> " 'By taking over the government?' he was asked.
>
> " 'Exactly that,' declared Owsley. 'The American Legion is fighting every element that threatens our democratic government—Soviets, anarchists, I.W.W.'s, revolutionary socialists and every other "red".'
>
> " 'Should the day ever come when they menace the freedom of our representative government, the Legion would not hesitate to take things into its own hands—to fight the "reds" as the Fascisti of Italy fought them.'
>
> "The Legion commander said the world spread of revolutionary doctrine had to be taken seriously. He said patriotic Italians had been forced to take extreme measures which probably would never be necessary here. But he emphasized the significance of what the Fascisti had done.

" 'Do not forget,' he said, 'that the Fascisti are to Italy what the American Legion is to the United States. And that Mussolini, the new premier, was the commander of the Legion—the ex-service-men—of Italy. . . . The Legion is not in politics. . . . But there is plenty of politics in the Legion—potential power, I mean.' "

In 1937 this writer was editor of a new magazine, *Ken,* owned by David Smart, owner of *Esquire.* Smart agreed to publish a series of articles on the Legion until he found out that one of its commanders, Franklin D'Olier, was also head of the Prudential Insurance Company, and would refuse him advertising if the truth were told. He suppressed the entire series of articles.

In order to document the charge of Fascism against Owsley and to give him a chance to retract his fascist views, if he had changed his mind during the course of fifteen years, *Ken's* editor wrote Owsley, who was then U. S. Minister to Ireland. The letter concluded: "I write to question you whether there has been any change in your opinion, or whether you wish to make any changes, before (N.E.A.) gives me permission to quote copyright article."

By the time he answered, the Honorable Alvin Owsley was U. S. Minister to Denmark. Here is his reply:

"(U. S. Seal)

"Legation of the United States of America

"Copenhagen, January 6, 1938

"You have been good enough to refer to my comment, the contents of which is reported as an interview to the news service of the N.E.A. in 1922, during the time I was privileged to serve as National Commander of the American Legion.

"While not recalling independently the interview, no doubt I at the time reflected the real sentiment of the hopeful and confident legionnaire in the light of history then before us. We shall ever keep in mind the American Legion is pledged to uphold and defend the Constitution of the United States of America. Hence any action taken by the Legion will be within the Constitution.

"Now only the newly elected National Commander is authorized to speak for the Legion.

"You recall that the instructions and regulations of the Diplomatic Service deny me the privilege of expressing an opinion in regard to the public affairs of any foreign government or discussing, outside the State Department, any issue of national or international significance.

"With cordial regards,

"Yours very truly,

"Alvin Mansfield Owsley

"American Minister."

Mr. Owsley has never repudiated his endorsement of Mussolini and Fascism.

On May 4, 1935, the New England Methodist Council met at Lowell, Mass., where a member of the American Legion, and a former state chaplain, introduced the following resolution:

"We warn our people against the approaching menace of Fascism . . . sponsored quite noticeably by the American Legion, which attempts to disguise itself in the terms of patriotism." The resolution was adopted.

But, almost every year from 1922 on, when Mussolini was invited by the San Francisco convention, new invitations were sent to him, and many Legion delegations visited him and returned to America filled with praise of the Duce, Fascism, and trains running on time.

Again in 1930 the Boston Legion convention invited Mussolini to attend. Labor unions protested and forced a withdrawal.

In 1931, Ralph T. O'Neill, national commander, presented to the fascist ambassador de Martino resolutions passed by the National Executive Committee of the Legion in favor of Mussolini.

In 1935 Col. William E. Easterwood, national vice-commander of the Legion, invited Mussolini to the Chicago convention, made the Duce an honorary member of the American Legion, and pinned a button on him. (Since the Legion has no honorary members, this action was later declared unconstitutional.)

But the most important documentary evidence of all exists

in the files of the first un-American Committee, the predecessor of the Dies Committee. This story was distorted or suppressed in 99% of the American press, and is therefore dismissed with a printed shrug in all official Legion publications. Here is a small part of the evidence:

In 1934 leading members of the Legion conspired with Wall Street brokers and other big business men to upset the government of the United States and establish a fascist regime. They asked Smedley Butler, noted former commander of the U. S. Marines, to head the American fascist march on Washington. Butler not only refused, he insisted on exposing the plot, and when newspapers refused to print the truth, he spent several years telling it from the lecture platform.

General Butler testified:

"Shortly after MacGuire [Gerald G. MacGuire, employee of the brokerage firm of Grayson M.-P. Murphy, and one of the founders of the American Legion] first came to see me he arranged for Robert Sterling Clark, a New York broker, to come to my house. . . . [MacGuire proposed Butler raise several hundred thousand Legionnaires to take over Washington]. To be perfectly fair to Mr. MacGuire he didn't seem bloodthirsty. He suggested that 'We might go along with Roosevelt and do with him what Mussolini did with the King of Italy.' "

Butler thought this was treason. He arranged to have a friend, the newspaper reporter Paul Comly French, present at subsequent talks with MacGuire. French testified before the McCormack-Dickstein Committee:

"He (MacGuire) shoved a letter across his (Butler's) desk saying it was from Louis Johnson of West Virginia, former national commander of the American Legion. MacGuire said Johnson wrote he would be in 'to discuss what we have talked about.'

" 'That's just what we are discussing now,' he told me.

"During our conversation he mentioned that Henry Stephens of North Carolina, another former national commander of the American Legion, was interested in the plan."

The Congressional Committee also heard testimony from

James Van Zandt, commander of the Veterans of Foreign Wars, which completely supported that of General Butler and admitted knowledge of this plot. Butler concluded his own testimony by suggesting that the Committee question several persons on the subject of the plot to lead a Legion army to establish a fascist regime in Washington, and notably: Grayson M.-P. Murphy, Governor Ely of Massachusetts, William Doyle, former department commander of the Legion in Massachusetts, and Commander Frank N. Belgrano of the Legion. Belgrano was called to Washington but secret pressure was exerted and he was never called to testify. Murphy was a director of Guaranty Trust, a Morgan bank; also director of Anaconda Copper, Goodyear, Bethlehem Steel. He was treasurer of the DuPont-financed Liberty League. He was decorated by Mussolini and made a Commander of the Crown of Italy. It was Murphy who raised a large part of the big money which started the Legion in Paris in 1919.

Clark, broker at 11 Wall Street, was also one of the Liberty League financiers. Butler testified that Clark said: "I have got $30,000,000 and I don't want to lose it. I am willing to spend half of the thirty millions to save the other half." In Butler's presence Clark phoned MacGuire to go ahead with a $45,000 fund to use at the American Legion convention to put through a resolution in favor of maintaining the gold standard. Such a resolution was passed.

When finally the McCormack-Dickstein Committee published its findings, it suppressed certain parts of General Butler's testimony, notably the phrase "and in about two weeks the Liberty League appeared," thus connecting the Liberty League with the Legion plot. Also suppressed: French's testimony that MacGuire said he could get financing for a fascist putsch from John W. Davis, Morgan attorney, or Perkins of National City Bank; and that the guns would come from the Remington Arms; and that "one of the DuPonts is on the board of directors of the Liberty League and they own a controlling interest in Remington Arms Co."

Some of the most sensational parts of the testimony were suppressed. Most papers suppressed the whole story or threw it down by ridiculing it. Nor did the press later publish the McCormack-Dickstein report which stated that every charge Butler made and French corroborated had been proven true. The official report concludes:

"Evidence was obtained showing that certain persons had made an attempt to establish a fascist organization in this country. There is no question but that these attempts were discussed, were planned, and might have been placed in execution when and if the financial backers deemed it expedient."

All the principals in the case were American Legion officials and financial backers.

The evidence of actual Fascism in the Legion is endless. Its record of anti-labor activities is one of the most violent chapters in American history. No less than 50 illegal acts of violence were committed in 1920, according to the 1921 report of the American Civil Liberties Union. Farmers Non-Partisan League speakers were tarred and feathered, crusading editors were beaten up, a concert by Fritz Kreisler broken up and strikebreaking in uniform was a commonplace. Kidnapping is a major crime but in 1935 Nick Bins, a racketeer, and several of his fellow members of the Racine Legion committed this crime. A newspaper man, posing as a customer, got Nick Bins to agree to do another kidnapping. Bins said (before a hidden microphone) that he would not murder the victim, but break his legs. There would be no difficulty if he were caught, said Bins, because all Racine judges are "100% OK" and especially Judge Belden, "a brother Legionnaire." For references for kidnapping and slugging, Bins suggested phoning "Chief Lutter of Racine." A $10 bill was handed Bins. Despite all this evidence it was almost impossible to get the law to act but when Bins was finally jailed a group of Legionnaires kept him company in his cell and shouted they had "fixed" the case. A defense fund for Bins, "a fellow Legionnaire," was supported by the Chamber of Commerce. National headquarters of the Legion took no action except to expel Rahman-De Bella and John Philip Sousa posts for supporting a labor union at the very same time.

In 1937, however, the national commander, Harry Colmery, issued an order warning the Legion that in the future no strikebreaking was to be done in uniform. This was, of course, an admission that from 1919 to 1937 the Legion had been one of the main anti-labor strikebreaking forces in the nation. Vigilanteism was endorsed, and the Legionnaires were not told to be neutral in strikes, but to leave off their uniforms, buttons and caps when they became strikebreakers.

The American Legion hasn't changed its fascist spots since Pearl Harbor. Since it was organized by big business in 1919 it has become the leading agency of the members of the National Association of Manufacturers. It has repaid its organizers, subsidizers and owners by becoming the main anti-labor and strikebreaking agency in the country.

When Roane Waring, Memphis utility executive, was chosen national commander of the Legion in September, 1942, he pledged that body's full support to the President and fulsomely urged that capital and industry as well as labor and agriculture be conscripted. The Legion has long been on record for equality of sacrifice in winning a war, conscription of money as well as of human life. Less than two months later, Waring, at an informal luncheon given to New York publishers, accused the administration of introducing "regimentation" and "communism." The $25,000 salary limitation, he declared to his picked and sympathetic audience, was communistic and would "stifle personal endeavor, private enterprise, free initiative, ambition and the right of a man to earn what he can." He apparently had no objections to wage stabilization for workers. The Justice Department's monopoly suit against the A.P. he described as "stifling freedom of speech, freedom of contract. . . ." And of course he added to these stiflers the usual NAM refrain of private energy, private ability and private interest.

Since then Waring has been touring the country denouncing

unions and threatening to shoot strikers, delivering a particularly anti-labor, anti-democratic diatribe to the soldiers at Fort Bragg. In words of NAM vintage he began by attacking those people concerned about the future of "Sandwich Island Hottentots or the Patagonians" and warned the soldiers that if they want to live in a better post-war world they must be prepared to return from this war and fight social reform. "The Legion has fought and will continue to fight these un-American tenets. When this war is over there will be more freak Isms, more Utopian crackpots, social politicians . . . who will trot out schemes for bringing on the millennium. . . . Your job will be to fight them to the last ditch. . . ."

Post Commander Jack Carrier of Minneapolis has taken Waring to task for violating the Legion constitution, which forbids not only strikebreaking but oratorical anti-labor activities. Carrier wrote Waring:

"The daily press currently carries stories of speeches made by you . . . saying that all strikers should be shot, etc. It seems to the writer that you have strayed a long way from the preamble of our constitution and the stand of the Legion as mandated at the Cleveland convention.

"In fact, your rantings smack a great deal of the diatribe currently being put out by Hitler, Goebbels, et al. Their move was to destroy the organized labor movement in Germany, and your mouthings bear a startling resemblance to their tactics.

"No one . . . denies you the right to do or say anything you may desire as an individual, but I do challenge your right to make such statements while wearing the uniform of the American Legion. Take off your Legion cap and put on the uniform of the National Association of Manufacturers.

"If you are the man and citizen that the American Legion pictures you to be, you will resign as national commander of the American Legion and cease fomenting disunity, intolerance and class hatred."

In May, 1943, meeting in Indianapolis, the executive committee of the American Legion continued its anti-American, Big Business, pro-NAM, anti-labor program by taking the following steps:

1. Endorsing the anti-labor program of the new Ku Klux Klan movement which started in Texas and which calls itself the Christian American Association.

2. Approving the proposal to accept $20,000,000 from the corporations for an "Americanism program" which is nothing more than the "Free Enterprise" or "The American Way" program of the NAM (which incidentally caused the collapse of 1929, with 13,000,000 unemployed in 1933, and which fought the New Deal and opposes all new deals, square deals and the Century of the Common Man).

Suppressed generally in the newspapers—but reported by Federated Press, which serves the liberal-labor press—was the action of the Legion committee in joining the fascist Christian American Association campaign for laws to prohibit the closed or union shop in the United States.

The Legion has now organized a World War II committee whose purpose will be to get the 10,800,000 veterans of the present war against Fascism to join the organization whose most notable act in more than 30 years is an act of omission: failure and refusal to fight Fascism. It was this new committee which introduced a resolution at executive session which states that "the American way of life has always endeavored to see to it that every citizen" enjoyed "free and unimpaired opportunity to accept gainful employment." This itself is cockeyed because no such opportunity exists for long periods of time.

The resolution then charges that "certain laws, regulations and contracts . . . may limit that opportunity" for the returned forces. This is aimed at the Wagner Act, the Magna Carta of labor, the most important success of the New Deal, which has curbed the profiteers, anti-labor employers and native Fascists (who were exposed by the La Follette Committee as employing tens of thousands of spies, thugs, and murderers, poison gas and Thompson machine guns, and spending millions annually in illegal ways to keep American labor underpaid, terrorized, and non-union).

The Legion resolution concludes that "we recommend to the national executive committee that they take such steps as are necessary" so that no veteran of this war "shall be forced to join any trade union or other organization in order to gain employment." This is the same program the K.K.K. Christian Americans introduced in Texas.

The National Association of Manufacturers, through its affiliate, the National Industrial Council, is spending $1,000,000 a year propagandizing America against labor, against unions, against the New Deal, against any social security plan, against the $25,000 or any other salary limitation, against the Wagner Act, against human progress.

It employs "secrecy and deception" according to the final report of the La Follette investigation—also college professors, newspaper columnists, journalists, clergymen and other propagandists whose aim is to pervert American public opinion.

Now the NAM has sent two of its subsidizers, representatives of the Owens-Illinois Glass Company and the General Tire Company, to arrange a $20,000,000 Americanism campaign through which the NAM propaganda will be spread by the Legion.

In the La Follette Report of the 76th Congress, 1st Session, the Owens-Illinois Glass Co. is listed among the employers of spies, detectives and racketeers to prevent labor from organizing; also as a large contributor, along with the General Tire Co., to the NAM.

Since January, 1943, the Legion "Royal Family"—as the ruling clique is called—has been discussing the $20,000,000 fund in secret with Big Business. Hugh O'Connor revealed in the *New York Times* in May that if other corporations do not contribute their full share of the millions, W. E. Lewis, chairman of the Owens-Illinois Glass Co., promises that his $150,000,000 corporation will "absorb the cost."

The $20,000,000 offer was made to the Legion by R. H. Barnard, vice-president of Owens-Illinois. His firm, along with eight other glass manufacturers, was indicted as a monopoly and violator of the Sherman anti-trust law. He wants to preserve "the American Way of Life," as James F. O'Neill, chairman of the Legion executive committee, put it in announcing the offer. Lewis explained that all the backers of the fund are interested in the future of "Free Enterprise" and "American initiative." All of these impressive phrases were coined by the NAM, whose real and main purpose, according to Congressional investigations, is to fight labor.

Labor Shows the Way to Save the Legion

It is evident that the Legion will continue to be a reactionary force unless veterans with democratic American views join it and steer it away from its past native-fascist line.

Labor has been slow to take action. But now it is on the march, and it is the present move by labor which can provide the solution of the fascist ideology of the Legion.

A national convention of the American Legion consists of about 1,300 delegates. Of these 1,300, probably not 15 carry union cards, and yet there are tens of thousands of union men in the Legion. If they were in touch with each other, acting and speaking together in the interests of labor and against the reactionary top clique that has generally run the Legion, they could be a great democratizing and liberalizing influence. One post commander, an active union man, told the writer that if 2% of the organized workers of the country were in the Legion and thinking and acting in it like union men, they could control it.

Efforts to unify the trade union membership of the Legion have been made for years. In 1938 an advertisement in a Legion paper asked all labor posts to get in contact with the labor posts in Los Angeles. A few posts did, and a semi-organization was formed. President Green of the A. F. of L. urged the millions of workers who are veterans of the first World War to join the 31 labor posts of the Legion and form new posts for the purpose of fighting the pro-fascists and NAM agents in control of the Legion.

But it was not until June, 1942, that a real conference of trade union posts was held in Chicago. A permanent organization was effected by the 31 posts represented in this National Conference of Union Legionnaires. The conference made its position known in a series of resolutions advocating a Second Front in Europe; approving Vice-President Wallace's Century of the Common Man speech; urging the Legion paper to carry the speech (which it didn't) —and condemning Westbrook Pegler and asking that his labor-baiting column be dropped from the army paper, *Stars and Stripes.*

One of the main objectives of the next conference of union Legionnaires will be to get the Legion to appoint a new standing committee, a National Labor Relations Committee. A resolution calling for the appointment of such a committee was passed by two national conventions, but the brass hats in control have ignored this mandate.

The most important fact about the present Legion activity is its move to enroll all it can of America's 10,800,000 men of our war against Fascism into the old Legion. Veterans are generally democratic; they never joined the Legion. They are workers, not corporation heads, and those in the Legion have never been permitted to hold office. The policy of liberal leaders and publications for years has been to attack the Legion. But labor leaders now favor another plan: every eligible veteran and every man now in uniform should join the Legion and throw out the reactionaries who have perverted its program.

DOCUMENTATION AND REFERENCES:

Congressional Committee report: "Nazi and Other Propaganda," February 15, 1935. 74th Congress, 1st session; House of Representatives, pp. 9, 10, etc.

The American Legion as Education, by Professor William Gellermann, Columbia University.

King Legion, by Marcus Duffield. Cape and Smith.

The Truth About the American Legion, by Arthur Warner, *The Nation,* vol. 113.

Senate, Report No. 6, 76th Congress, 1st Session, Violations of Free Speech and the Rights of Labor (La Follette Report), page 151.

CHAPTER II

FASCISM IN U. S. INDUSTRY: THE FORD EMPIRE

HENRY FORD's picture for years hung over Hitler's desk in the Brown House in Munich. The Nazis in their early days boasted that they had the moral and financial support of the richest man in America.

The great democratic ambassador William E. Dodd saw the relationship between the big business interests which financed Hitler and the big business interests which financed the Liberty League and other early fascist organizations in America. Dodd had protested the deal whereby the Standard Oil Company of America and I. G. Farben of Nazi Germany became members of the same cartel; Standard advanced millions to I.G.F. for the manufacture of high octane gasoline from coal, and both split the world into sales zones for certain products, one of which was synthetic rubber. (Standard Oil suppressed the use of this patent.) Dodd also knew of the relationship of Henry Ford to Hitlerism. On returning to the United States, after a stormy relationship with the President, Ambassador Dodd said in an interview:

"Fascism is on the march today in America. Millionaires are marching to the tune. It will come in this country unless a strong defense is set up by all liberal and progressive forces. . . .

"A clique of U. S. industrialists is hell-bent to bring a fascist state to supplant our democratic government, and is working closely with the fascist regime in Germany and Italy. Aboard ship a prominent executive of one of America's largest financial corporations told me point-blank that if the progressive trend of the Roosevelt administration continued, he would be ready to take definite action to bring Fascism to America.

"Certain American industrialists had a great deal to do with bringing fascist regimes into being in both Germany and Italy. They extended aid to help Fascism occupy the seat of power, and they are helping to keep it there.

"Propagandists for fascist groups try to dismiss the 'fascist scare.' We should be aware of the symptoms. When industrialists ignore laws designed for social and economic progress, they will seek recourse to a fascist state when the institutions of our government compel them to comply with the provisions."

Dr. Dodd did not name Henry Ford as chief of those certain millionaire industrialists who were working for Fascism, but it was not only generally believed at the time, but the Left press declared openly that Dodd was aiming at Ford.

To many persons Ford has always been our No. 1 Fascist. (Newspapermen usually give that spot to William Randolph Hearst, and there is an unending argument as to which of the two has done more harm to the mind of America, but no one doubts that both have spread more fascist poison in this country than any other pair of prominent men.)

"The Kingdom of Henry Ford," wrote Michael Sayers, "is a fascist state within the United States. All the characteristics of Fascism—Jew-baiting, corruption, gangsterism—exist today wherever King Henry Ford reigns over American workers. But Fordism and Americanism cannot long continue to exist side by side. Already in more than half a dozen states the National Labor Relations Board has found the Ford Motor Company guilty of maintaining 'a regime of terror and violence directed against its employees.'"

At the hearings in Dallas, Texas, Trial Examiner Robert Denham, who learned of almost unbelievable violence and sadism paid for by Ford, said in his report (April, 1940): "No case within the history of this board is known to the undersigned in which an employer had deliberately called and carried into execution a program of brutal beatings, whippings and other manifestations of physical violence comparable to that shown by the uncontradicted and wholly credible evidence on which the findings are based." Between June and December, 1937, 30 to 50 persons had been beaten up in the streets of Dallas by thugs, racketeers, gunmen and murderers on the payroll of Henry Ford, men hired by Harry Bennett for his service department. "Shocking brutalities" had been reported from every part of America where Ford had a plant and where the unions tried to exercise their constitutional rights to organize the men.

In the case of Ford, as in the case of Hitler, it was violence and bloodshed for profits. It was again the universal pursuit of money.

Strangely enough, the La Follette Committee investigating the terroristic systems of American Big Business—the use of spies, stoolpigeons, thugs, gangsters, racketeers, gunmen, and murderers and the employment of Thompson machine guns and poison gas—fails to mention Ford. It goes into detail on Lieut. Gen. William E. Knudsen's, Alfred P. Sloan's and the DuPont brothers' General Motors, for example, but there is no mention of Ford although it is generally known that Ford's Mr. Bennett had one of the biggest spy and thug services in America.

The many volumes of La Follette reports on American industry's hatred of the American workingman and its efforts to keep him down tell these facts:

1. that American business employs a vast espionage system whose purpose is to fight labor;

2. that 200 agencies employ 40,000 to 50,000 spies in industry;

3. that $80,000,000 a year is spent by the big corporations in fighting labor, employing spies, buying gas and guns, hiring gangs;

4. that almost all the great corporations are in the spy racket, including Ford, General Motors, U. S. Steel, Bethlehem Steel, Consolidated Edison, Weir, Frick Coke, etc.

5. that 2,500 companies, comprising what Senator La Follette called "the Blue Book of American Industry," are part of the American Gestapo;

6. that the National Association of Manufacturers, U. S. Chamber of Commerce, Merchants and Manufacturers Association,

National Metal Trades Association, are the chief organizations engaged in native Fascism.

7. that the American press, which still gives its front page and its approving editorials to the smears, exaggerations and falsehoods of the Dies Committee and similar committees, and which employs reporters to attack labor, and especially those labor unions which are progressive and militant and put up a strong fight for the rights of labor, suppressed almost all the hearings and findings of the La Follette Committee, which constituted an exposure of Fascism in American industry.

Unfortunately, also, our book publishers (who do not live on automobile company advertising, but who are nevertheless afraid of the goodwill or evil notice of newspapers which do), are none too anxious to print books exposing our own brands of Fascism.

A man named Ralph Rimar, who was in Harry Bennett's department for many years, and during the great strike which preceded the C.I.O. unionization, and who was second in command to Norval Marlette, chief of the so-called Intelligence Department of the Ford Empire, and therefore fourth man in the hierarchy from Ford himself, wrote a book which he called *Heil Henry!—The Confessions of a Ford Spy.* No publisher would take it. I have read the entire manuscript and have obtained permission from Rimar's agents to quote from it.

The Ford Empire, Rimar shows, is ruled by a triumvirate for its owners, the Ford family. The triumvirs are: Harry Bennett, who bosses 130,000 men in peacetime, more in wartime; Charles Sorensen, an admirer of Hitler's, who bosses production; and W. J. Cameron, who directs public relations and who until recently spoke over the Ford Radio Hour. It was Cameron who published the notorious forgeries called "The Protocols of Zion" in Ford's anti-Semitic publication called the *Dearborn Independent,* and when Ford in 1927 recanted his anti-Semitism (at least officially) it was Cameron who continued his anti-Semitic activities through the Anglo-Saxon Federation of Detroit and Boston.

Thus we get a picture of Ford, Bennett, Sorensen and Cameron, each representing a different facet of a transplanted European Fascism.

Rimar is not an ordinary person. In his documents, which the present writer has examined, there are letters from Frank Murphy, governor of the Philippine Islands, governor of Michigan and a justice of the Supreme Court of the United States. One of them says:

"I recall very pleasantly the happy hours we spent together in philosophical discussion and exchange of views of man's endless quest for social and economic justice. I trust you are still interested. I am sure you would look upon my current effort (in the Philippines) to break down social inequalities in the Orient approvingly."

Here, then, are extracts from the amazing unpublished manuscript:

Extracts From Rimar's Confessions

"Perhaps in telling my story [Rimar begins] I can undo some of the many wrongs I have helped to accomplish. . . .

"It is not a pleasant story. . . . It is a tale filled with violence and brutality, with human baseness and deceit, with greed, depravity and ruthlessness. It is a tale of the underworld, a tale describing the inner and furtive workings of the greatest individual industrial empire in the world, the Ford Motor Company.

"International fascist tieups, gangsterism within the plant as well as support of the Fifth Column without; connections between Ford Company officials and vice rings; relationships between Ford henchmen and city, state and government authorities; the use of criminals by the company, the protection of Nazis, the bribery of government witnesses; the torture, mutilation and murder of union men; the efforts to instigate race riots; the constant relentless plotting against tens of thousands of Ford workers."

[This is Rimar's introduction. The manuscript bears out these promises. All the fascist actions and horrors are described in the book.]

"For years I have been one of the key men in the Ford Gestapo. . . . Within Ford's domain I soon found there was no liberty, no free speech, no human dignity . . . the vast power of Ford extended into courts, schools, prisons, clubs, banks, even into the national capital, enveloping us all in a black cloud of suppression and fear.

"To those who have never lived under dictatorship it is difficult to convey the sense of fear which is part of the Ford system."

The part of the chapter describing industrial espionage and counter-espionage, every man spying on another, every man suspecting his neighbor, is no different from the spy system in General Motors, Bethlehem Steel and other industrial empires, as described by the La Follette Civil Liberties reports. These corporations, however, never pretended they were paternal, or that they were operated by a humanitarian. They were out to make money at all costs and, until the government took a hand, every legal and illegal means was used. Ford, however, posed as a friend of labor. According to Rimar he was in truth a worse enemy than all other corporation heads. Rimar describes how hatred was encouraged between racial, national and color groups, how Protestants and Catholics were encouraged to hate each other, and to spy on each other and report to superiors; how foreign-born and children of foreign-born were encouraged to keep alive European national hatreds, how Negroes and whites were stirred to enmity, how even high officials were made suspicious of each other. "Between Cameron and Bennett, between Bennett and young Edsel Ford, between Hogan and Deenan, between John Koos and myself there was a constant strife," continues Rimar.

The Bennett system approximated Himmler's.

"Our Gestapo," writes Rimar, "covered Dearborn with a thick web of corruption, intimidation and intrigue. The spy net was all embracing. My own agents reported back to me conversations in grocery stores, meat markets and restaurants, gambling joints, beer gardens, social groups, boys' clubs and even churches. Women waiting in markets buying something might discuss their husbands' jobs and activities; if they did I soon heard what they said. . . ."

Bennett, Marlette and Rimar collected all this evidence and acted on it. Men were fired and blacklisted. Rimar confesses: "Prior to 1937 and the rise of the C.I.O. . . . I was responsible for the firing of close to 1,500 men. During the year 1940 alone I named over 1,000 union sympathizers and they were all fired." Every man who bought other than a Ford car was fired. Rimar used a Dodge so he could give the impression he was not a Ford employee. But spy evidence to get union sympathizers fired was only part of the anti-labor system. There was also a gangster outfit to break unions. "The service men were professional athletes, former policemen, gangsters, criminals and ex-convicts . . . ready at a moment's notice to handle union organizers . . . to break up union gatherings . . . they were the Storm Troops of Ford." Rimar lists names of men guilty of second degree murder, rape, felonious assault, armed robbery and "indecent liberties." Bennett is a member of the Michigan State Parole Commission, and among the convicts paroled to the Ford Company was Kid McCoy, the wife-murderer, who taught the other members of the goon squads how to use the third degree, how to handle tear gas, pistols and machine-guns. Many persons, Rimar alleges, joined Bennett's Storm Troops in order to escape going to jail because, Rimar says, no law could reach them once they were in Bennett's care. Rimar thus blows up the myth that Henry Ford, great humanitarian, employed a number of convicts to give them a chance to earn an honest living when they went straight. He employed the worst criminals because Bennett needed gangsters to break unions.

In the 1932 Ford hunger march Bennett took motion pictures of the marchers, Rimar discloses. Every worker recognized on these films was fired.

Bennett, for reasons connected with Dearborn politics, ordered Rimar to get a sensational exposé of prostitution and gambling in the district. There were 30 disorderly houses, a dozen major gambling joints run by two rival gangs in Dearborn. The most notorious was May Irwin's. Rimar writes that May Irwin told him she paid $800 a month to the police. Rimar turned in a sensational report on the vice situation, naming the police heads who got the money from prostitution and gambling. Rimar says

Bennett then told him to shut up because the police heads were Bennett protégés.

Another scandal which he uncovered was the theft of $5,000,000 worth of Ford parts every year by a ring of 90 thieves, some within, some without the plant. Rimar found one man with $100,000 worth of stolen materials, but couldn't get a warrant for his arrest. Rimar writes:

"Relatives of every key man in the Ford plant were involved in this very ring. Whenever we caught these thieves we had to let them go."

In 1935 a ring of thieves was discovered at General Motors. The *Detroit News* admitted that the police department had given "fences" protection, and demanded an investigation. Among those indicted was Rimar. He relates that he went to see Judge Scallins, who said it was a strange situation (that a man working against the thieves, but secretly, should be among those indicted) but said that Rimar's innocence would be established. Rimar then got orders from his superiors to say he was not working for Ford, but for Chief of Police Brooks. The attorney, supplied by the Ford Company, told Rimar not to go on the stand to testify. Lies were told in court, but Rimar's lawyer told him not to answer, and he refused to cross examine. The plan was to keep the Ford name out. So Rimar was found guilty. He became angry. He threatened to "blast the whole story in the papers." But Ford officials said, "Who do you think is going to print it?" All the newspapers were subservient to Ford, and Bennett and his service hoodlums boasted they had the press in hand. Rimar kept quiet. A few days later he was probationed as had been promised him by company officials, who also boasted they had the judiciary in hand.

The story of how Father Coughlin worked for Ford and against the labor unions in the Ford plant has been told from many angles. It is now an established fact. Rimar adds his own testimony. He tells how Father Coughlin got orders from Bennett to invite Homer Martin, head of the United Automobile Workers, to dine at the Shrine of the Little Flower. Coughlin began the conversation by deploring the spread of radical influences in the union, suggested that Martin "strike out on his own," become an independent labor union leader who "could do more for the working man than by taking orders from (John L.) Lewis and his red henchmen."

Coughlin suggested unionizing Ford. Martin said, "That's a tough nut to crack." Coughlin replied, "I wouldn't be too sure. I know Mr. Bennett personally . . . a man with vision . . . I am sure he could be made to realize the advantages of a union with honest intentions and no red influences, a union with a fine and dependable leader like yourself organizing his plant."

Coughlin arranged a conference between Martin and Bennett. Bennett said he wanted a "reliable" union in the plant. Rimar continues:

> "Bennett played his cards carefully. Early in 1938 Martin was already taking cash from him. . . . Bennett simply suggested he be allowed to help out—for the good of 'honest unionism.' The money advanced could be considered as a loan."

Homer Martin was flattered into betraying the union. Between Coughlin and Bennett the attempt was made to organize a Ford company union under Martin which would divide labor and prevent either the C.I.O. or A. F. of L. from coming in.

Henry Ford, who believes he is a benefactor of mankind, and who is considered now the worst anti-Semite, hate-spreader, and labor-baiter in America, employed men who employed other men who on orders from Ford Company officials committed all sorts of violence including murder. All to keep wages low, unions out of the plants, and more money going into the Ford Empire.

Rimar writes that Bennett employed a gangster by the name of Elder to beat up three union men for $250; he also describes the beating of Attorney W. A. Houston of Dallas. The labor lawyer was almost killed but not one Dallas newspaper reported the incident. "That," continues Rimar, "gives you some idea of the influence Ford exerts over the press in those cities where the company operates." The Dallas gangsters employed by the Ford Company are named and pictured. The Dallas gang murdered Archie Lewis, mistaking him for his twin brother, a labor union man.

When the great strike began, Rimar writes:

"Bennett was not caught completely napping . . . (he) was quoted in headlines throughout the city's press that the strike was a 'gigantic communist plot threatening national defense.' All of us went to work on the strike as red. The Little Fellow (Bennett) had said, 'Discredit it and it will be easy to break. Smear it. Say it is communist-inspired.' We spread the word far and wide. We had excellent support from Detroit papers. They always back up Ford 100% and in this case they outdid themselves. We plugged the red theme on the radio as well. The Rev. Gerald L. K. Smith and Rev. Frank Norris were ready for the job. In their broadcast they said the Bolsheviks were trying to take over. Norris, the same preacher who was once tried in Texas for shooting a man, gave a long sermon in which he described the strike as a 'revolution.' The *Detroit Times* printed the sermon in full, frontpaging it."

Rimar tells the inside story of the strike. There was a raid on Detroit Communist headquarters where police picked up a map of the Ford plant. Rimar alleges that Norval Marlette, his superior, admitted this was the official map handed every tourist at Ford's plant. Nevertheless, "not only the newspapers in Detroit, but the press throughout the country as well, carried the stories of the raid on Communist headquarters, the 'discovery of the map.' . . . We were getting clippings from every state. We knew they must be influencing public opinion. The strategy seemed to be working well." The map, of course, was linked to a charge of plots, revolution, dynamite.

"But the red scare was by no means our only tactic to break the strike. We used that to discredit it. We had other methods for demoralizing the workers." One way was to pass around Detroit newspapers which were shouting all over the front page that the men could never win the strike because "public opinion"—which is something the newspapers boast they manufacture and control —was against them. The press, which lives largely on Ford ads, said public opinion favored Ford. Ford men started the rumor that the governor would ask Roosevelt to send in the U. S. Army to break the strike. "The *Detroit Times,* Hearst paper, was the first to carry the headline: 'CAMP CUSTER SOLDIERS MAY GO TO FORD'S.' That headline appeared in six editions of the *Detroit Times.* Then newspapers throughout the country carried similar leads to their Ford stories.

"Naturally, we promoted a 'back to work' movement. . . ." This is part of the Mohawk Valley strikebreaking formula, sponsored by the NAM.

> "We did everything we could to provoke trouble at the plant, especially in the picket line. We knew that if there were enough disturbances, perhaps even a few riots, public sentiment against the strike would rise.
>
> "Inside the plant we had our gang of strikebreakers. We saw to it that they were well provided with liquor. Almost all of them had weapons."

Rimar describes violence organized by Ford officials and started by strikebreakers while other officials issued "public demands" for troops to stop these same violences. Rimar tells how Bennett's men hired hundreds of Negroes and inflamed them against white workers. Rimar charged that Donald T. Marshall, Negro assistant to Harry Bennett and Homer Martin, is responsible for this spread of race hatred. Bennett men also distributed a circular saying "Henry Ford is the next man to Abe Lincoln in helping the colored race. . . . Henry Ford has done more for our race than the union." At the same time Ford men were stirring up the freshly hired Negroes against the white men on strike.

Rimar also charges Ford service men with spreading anti-Semitism.

"We told the Negroes the Jews were leading the union. . . . We tried to divide the men, not only White against Black, but also Jew against Gentile.

"Bennett was counting heavily on the tactic of pitting the Negroes against the Whites. We all knew that, if he thought it necessary, he was willing to provoke race riots. As a matter of fact he was already laying the groundwork for such riots. He knew that once the workers started killing one another, once they split into armies of Black and White, he would have the strike licked. But even here I felt that he was underestimating the strength of the union. The U.A.W. had already won over thousands of Ford Negro workers and they were marching in the picket line. . . . Prominent Negroes in Detroit and throughout the country were issuing public statements giving their support to the strike.

"For years his (Bennett's) system had worked out. The Homer Martins had come across. He had believed that all union men could be bought in the same way. . . . 'I can buy them for a dime a dozen,' he would say; 'Hell, they've all got their price.' He felt the same way about the rank and file in the plant. 'I can pay half of them to kill the other half,' he used to tell us. . . . After the men marched back to work (Bennett said) 'they think they've won but the fight's just beginning.' "

When Rimar wrote six articles, "I Was A Ford Spy," Bennett did everything to discredit his former associate. He arranged that the Detroit newspapers, notorious for their venality, feature the story of Rimar's framed arrest years earlier. The newspaper reporters knew that the reason Rimar had been found guilty and immediately pardoned was because a deal had been made between the Ford Co., the police, and the courts of justice, to have this happen so that the Ford name would not be dragged through the mud. But the newspaper proprietors chose to forget that fact. Rimar says the *Detroit News,* the *Detroit Free Press* and the *Detroit Times* all joined in Bennett's smear campaign, revived the old story, heaped new mud on him, tried to whitewash the Ford Empire.

Rimar ends his book with this line:

"Fordism is American Fascism."

Ford's Profits in Fascism

Like Hitler-Germany and Mussolini-Italy, Ford himself has been able to earn a profit on his Fascism. The swastika decoration which Hitler sent him was only a symbol of the aid he had given the Nazis. The Ford factory in Cologne, operated with the aid of the Nazi authorities, who kept the workmen in line—on low wages—also paid dividends. But the big money Ford made was by employing violence and terrorism (fascist tactics) to keep labor from organizing. When finally the C.I.O. swept the Ford empire it was estimated that Harry Bennett, known as Ford's personnel director but actually his lieutenant of private militia, had saved Ford no less than $140,000,000 in the three years they had defied the National Labor Board.

If the fascist dictators resort to lies, so does Ford. One of the great Ford lies actually created the myth that Ford paid higher wages than anyone in America. The United Autoworkers, in their 1940 campaign, opened the eyes of many Americans when they printed tables showing that Chrysler and Briggs (General Motors) paid higher wages in every category, from arc welder to water sander. Ford wages ranged from 75c to 95c an hour minimums, the rivals from 98c to $1.38 for the same work, and in many cases the Ford maximum wage was below the union minimum.

The first union contract which Ford was forced to sign brought an immediate gain of $30,000,000 a year to his 130,000 employees. Even with the family worth more than $2,000,000,000—the T.N.E.C. report listed its stock ownership alone at $624,975,000—a matter of thirty millions is something.

Ford has never been known for any charities, nor has he been known to contribute any considerable sum to anyone, but one of the few outfits which got something from Henry and Mrs. Ford is the Moral Re-Armament Movement, better known as Buchmanism. Dr. Frank Buchman is a notorious Fascist, who had endorsed Hitler many years ago, and who made an excellent living getting money from big business men to preach a "philosophy" of appeasement to labor. Everyone was to co-operate, there were to be no strikes, the lion and lamb were to lie down together, and if the labor-lamb frequently was inside the belly of the capitalist-lion, it could only result in more contributions to Buchmanism. Leading Buchmanites: Himmler, the chief murderer of Nazidom—this is attested by Fritz Thyssen in his book *I Paid Hitler*; Rudolf Hess, the No. 3 Nazi who made the flight from Germany to the estate of the Duke of Hamilton—another Buchmanite—with Hitler's proposals for a patched up peace between Germany and Britain and a united war against Russia; David Dubinsky, a labor leader well known and liked by employers; Harry Chandler, the notorious reactionary publisher of the *Los Angeles Times,* most bitter anti-labor paper in the nation; Louis B. Mayer, the notorious movie producer who faked movies in order to smear Upton Sinclair in the California gubernatorial election; and assorted native and foreign Fascisti, all enemies of labor and the general welfare.

Ford and Early Hitler Money

It was general knowledge in the early 1920's, when it was not treason to aid Hitler, that Henry Ford was one of his spiritual and economic backers. Ford was for Hitler because both were anti-Semites, whereas Fritz Thyssen, who later took over the financing of Naziism, was not an anti-Semite and was not attracted to Hitlerism until he realized that the crackpot could be made into a tool of Big Business.

The most credible evidence regarding Ford's financing of early Naziism was given in the treason trial of Herr Hitler himself. On November 8, 1923, Hitler had made the now famous Munich Beer Hall Putsch—he rushed into the Buergerbrau cafe, leaped on a table, screamed, and when people began to laugh, fired three revolver shots into the ceiling and announced the Nazi revolution. On February 7, 1924, Herr Auer, vice-president of the Bavarian Diet, testified in the Hitler trial as follows:

"The Bavarian Diet has long had the information that the Hitler movement was partly financed by an American anti-Semitic chief, who is Henry Ford. Mr. Ford's interest in the Bavarian anti-Semitic movement began a year ago when one of Mr. Ford's agents, seeking to sell tractors, came in contact with Diedrich Eichart [Note: Eckart is correct] the notorious Pan-German. Shortly after, Herr Eichart asked Mr. Ford's agent for financial aid. The agent returned to America and immediately Mr. Ford's money began coming to Munich.

"Herr Hitler openly boasts of Mr. Ford's support and praises Mr. Ford as a great individualist and a great anti-Semite. A photograph of Mr. Ford hangs in Herr Hitler's quarters, which is the center of the monarchist movement."

Shortly after Herr Auer made this accusation, Mr. Ford's European agent, W. C. Anderson, resigned, and the Ford company experienced great difficulties in doing business in the German Republic.

There was nothing illegal about subsidizing Hitler—that is, until Pearl Harbor, when such an action would be treason, punishable by death. From 1922 on it was frequently reported in the press and it was common knowledge that Ford was subsidizing Hitler, and Ford never denied it.

The *Manchester Guardian,* leading liberal newspaper of the world, reported that Hitler received "more than moral support" from two American millionaires. In his biography of Hitler, Konrad Heiden says:

"That Henry Ford, the famous automobile manufacturer, gave money to the National Socialists directly or indirectly, has never been disputed."

The *Berliner Tageblatt* made an appeal to the American ambassador to investigate the report that Henry Ford was financing Hitler, the *New York Times* Berlin correspondent cabled (*Times,* December 20, 1922, p. 2, col. 3). The correspondent added that Hitler had money to spend—and this was in the midst of the inflation when marks were becoming worthless. The *Times* continued:

"The wall beside his desk in Hitler's private office is decorated with a large picture of Henry Ford. In the antechamber there is a large table covered with books nearly all of which are a translation of a book written and published by Henry Ford. [These are anti-Semitic books]. . . . In Nationalist circles in Berlin too, one often hears of Ford's name mentioned by people who would seem the very last in the world with whom an American respecting the Republican Constitution would seek any association.

"The *New York Times* correspondent is in a position to say that certain circles who make Hohenzollern propaganda their business addressed Henry Ford, whose name was given to them as being that of a man likely to respond favorably—for financial aid. . . . Mr. Ford has not invested in the monarchist propaganda. Indeed he has made that quite clear to those who long for Wilhelm's return. And this fact may be responsible for the pains Hitler takes at every occasion to state that he is not supporting a monarchist movement."

Early in 1923, seven months before the Beer Hall Putsch, Raymond Fendrick, an honest and reliable foreign correspondent (despite the fact he was employed by the *Chicago Tribune* Foreign News Service, an organization which included professional falsifiers such as Donald Day who is now in the Finnish army), had an interview with an almost unheard of man who had been referred to once or twice as "Otto" Hitler.

"We look on Heinrich Ford as the leader of the growing Fascisti movement in America," Adolf told the journalist; "we admire particularly the anti-Jewish policy which is the Bavarian Fascisti platform. We have just had his anti-Jewish articles translated and published. [It] is being circulated to millions throughout Germany."

If Ford were to deny that he ever sent money to Hitler it would not at all alter the charge that Ford's writings and anti-Semitic views were a great force in the Hitler movement in Germany.

In his book, *I Knew Hitler,* published here in 1938, the Nazi agent Kurt K. W. Luedecke tells of his first trip to America in 1924 for the purpose of obtaining funds from Henry Ford. He insists that he was sent on direct orders from Hitler. Luedecke got along well with Ford's editor. He writes:

"During my visit to America I found time for several talks with the editor of the *Dearborn Independent.* That publication has now embarked on an anti-Jewish campaign, with William J. Cameron writing most of its articles. . . . Cameron, a capable journalist who successfully phrases Henry Ford's inarticulate racial uneasiness, was receptive when I went to see him. He appeared eager for outside assistance."

[For many years after Ford admitted that the Protocols of Zion and other material he published in his Dearborn *Independent* were forgeries, his editor, Cameron, continued to reprint them in *Destiny,* publication of his Anglo-Saxon Federation.]

The Ford Empire is the biggest industrial undertaking in America owned by one family. Edsel Ford was said to be a man with no political leanings and no social conscience. But both Mrs. and Mr. Henry Ford are true Fascists. It was Mrs. Ford who first came under the influence of anti-Semitic preachers and who was favorable to the Tsarist terrorist agent Boris Brasol, who brought the first forgeries known as "The Protocols of Zion" to America. Henry Ford, who at the libel suit against the *Chicago Tribune* proved himself a complete ignoramus on history, philosophy, economics, literature, and everything else except auto engines, has the typical hoodlum mind of the Fascist. Another is Pegler. Still another is Lindbergh. Both Ford and his wife endorsed Buchmanism, which is a highclass form of Fascism, subsidized by big business men for the purpose of propagandizing working men into subservience. Ford, however, proves himself the real Fascist in his employment of the Bennett system of violence (including murder) as a means of maintaining business interests. The Ford Empire is the Hitler Nazi empire on a small scale.

DOCUMENTATION AND REFERENCES:

Dodd interview: Federated Press, January 7, 1938.
The Tragedy of Henry Ford, by Jonathan Norton Leonard.

CHAPTER III

LINDBERGH: SPREADER OF HITLER'S LIES

"For the combating of 'racism' before it sinks its poison fangs deep into our body politic, the scientist has both a special motive and a special responsibility. . . . Only he can give the people the truth. Only he can clean out the falsities which have been masquerading under the name of science in our colleges, our high schools and our public prints. Only he can show how groundless are the claims that one race, one nation, or one class has any God-given right to rule."

—Henry A. Wallace.

"The deepest sin against the human mind is to believe things without evidence."

—Thomas Huxley.

ONE OF THE truly important features of Fascism which neither the great psychologists nor the newspaper vulgarizers have mentioned is the hoodlum minds of so many of its leaders. It is of course natural for all the gangsters of both Germany and Italy to gravitate to a Duce or Fuehrer who proclaimed the greatness of lying and the moral virtues of street fighting, and it is just as natural for the mental criminals to join movements led by these types. In America, however, Fascism has been propagated by persons who may be brilliant, even geniuses in their own field, but political, economic and social hoodlums.

We have had Ford exposed as a mental hoodlum; Westbrook Pegler had been a good sports writer before he developed mental ulcers; and Charles A. Lindbergh, Jr. was an excellent mail pilot and had the good luck to land his plane in Paris and capture the emotions of the world although his feat was not nearly as perilous as that of Hawker and Alcock and Brown who flew the Atlantic before him.

One may even grant Lindbergh the right to enjoy the title of genius for his flight, and sympathize with him on the raw deal the yellow press gave him on later occasions, notably his marriage and honeymoon, and the kidnapping of his baby, and the Hearst campaign which drove him out of the country for several years, but there can be no forgiveness for Lindbergh as a mental hoodlum who spread the three following Hitler lies in America:

1. The Nazi-Coughlin lie of the Jewish ownership or control of the American press.

2. The lie of Nazi air invincibility, and general military supremacy.

3. The Nazi lie of race, color and blood superiority.

The word "lie" in this case is used advisedly. Hoodlum minds cannot be excused. Ford and Pegler and Lindbergh have done America untold harm by spreading falsehood, and thereby confusing the American people at a time the one clear issue—the democratic world against Fascism—should have been stated.

No one, not even Machiavelli, has recognized the value of outright lying as a social, economic and political weapon, as deeply as Adolf Hitler. In the original 1935 German edition of *Mein Kampf* Hitler wrote a passage which begins:

"In der Groesse der Luege liegt immer ein gewisser Faktor des Geglaubtwerdens, da die breite Masse eines Volkes . . ." etc. The reader will find it on page 252. [Here is the passage in translation:]

"The size of the lie is a definite factor in causing it to be believed, because the vast masses of a nation are in the depths of their hearts more easily deceived than they are consciously and intentionally bad.

"The primitive simplicity of their minds renders them more easy victims of a big lie than a small one, because they themselves often tell little lies but would be ashamed to tell big ones.

"Such a form of lying would never enter their heads. They would never credit others with the possibility of such great impudence as the complete reversal of facts. Even explanations would long leave them in doubt and hesitation, and any trifling reason would dispose them to accept a thing as true.

"*Something therefore always remains and sticks from the most impudent lies,* a fact which all bodies and individuals concerned in the art of lying in this world know only too well, and therefore they stop at nothing to achieve this end."

Hitler not only admits "the value of the big lie" but admits aiming Nazi propaganda at the lowest, or moron intelligence. He writes in *Mein Kampf* (the numbers are the pages in the 14th German edition):

"All propaganda must be so popular and on such an intellectual level that even the most stupid of those toward whom it is directed will understand it. Therefore the intellectual level of the propaganda must be the lower, the larger the number of people who are to be influenced by it." (197)

"Propaganda must not serve the truth, especially not insofar as it might bring out something favorable for the opponent." (260)

"Through clever and constant application of propaganda people can be made to see paradise as hell, and also the other way round, to consider the most wretched sort of life as paradise." (376)

1. The Lindbergh Lie About the Press

Proof that Lindbergh lied regarding Jews and the press is given in *Editor & Publisher,* unofficial spokesman for the publishers of America, its statistical publications and handbooks. The weekly is reactionary, as venal as the newspapers it defends, but its statistics, facts and figures are authoritative. For many years Arthur Robb, liberal Catholic editor of *Editor & Publisher,* has been exposing Coughlin and other falsifiers so far as the press is concerned. According to *Editor & Publisher,* there are some 1,900 dailies, published by 1,700 men and corporations, of whom just 15 are Jews—or less than 1%. No Jew directs the three national news services. So far as editorial policy is concerned, Mr. Robb says, the department stores and other advertisers do not control it. It is true that advertisers, department stores and others suppress news unfavorable to themselves, as for example, during the Gimbel strike in New York. But there is no evidence that department store owners, Jews, Catholics or Protestants, have ever used their pressure for religious or racial purposes. All they are after is money.

Following Lindbergh's Des Moines attack on the Jews, Mr. Robb wrote in *Editor & Publisher*:

> "War hysteria has created the opportunity for the malicious and wicked crackpots who revel in race prejudice to get their faces out of the mud which is their natural habitat. Determined efforts have been noted to inflame the American people against the Jewish race and religion, charging that through the 'control' exercised by Jewish people over the press, the radio, and the films, the country is being drummed to war. As *Editor & Publisher* has demonstrated by citing the facts, it is absolutely false that there is any Jewish control of the daily newspapers. [Here statistics are given.] The case for control of news and editorials by Jews is a chimera. (October 14, 1940.)
>
> "This page has often expressed detestation for intolerance and for propaganda against any race or religion in America. There is no 'Jewish question' of any importance except in the minds of the bigoted, the ignorant and those who use anti-religious agitation of all kinds as a cloak for even less creditable aims. We have stated, and proved, that there is no Jewish control of the American press. The facts on that are easily ascertainable by anyone who wants to know the truth; the repetition, after repeated disproof, of the lie about 'Jewish control of the news,' has come from many sources with many possible motives. Whatever their motives, and no matter how great their sincerity, their promotion of this falsehood tends toward one result—the forwarding of Fascist-Nazi propaganda in a land where it can have no place." (June 15, 1940.)

The second quotation was occasioned by the exposure by the *Birmingham News* of a letter from the Deutsche Fichte-Bund, Hamburg, sent to many Americans in which the phrase "Jew-controlled American press" is used; also the distribution of a sheet signed "Francis P. Moran, director Christian Front," during the Yankee Division parade, Boston.

La Follette's *Progressive* pointed out (March 11, 1939) that an examination of the facts disproves Father Coughlin, then using the radio for anti-Semitism. "Father Coughlin," said the *Progressive,* "is too realistic to believe that statement [that Jews control the press] but he finds the attack useful in his plan of utilizing anti-Semitism to attain his ends."

Going down the list of cities, it is found that New York, the metropolis, with a larger Jewish population than any other city, has 2 out of 9 papers owned by Jews, the *Times,* which is Tory, and the *Post,* pro-New Deal. The biggest paper is the *News* with a circulation more than three times that of the *Post* and *Times* combined. The *News* was isolationist, has been pro-Japanese. Hearst's *Mirror,* with more than *Times* and *Post* circulation combined, has urged a Mussolini for America. Most embattled win-the-war newspaper is Reid's *Herald Tribune.*

"In Chicago," continues the *Progressive,* "there is not a single daily newspaper which is controlled by Jews. . . . In St. Louis one . . . out of three is owned by Jews. . . . There is no Jewish newspaper owner in St. Paul or Minneapolis. Ditto for Kansas City. In Washington, the national capital, where if what Father Coughlin says is true, Jewry would attempt to dominate the newspapers, there is only one newspaper out of five which is owned by a Jew. This is the *Washington Post,* whose proprietor is the wealthy financier Eugene Meyer. But the circulation of the *Post* represents a small minority. . . . The cities outlined above are typical of the general situation throughout the country."

In Lindbergh's Des Moines speech, his most anti-Semitic, he used the same phrase which the Columbia shortwave listening station had picked up in a Berlin Propaganda Ministry broadcast at the same time. The Berlin propaganda said: "There are too many Jews who control the North American radio and the North American press. . . ." Lindbergh said that "the British, Jewish and Administration groups" are the only important interventionists in America, and that "the greatest danger to this country lies in the large Jewish ownership and influence in our motion pictures, our press, our radio, and our government."

Are both statements true, or are they false?

Miss Dorothy Thompson (whose politics are no concern here but whose record as a journalist publishing facts is unequaled) has taken every line of Lindbergh's quoted above (which is also the content of the Nazi broadcast) and shown in her syndicated column that Lindbergh spoke falsehood and propaganda rather than facts.

"Among the more influential radio commentators," she writes, are "Raymond Gram Swing, H. V. Kaltenborn, Elmer Davis, Walter Winchell, William B. Shirer. Among journalists: Leland Stowe, H. R. Knickerbocker, Edmond C. Taylor, Edgar Ansell Mowrer, John Gunther, Vincent Sheean, John Whitaker, William Stoneman, Quentin Reynolds . . . Hamilton Fish Armstrong. Among columnists: Walter Lippmann, Jay Franklin, Raymond Clapper, Samuel Grafton and myself. Of these 30 names [including government officials] who would certainly be the first people to be suppressed if interventionism were being suppressed, exactly three are Jewish. The others are racially of Dutch, British, Irish and German extraction—there are three of pure German extraction to two of Jewish."

Of the movies, the ownership "is in the hands of banks, and there are few Jewish banks in America. None of the big three is Jewish: Chase National, Guaranty Trust, National City."

Of the press:

"There is an amazingly small amount of Jewish ownership of newspapers. The big news services, A.P., U.P., I.N.S., are not Jewish. The largest chains are Scripps-Howard, and Hearst—not Jewish. . . . The most powerful interventionist newspapers in the country are the *New York Herald Tribune, Chicago Daily News, Baltimore Sun, Louisville Courier-Journal, Denver Post, Atlanta Constitution, Kansas City Star, San Francisco Chronicle, Des Moines Register, Washington Post* and *New York Post.* Only the last two are Jewish-owned. The most powerful interventionist weekly press is the Luce press. Not Jewish. The two monthly magazines with the strongest interventionist policy are the *Ladies Home Journal* and the *Atlantic Monthly*. Not Jewish."

Only a very small percentage of the advertisers is Jewish. It could be added that the richest and biggest papers in America, the *New York Daily News* and *Chicago Tribune,* were isolationist. It is true that bankers, advertisers, big money, control the press, causing suppression, distortion, anti-labor bias, venality and corruption. But no one except the Coughlinites and other anti-Semites has tried to propagate a falsehood that department store advertisers dictate the politics of papers. They merely look after their profits.

2. The Lie of Nazi Invincibility

From June 22, 1941, to Stalingrad, the newspaper headlines told the story of Hitler's attack on Russia. The historic fact has already been written and officially admitted by the Germans, that the foe was strong, stubborn, brave, knew no fear, and returned blow for blow. By October 24, 1941, the Germans had claimed 14,000 Russian airplanes destroyed and on that same day they reported Russian air attacks. Both sides admitted that the Germans were superior in numbers of men, guns, tanks and planes but the Germans never claimed that the Russian air force was inferior, the airplanes worthless, the fighting capacity of Russian aviators not worth mentioning, the personnel untrained, and the whole Russian air service a walkover for Germany.

Lindbergh had done just that.

Lindbergh was decorated by the Nazis. He stated he received the medal merely as a gesture. Those who years ago warned against Lindbergh said he received the decoration for services to the Nazis. The official citation which goes with Nazi medals (such as Henry Ford and other pro-Nazi Americans have received) shows it is for help to the Hitler regime. No one but Lindbergh himself can answer the question whether he got the medal for spreading the Hitler propaganda lie of the invincibility of the German air force and the uselessness of the Russian air force. The facts about his spreading this lie appeared in the daily press of Britain in 1938.

1. In the House of Commons, October 10, Ellen Wilkinson, Labor member, said:

"It is a very serious thing that when a very prominent American airman was being lunched by these people [Lady Astor and Clivedeners] and all sorts of official people invited to meet him, he assured them it was impossible for this country to do anything because Germany's air force was better than the Russian, British and French combined."

2. *London Sunday Times,* October 2:

"Colonel Lindbergh has recently returned from a visit to Russia and apparently he was not favorably impressed by the rate of progress there."

3. Lord Beaverbrook's *Express,* October 16:

"What is the mysterious, secretive, over-publicized Col. Lindbergh up to? Always when trouble has been bubbling, his black and orange airplane has flown him to the storm center. . . . He paid another visit to Germany early this year and in between these visits he has busied himself spreading alarming stories here about Germany's air strength compared with ours.

"Germany's machines, he tells all ears that listen here, are better than ours. She has more of them. Her production is fivefold ours. And when these facts are firmly planted in the listener's mind, the Colonel will then, it is said, strongly advocate some sort of pact between Britain and Germany as the only way Britain can avoid disaster.

"He always insists firmly that he is anti-Nazi himself, but those who are favored with his views say that he never hesitates to voice his glowing admiration for Hitler and the German State.

"Early this year he was in Russia as an honored guest and he was given unusual facilities to see the Russian air force, Russia's flying men took him fully into their confidence.

"Then he returned to Britain and began to spread the story that the Russian air force was useless.

"When the crisis was developing, too, he took himself to France and spread the same story there. That story shook France and may have considerable influence on the vital decisions that France in common with Britain had to make."

4. *The Week*, October 13, declared that Lindbergh called on Lloyd George to persuade him that the Russian air service was useless. *The Week* reported that Lloyd George asked Lindbergh if he had talked with War Commissar Voroshilov, and that Lindbergh replied:

"No. Voroshilov? Who's Voroshilov, anyway?"

It was also reported that Lloyd George found Lindbergh personally "quite a charming fellow."

The Hitler decoration to Lindbergh, a "distinguished foreigner who has deserved well of the Reich," was presented October 19, about a week after Lindbergh's Russian hosts, eleven noted aviators, signed a statement accusing Lindbergh of "providing Chamberlain with arguments for handing over parts of Czechoslovakia to Adolf Hitler." The statement also accused Lindbergh of "calumnies and insolent attacks" and quoted Lindbergh as telling Lady Astor: "Germany possesses such a strong air force it is capable of defeating the combined air fleets of England, France, Russia and Czechoslovakia." This is called "a colossal lie. . . . Another unbridled lie followed. Lindbergh declared the Soviet air fleet is without leadership and is in a chaotic condition. . . . Lindbergh plays the role of stupid liar, lackey and flatterer of German Fascists and their English aristocratic protectors. He had an order from English reactionary circles to prove the weakness of Soviet aviation and give Chamberlain an argument for capitulation at Munich in connection with Czechoslovakia.

"The bribed liar, Lindbergh, fulfilled the order of his masters. That explains everything."

Who was lying, Lindbergh or the Russians?

Here is what the Nazi official handbook of contemporary military science (*Handbuch der Neuzeitlichen Wehrwissenschaften*), issued in Berlin in May, 1939, said half a year after Lindbergh's propaganda trip to the British Clivedeners and Hitlerites, and before the attack on Russia gave final proof:

> "In the past 16 years the Russians have built up a military air force which leads the world in numbers. . . . The powerful Soviet aviation industry is based on some 50 factories producing planes and engines and another 50 spare parts. These factories furnish six to seven thousand planes annually and 7,000 engines.
>
> "In a short time Russia has become an air power of the first order."

Major Al Williams of the Scripps-Howard newspaper chain endorsed Lindbergh. Major George Fielding Eliot said the opposite. Captain Bossoutrot, who had inspected Russian aviation as head of a delegation of the air commission, French Chamber of Deputies, said regarding Lindbergh's statement that: "I can only repeat that in 1936 the Soviet air force was the most powerful in the world, and since then even German technicians agree that its production has increased."

C. C. Grey, editor of *Aeroplane* (London), agreed with Lindbergh. Grey also came out for Hitler and Mussolini politically.

These are the facts in the case. In view of the written pages of history of the Global War, there can now be no question that Lindbergh carried the Nazi air invincibility lie to Britain. Of course, the fact that the inferior British air fleet in September, 1940, held its own against—and some say it defeated—the German air fleet, is further evidence that Lindbergh was just another agent of the Hitler theory of the colossal lie when he mingled with the Cliveden Set. The purpose, of course, was to help defeat the democracies, to help the triumph of world Fascism.

3. The Race, Blood and Color Lie

Regarding the myth of superiority of blood, race or color, the ancient saying that "a lie can travel half way round the world while truth is putting on her shoes" also holds good. The men whose writings Hitler and Lindbergh have adopted are not scientists; they are: Houston Chamberlain, a renegade Englishman who worked for the Kaiser in the first World War; the Count de Gobineau, a fiction writer; Madison Grant and Lothrop Stoddard, two American journalists whose writings are absolutely without scientific backing. German scientists since the coming of Hitler and Italian scientists of the past two years have on orders revised their views. But free scientists have denounced as lies, frauds and myths the entire output of the race, blood and color superiority propagandists.

Lindbergh's adaptation of the Hitler-Mussolini Nordic myth is expressed by him in his article, "Aviation, Geography, and Race" (*Reader's Digest,* November, 1939), in which he says:

"Aviation . . . is a tool specially shaped for Western hands, a scientific art which others only copy in a mediocre fashion, another barrier between the teeming millions of Asia and the Grecian inheritance of Europe—one of the priceless possessions which permit the White race to live at all in a pressing sea of Yellow, Black, and Brown. . . .

"While we stand poised for battle, Oriental guns are turning westward, Asia presses towards us on the Russian border, all foreign races stir restlessly. It is time to turn from our quarrels and to build our white ramparts again. . . .

"Our civilization depends on a united strength among ourselves; on a strength too great for foreign armies to challenge; on a Western wall of race and arms which can hold back either a Genghis Khan or the infiltration of inferior blood; on an English fleet, a German airforce, a French army, an American nation, standing together as guardians of our common heritage, sharing strength, dividing influence. . . .

"We can have peace and security only so long as we band together to preserve that most priceless possession, our inheritance of European blood, only so long as we guard ourselves against attack by foreign armies and dilution by foreign races."

This is the stuff that Hitler's Rosenberg wrote and Hitler and Hess adapted in *Mein Kampf.* But scientists before and after this publication have united in showing up this nonsense and falsehood.

In August, 1934, the Congress of Anthropological and Ethnological Sciences discussed racial theories and political action. Sir Grafton Elliot Smith, J. B. S. Haldane, Professor of Genetics in the University of London, and scientists from many parts of the world, united in showing scientifically that the Hitler theory, now propagated by Lindbergh, was a total falsehood. One of the most interesting statements was that of Professor Haldane from which the following is a quotation:

"Whatever innate differences in ability may exist between races, they are clearly of an overlapping type.

"If South African Negroes are ever afforded equal cultural opportunities with Whites, it may be found that a smaller proportion of them can reach a given standard, but it is already certain that some Negroes can reach higher cultural levels than most of the Whites.

"The doctrine of the equality of man, although clearly untrue as generally stated, has this much truth: that on a knowledge of their ancestry we cannot yet say one man will and another will not be capable of reaching a given cultural standard.

"The so-called races within Europe have a much more dubious status. In respect to physical characters, they overlap to a considerable extent. Any population may be 'racially homogeneous' in the sense that its genes have been thoroughly mixed by random mating, but there is no reason to believe such populations differ in any but a statistical sense—the same genes being found throughout, though in different proportions.

"Within such a population a man of a given type—for example, a 'Nordic' with a long head, blond hair and blue eyes, is no more likely to have a high proportion of Scandinavian ancestry than a relative not possessing those characters. Nor is it possible in the present state of our knowledge to determine the proportions of ancestry in a given population which belonged to various hypothetical races in the past."

The European race theory was studied by two noted scientists, Julian S. Huxley and A. C. Haddon. In reviewing their work (*We Europeans*), H. S. Jennings, professor at Johns Hopkins, states:

"The keystone of modern genetics is the gene. Genes are substances present in small amounts which are precisely located in certain structures (chromosomes) of every cell in the body and are transmitted from parent to offspring. . . .

"Apparently man developed in early times by alteration of some of his genes . . . some three or four or five geographical varieties . . . the white, black, yellow and brown varieties. . . .

"Almost, or quite from the beginning of differentiation, these different varieties began to intermingle; to exchange genes; so that it is doubtful if any human group now represents any one of these varieties in 'pure' condition—without admixture of genes from another. Whether the genes of these different primary varieties differ in their capabilities for mental and cultural development has never been demonstrated.

"In Europe . . . they have exchanged genes to such an extent that it is doubtful whether there exist any 'pure' representatives of any of them. Every nation in Europe is an inextricable mixture of the genes of these secondary varieties. . . . In Germany Nordics and Alpines are intermixed. . . .

"These conditions apply to Jews as well as to existing nations. The Jews are shown both in history and by anthropological evidence to be a much mixed group, carrying genes from many diverse sources."

There is no evidence, the scientists find, that the chief European groups differ in cultural capabilities; "the nations of the present time are not racial units."

The eminent scientist, the late Professor Franz Boaz of Columbia, wrote that there is no Aryan people or race, there is only an Aryan language. . . . It is fiction to speak of a German race. . . . The East German is close to his Polish neighbor. There is no more a Semitic than there is an Aryan race, since both terms define linguistic groups, not human beings. . . . In some cases the Tyrolese (Hitler folks) and the Armenoid (Jews) can hardly be distinguished with certainty.

The word "Aryan" dates from 1794 when Sir William Jones introduced the word "Arya" for people who spoke one of the Indo-European languages. Professor Max Mueller, German professor of Philosophy at Oxford, in 1853 promulgated the theory that Aryan languages must have originated with an Aryan race. Many Germans leaped upon this idea to boast of a superior Aryan German people. By 1888 Prof. Mueller, who was a scientist and therefore open-minded, confessed his error. He wrote:

"I have declared again and again that if I say Aryan I mean neither blood nor bones nor hair nor skull; I mean simply those who speak an Aryan language. . . . To me an ethnologist who speaks of Aryan race, Aryan blood, Aryan eyes and hair, is as great a sinner as a linguist who speaks of a dolichocephalic dictionary or a brachycephalic grammar."

Professor Mueller protested for years, but nothing could stop the falsehood. Again it was proven that a lie can travel half way round the world while truth is putting on her shoes. It also proved that whereas the quest for knowledge and scientific truth produces great enlightenment, and this truth is placed in books and kept in libraries, it does not prevail against something like a Goebbels propaganda machine when a cog as famous as Lindbergh is placed in it. Readers will find every scientific book denies the Hitler-Lindbergh myth, and that its only supporters are crackpots, fiction writers, and hired journalists.

If Lindbergh, as his friends claim, is not a pro-Nazi, it is very easy for him to say so and to prove it by action. The following open letter to Lindbergh is a fair challenge. A similar challenge was made to Wendell Willkie by this writer when Coughlin and other anti-Semites endorsed him and he immediately repudiated them and *Social Justice,* naming them by name. This one was written by L. M. Birkhead, national director, Friends of Democracy, Fidelity Building, Kansas City, Missouri; it is the concluding page of the pamphlet *Is Lindbergh a Nazi?*:

"Dear Mr. Lindbergh:

"On the basis of the evidence presented in this pamphlet we are forced to believe that you accept Hitler's 'New Order' as the future pattern of the world. Moreover, the evidence indicates that you are attempting to extend the 'New Order' to the U. S.

"If it is not true that you are working toward a Hitlerized world, you are the victim of the most gigantic coincidence in the history of the world, for in your speeches and writings you have repeated almost word for word the Nazi propaganda line.

"So great has been the coincidence, if it is coincidence, that you have fooled a majority of American Nazis. They look upon you as their 'leader.'

"If you are the victim of a coincidence, and if you wish to clear up the matter, once and for all, you must do these things:

"1. Return your Nazi decoration to Hitler.

"2. Repudiate Naziism as forthrightly as you have condemned Communism.

"3. Condemn Nazi aggression.

"4. Disavow the support of those American Nazis who have declared you to be their 'leader.'

"5. Insist that the America First Committee, under whose auspices you speak, dissociate itself from the pro-Nazi, anti-Semitic elements which make up a large part of its membership.

"6. Repudiate as Nazi propaganda all theories of racial or 'Aryan' supremacy.

"7. Declare anti-Semitism to be a Nazi propaganda trick, a device of power politics.

"8. Reaffirm your faith in democracy and declare your willingness to fight for its preservation.

"In order to counteract the effects of the extensive distribution of your speeches and writings by Nazi propagandists, and their repeated assertion that you are in agreement with them, you must see to it that your repudiation of Naziism is widely publicized. Otherwise your name will continue to be used to sell an un-American, anti-democratic ideology. No single American must be left in doubt concerning your choice between democracy and Naziism.

"If you do not see fit to speak, Mr. Lindbergh, your silence will testify that you are, indeed, a disciple of Hitlerism."

Lindbergh remained silent.

International Bankers Are for Fascism

Another colossal Hitlerian lie which Goebbels, Coughlin and other falsifiers of fact have spread for decades is the charge the international bankers are Jews. Curiously enough it was one of the leading America Firsters, Senator Nye, who proved conclusively who the international bankers were and what part they had in bringing America into the World War. Nye proved it was the House of Morgan which must take most of the blame.

Nye's partner in America First leadership, Senator Wheeler, in one of his pre-war speeches said: "Now we find these same international bankers . . . with the Sassoons of the Orient and the Rothschilds and Warburgs of Europe in another theme song . . . 'Our investments in India, Africa and Europe must be preserved.' "

Wheeler apologized. "I have repeatedly called attention to . . . the Morgans and the Chase and other international bankers and particularly Tom Lamont . . ." he said in his apology. Nevertheless the listing of Jewish names was heard throughout the nation, the apology appeared in a small Jewish newspaper.

Every intelligent person knows that bankers are bankers, that their object is to make money, and that "race, religion, blood," nationality, patriotism, etc., etc., have never interfered with international or national banking. The fact that J. P. Morgan had no Jewish partner and was an Episcopalian does not indicate an "Episcopalian plot" in the First World War to anyone but crackpots. And because there was money in it, Zacharoff, a Greek Catholic who was incidentally a director of the Chase National Bank, armed Turkey to fight Greece. (The love of money is the root of all evil.)

The Jewish bankers are no better and no worse than the Episcopalian bankers or the Catholic bankers or the Mohammedan bankers.

For a long time several Jewish bankers dealt with Hitler and the Nazis. They said anti-Semitism was all right because it was directed against the poor, the refugees, the Jewish workingmen, not the rich bankers. They showed no "race" or "blood" ties with the poor. To this day a Jewish banker works for Hitler. (Baron Max von Oppenheim, who said Hitler was fighting only Bolshevism, that nice people need not be afraid of him. Hitler has raised Baron Max to Honorary Aryan status. —*Time,* June 16, 1941.) Banker Giuseppi Toeplitz of Milan collected funds which paid for Mussolini's blackshirt army and put the Duce in power. He too was a Jew.

For the sake of the factual record, here is a list of the leading American international bankers and the money they have out in international loans:

J. P. Morgan & Company	$1,514,000,000
National City Bank	892,000,000
Dillon, Read & Company	872,000,000
Chase, Harris, Forbes	643,900,000
Guaranty Trust	509,000,000
Bancamerica-Blair	471,500,000
Lee, Higginson	322,000,000
Kuhn, Loeb & Company	220,700,000
Speyer & Company	207,000,000
Hallgarten & Company	194,400,000
Brown Brothers, Harriman	190,100,000
J. & W. Seligman	118,900,000
White Weld & Company	88,300,000
Bankers Trust	78,500,000
First of Boston Corp.	55,400,000
Halsey Stuart & Company	30,000,000
Miscellaneous	1,212,900,000
A total of more than	$7,000,000,000

Any person able to read a book can obtain *Poor's Register of Directors* and other financial manuals which print the facts. *Poor's,* for example, lists some 80,000 persons as directors of American corporations of whom 3,825 or 4.8% are Jews. Of the 919 members of the Stock Exchange (according to *Fortune's* 1936 survey) 148 were Jews; of 420 listed directors of the New York Clearing House 30 were Jews. Kuhn Loeb is the only Jewish firm with any substantial international banking business, and had foreign loans outstanding March 1, 1935, amounting to

2.88% of the total compared to National City's 11.71% and Morgan's 19.87%.

It is a fact that J. P. Morgan financed Mussolini. One loan amounted to $100,000,000. On the other hand, the Jewish banker, Clarence Dillon of Dillon, Read, a firm including Catholics and Protestants, financed Thyssen, who in turn was the chief backer of Hitler. He also issued loans to Italian fascist cities.

Factual evidence shows that bankers, international or whatnot, are without exception on the side of money; they always invest to make profits, and they are without exception on the reactionary or fascist side, no matter what church, nation, "race" or "blood" they belong to. When Wheeler, Coughlin, Hitler, Goebbels and others make statements to the contrary such statements are propaganda, if not plain falsehood.

Curiously enough, no less an authority than Fritz Thyssen, the man who bought and paid for the Nazi Party, believes the rumor that Hitler is partly Jewish.

Every official trace of evidence concerning Hitler's ancestry has now disappeared. It has been destroyed by order, just as were Mussolini's police record in Italy and his record for forgery in Switzerland (as well as his political arrests). However, Thyssen writes: "According to the published records, Hitler's grandmother had an illegitimate son, and this son was to become the father of Germany's present leader." An inquiry by Chancellor Dollfuss of Austria "disclosed that the Feuhrer's grandmother became pregnant during her employment as a servant in a Viennese family . . . none other than that of Baron Rothschild." Thyssen insists that Hitler learned of this document and that it was one of the reasons for the murder of Dollfuss. Thyssen believes the British secret service has a copy. The original, he says, Hitler got from Chancellor Schuschnigg and destroyed.

If Thyssen's rumors turn out to be facts, it would appear that the world's greatest anti-Semite, the greatest liar and the greatest propagandist of the "international bankers" myth, is himself a Rothschild.

BOOKS ON THE RACE MYTH

We Europeans, by Julian S. Huxley and A. C. Haddon.
Race, by Jacques Barzan.
Man's Most Dangerous Myth: The Fallacy of Race, by Professor M. F. Ashley Montagu (with a foreword by Aldous Huxley).
Race: Science and Politics, by Ruth Benedict.
General Anthropology, Franz Boaz, editor.
The Mind of Primitive Man, by Franz Boaz.
Race, Language and Culture, by Franz Boaz.
Heredity and Politics, by Professor J. B. S. Haldane.
The Genetic Basis for Democracy, by Vice President Wallace.

CHAPTER IV

THE READER'S DIGEST

IF IT IS true that five, six or seven persons read every copy of the popular magazines, then it is also true that the reactionary, anti-labor, and frequently fascist propaganda which the *Reader's Digest* passes off on an unsuspecting public influences no less than 50,000,000 persons. The *Digest* has 9,675,000 subscribers, 8,300,000 in America. It pretends to be an impartial reprint magazine, selecting the best items from all the others, but it is in fact a skillfully manipulated publication spreading the reactionary views of a powerful nobody named DeWitt Wallace.

A man who has so much power in his hands—the making of public opinion by reaching the majority of the people of this country who can read—should realize his social responsibilities. DeWitt Wallace is either a knave or a fool. Either he is so stupid that he does not know that he is spreading Fascism, or he is a Machiavellian knave who has devised a wonderful and sinister method, far superior to any known to Herr Goebbels.

Before presenting the evidence—most of which is visible to any person who will go to the public library and study the issues of *Reader's Digest* beginning with 1933, the year Hitler took over—I will permit Mr. Wallace himself to speak first. In reply to my indictment of himself and his publication as native-Fascist, he replied by saying my charges were "unadulterated lies." My three-part indictment was summarized as follows:

1. That DeWitt Wallace, owner and publisher of the *Reader's Digest,* told his staff he does not want Hitler defeated.

2. That beginning with the November, 1942, *Reader's Digest*

a new editor has been appointed who as editor of the *American Mercury* was first to publish native fascist propaganda in the United States. (Foreign fascist propaganda, written by Mussolini, Ribbentrop, Goebbels, Goering, etc., was first introduced to America by William Randolph Hearst in his magazine *Cosmopolitan,* and his 20-odd newspapers.)

3. That *Reader's Digest* has consistently published reactionary, anti-labor and native fascist propaganda, sandwiched in with pleasant human interest stories which have built up the largest circulation in the world.

Here is Mr. Wallace's form letter, sent no doubt to thousands of his readers who protested. Please note that there is no rebuttal of the second and third part of the indictment, the documented parts. Mr. Wallace wrote:

> "The statements attributed to me are unadulterated lies, as anyone knows who has ever talked to me. The magazine itself and the easily available record of its 25 senior and roving editors speak for themselves. The members of our staff feel that we should regard as laughable such complete drivel.—DeWitt Wallace."

More than a hundred persons sent me their copies of this letter. To many of these persons I wrote suggesting they write Mr. Wallace this simple question: "Is Paul Palmer a senior editor? Is this the same Paul Palmer who printed Dennis and other fascist propaganda in the *American Mercury?* If Wallace replies No, he is a liar; if he replies Yes, he is a native Fascist."

Mr. Wallace did not reply.

The evidence against the *Reader's Digest* as a fascist publication hinges somewhat on the most famous declaration about American Fascism ever made. Its author was the man who at one time appeared to be the logical demagogue who might take over the country. I was very much impressed with him when I met him in the lobby of the Senate because he was so clearly the Mussolini (rather than the Hitler) type: smiling (rather than frowning), affable, silver-tongued (rather than strident), apparently well-read and considerably cultured (rather than hoodlum-minded like Hitler) and crookedly demagogic. Fascism, said Huey Long, will come to America on an anti-fascist platform. A study of Wallace's expressions and deeds indicates that behind all his patriotic flagwaving Americanism and his declarations against Fascism here is indeed a man in the Huey Long tradition.

The statements which Mr. Wallace called "unadulterated lies" were reports of his views made to me by several members of the editorial and business staff of *Reader's Digest.* At least four of Mr. Wallace's employees are aware of his Fascism, and one of them quoted Mr. Wallace as saying:

> "We do not want Germany completely defeated. I think Germany should be beaten up a bit, and I prefer that the American army does it, so that Hitler will learn who is boss in this world.
>
> "But I do not want Germany smashed. What will become of the continent of Europe if Hitler is killed and Fascism completely eradicated? The Russians will conquer all of Europe. Therefore our policy should be to whip Hitler to the point where he recognizes we are the biggest power in the world, and then keep Hitler in Europe to police the continent and maintain order.
>
> "We also need a little Fascism in the United States to keep this country in order. We need a certain type of Fascism here to keep radicals out and radical systems and philosophies from making any headway, and even attempting to take over the government."

Shocking as this statement sounds in wartime, when we are fighting Hitler and Mussolini, and spending blood and treasure in vast amounts to preserve the anti-fascist or democratic way of life, it is a fact that just before Pearl Harbor this view was held by all the native Fascists who feared Hitler less than a victory of the people of all countries. William Randolph Hearst, Colonel McCormick, the appeasement Senators, the pro-Nazi Representatives led by Clare Hoffman and other anti-Semites, the large body of preachers led by Father Coughlin, Rev. Gerald L. K. Smith, Rev. Gerald Winrod, Rev. Bob Shuler and the like, and Lindbergh, were so anti-Russian that they preferred Hitler. Several expressed the hope that both nations would bleed them-

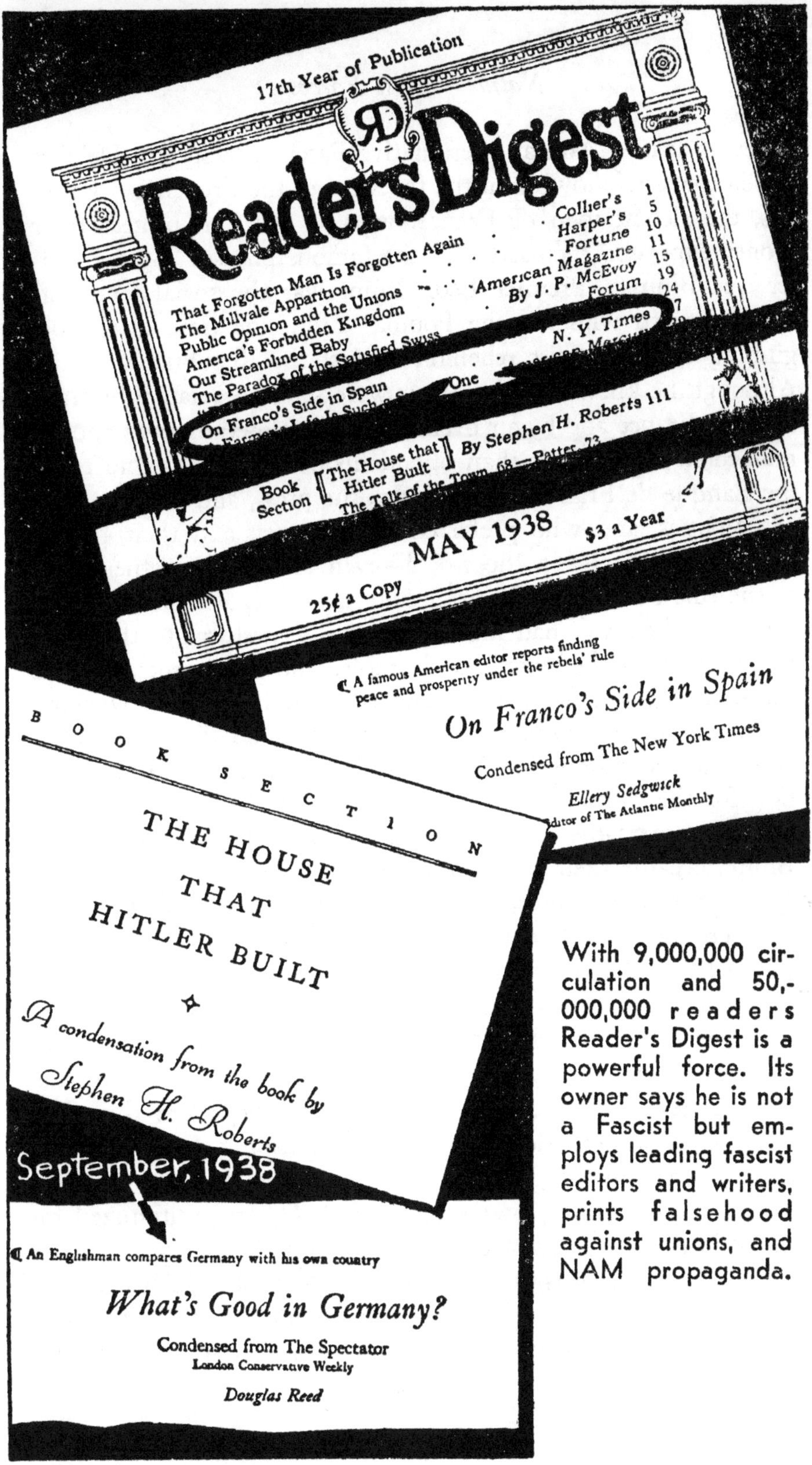

17th Year of Publication
Reader's Digest
That Forgotten Man Is Forgotten Again . . . Collier's 1
The Millvale Apparition . . . Harper's 5
Public Opinion and the Unions . . . Fortune 10
America's Forbidden Kingdom . . . American Magazine 11
Our Streamlined Baby . . . By J. P. McEvoy 15
The Paradox of the Satisfied Swiss . . . Forum 19
On Franco's Side in Spain . . . N. Y. Times
Book Section [The House that Hitler Built] By Stephen H. Roberts 111
MAY 1938
25¢ a Copy
$3 a Year
A famous American editor reports finding peace and prosperity under the rebels' rule
On Franco's Side in Spain
Condensed from The New York Times
Ellery Sedgwick
Editor of The Atlantic Monthly
BOOK SECTION
THE HOUSE THAT HITLER BUILT
A condensation from the book by Stephen H. Roberts
September, 1938
An Englishman compares Germany with his own country
What's Good in Germany?
Condensed from The Spectator
London Conservative Weekly
Douglas Reed

With 9,000,000 circulation and 50,000,000 readers Reader's Digest is a powerful force. Its owner says he is not a Fascist but employs leading fascist editors and writers, prints falsehood against unions, and NAM propaganda.

selves to death. And all these native Fascists, including DeWitt Wallace, were following in the footsteps of the French 200 Families, the richest men of France, who in order to protect their money expressed themselves in the famous phrase: "Mieux Hitler que Blum." Premier Leon Blum was the social-democrat-liberal-coward who ran the Popular Front the time of the beginning of the Fascist rebellion against the Republic of Spain. Although he knew that the Nazis were sending aviators by train through France and by air over France, he closed his eyes and remained neutral, rather than offend his own Fascists, who ruled the Banque de France, big industry, the press, and the Chamber of Deputies, and who preferred their money and their possessions above all else in the world—even to sacrificing their land to the rule of Hitler. Blum, despite his cowardice and appeasement and betrayal, had made some feeble gestures to the labor unions and to the poor and humble, and every such gesture meant a slight gain in the standard of living of the working class, a necessary slight increase in taxation on the rich. They would not stand for it. They would not even stand for taxation for the purpose of building up an air fleet and for armaments to meet the menace of Hitlerism. "Better Hitler than Blum" became their motto and their program.

Americans, of course, were not faced with this choice. But we were aware of two very important facts, first of which was the fact that the American labor movement was coming of age, and that the 13,000,000, out of a labor force of 52,000,000 in normal peace times, who belonged to unions were intelligent enough to demand something more than a few cents on the hour, a few hours less in the week. Labor, more than any other class in American society, was grasping for something better, that something which Vice President Wallace—no relation to the reactionary owner of *Reader's Digest*—epitomized for us all in his "Century of the Common Man."

The other fact was best expressed by Mussolini in his famous "We or They" speech in which he predicted, a decade ago, that the world was dividing itself between Fascism and Democracy, and that they would clash, and that Fascism would have to destroy Democracy to survive. America saw this conflict the day the Fascist International, the three signatories to the powerful Anti-Komintern Pakt, the Axis powers, turned on Russia, after attacking and conquering many small nations and threatening to invade Britain.

In the face of these two facts all native reactionaries (and you can use this word if "native-Fascists" offends your sensitive ears) were united in attacking and undermining labor, and in upholding the fascist nations in their attempt to overthrow the Union of Soviet Socialist Republics (better known as Russia). There were many in America, outside the Fifth Columnists who were indicted for treason and sedition, who changed the French "Mieux Hitler que Blum" to "Better Hitler than Russia."

DeWitt Wallace denies that he ever said he preferred Hitler. I have therefore printed his denial, although I can produce several members of Mr. Wallace's editorial and business staff who say otherwise. But Wallace's denial of this quotation is not enough because there is a volume of evidence that Mr. Wallace employs Fascists, prints fascist propaganda, has consistently attacked labor unions, has lied about one union and refused to print a retraction, has smeared labor, and has, generally speaking, followed the fascist rather than the anti-fascist line, and tried to indoctrinate 50,000,000 Americans who have read his propaganda against the general welfare of all the people, and especially against the Century of the Common Man. The evidence which follows has not been denied by Mr. Wallace.

America's First Fascist Editor

The evidence which Mr. Wallace dare not answer follows the charge that in the November, 1942, issue of his magazine he named Paul Palmer a senior editor. Paul Palmer is the first and foremost fascist editor in America. There is no getting around or explaining away of these facts.

Palmer introduced American Fascism in the *American Mercury* during his editorship. The publisher at that time and even now is Lawrence E. Spivak. Spivak was publisher of all the fascist propaganda which Palmer bought and remains publisher today with his new editor, Eugene Lyons, and the Spivak-Lyons *American Mercury* is the favorite place in which Wallace places some of his reactionary propaganda.

Palmer and Spivak appeared as editor and publisher of the *American Mercury* April, 1935. The amount paid is estimated at $25,000 to $40,000.

Previous to the Palmer-Spivak fascist regime there had been a liberal regime which permitted Lawrence Dennis to criticize the New Deal, but under Palmer's guidance Dennis, the leading native Fascist in America, came out in the December issue with "Portrait of American Fascism," which openly stamped the *American Mercury* as the foremost advocate of Fascism in this country. The *Mercury* also announced that Dennis was the author of *The Coming American Fascism,* which was about to be printed and which was recognized as a *Mein Kampf* for America.

March, 1936, Dennis wrote for Palmer and Spivak a review of Einer's *Mussolini's Italy* and *Sawdust Caesar* by the present writer. Dennis defended Fascism against all critics. Paul Palmer published this defense of Fascism.

Throughout the Palmer-Spivak regime the *American Mercury* published other Fascists also, but Dennis was the favorite. July, 1936, in *The Highly Moral Causes of War* Dennis repeated the propaganda for war which was put out by Mussolini; he also defended the Hoare-Laval betrayal of Ethiopia to Mussolini. February, 1937, in *Liberalism Commits Suicide* Dennis attacked any attempt to aid China against the aggressor Japan, or Loyalist Spain against the Fascist Axis—Germany, Italy and Portugal. Dennis defended fascist aggression in all countries. May, 1938, in *Propaganda for War: Model* 1938, Dennis not only pleaded for the cause of fascist aggression but asked American sympathy for it. January, 1939, in *After the Peace of Munich: Is Hitler a Madman?* Dennis exulted over Hitler's victory at Munich, heiled the rule of force in Europe and praised a coming world conquest by the Fascist Axis.

Early in 1942, when Dennis was applying for a commission in the U. S. Army, which most people believe is being trained to fight Italian Fascism and German Naziism, he was writing in his *Weekly Foreign Letter* that the U. S. A. would turn to a "brand of National Socialism (Naziism) of our own making, already emerging in its institutional pattern." Margolin and Conant exposed Dennis in *PM* of March 1 as having gone to Italy in 1936 when an official car of the fascist foreign office was placed at his disposal because fascist officials called him "an important American Fascist." Dennis is revealed telling Italian friends that Nazi Fascism is better than Italian Fascism, that it is necessary to do away with democracy in the U. S. It is also revealed that in the files of the Dies Committee (which notoriously has failed to do anything about native Fascists and Nazis in America) there is a note from Dennis to the Nazi agent Friedrich Auhagen, now in jail, with a notation by Auhagen saying "Had lunch with L. D.; paid him $50 on account."

On March 5 Conant published in *PM* copies of correspondence between Dennis and other Fascists: letter from Dennis submitting articles to Auhagen; letter from Ralph Townsend, Japanese agent now in jail, approving Dennis' May, 1938, article in *American Mercury;* letter from General Van Horn Moseley, who wanted to lead a fascist march on Washington; letter from Amerika-Institut, Berlin, to Nazi propagandist Zapp, telling him to see Dennis; letter from George Deatherage. Thanks to this exposure, Dennis was refused a commission.

How Paul Palmer worked as an editor was revealed by the *New Republic* (December 22, 1937): "A few months ago the editors of the *American Mercury* approached Henry F. Pringle . . . asked him to write an article about the *New Republic* and the *Nation*. . . . He was promptly paid. . . . (Later) he was told firmly that the *American Mercury* would not print his article. It was explained that what that magazine wanted was an article indicating that the liberal journals were tools of Moscow and constituted a great danger to the U. S. Mr. Pringle replied that he did not propose to stultify himself by writing things that he regarded as unfair and untrue. Thereupon the matter was dropped until Mr. Varney was persuaded to write the article." It appeared December, 1937. Harold Lord Varney was associate editor of another fascist magazine published by Dennis—*The Awakener.*

June, 1937, the American Civil Liberties Union sued the *American Mercury* for $50,000 for a libelous article by Varney entitled *Liberalism à la Moscow*. The annual report of the Liberties Union said: "The *American Mercury,* now a spokesman for the fascist viewpoint, published in December an article . . . by Harold Lord Varney, associate editor, formerly secretary of the Italian Historical Society, subsidized by Mussolini. Mr. Varney was personally decorated by the dictator. The article so libeled the Union that suit for $50,000 was brought. . . . When the Union offered to submit to an impartial referee the examination of Mr. Varney's charges, provided the *Mercury* would publish his findings, the publisher (Lawrence E. Spivak, who is still publisher) refused." *New Republic,* approving the suit against the Mercury, said "individuals and organizations of progressive outlook who are working for justice and fundamental human rights are made the targets of loose and irresponsible charges."

And just to round out the history of Palmer, Spivak, the *American Mercury,* Dennis and Varney: June 1, 1935, the *Guild Reporter,* official organ of the American Newspaper Guild, denounced the "arrogant public statements the *Mercury* publisher and editor, Lawrence E. Spivak and Paul Palmer, have been issuing" in the strike of seven editorial employees for decent living wages. The New York Newspaper Guild at a general meeting voted not to read the *Mercury* until it had recognized the right of its employees to organize. Spivak fought his employees until 1937 when the Regional Labor Board found him guilty of violating the law. Spivak and Palmer yelled freedom of the press, announced they would not obey the law, would fight to the Supreme Court. *The Nation* (May 22) called the *Mercury* owners reactionary.

One of the contributors to Palmer's *Mercury* and the present *Mercury* is George E. Sokolsky, exposed by the La Follette committee as secretly in the pay of the NAM, the most powerful and the most fascist organization in America.

During the Spivak-Palmer regime the partners quarreled over only one subject, anti-Semitism. Being a Jew Spivak spoke up against Palmer's bringing in anti-Semitism with his Fascism, but up to February, 1939, Spivak went along with Palmer, and helped introduce most of the fascist writers of the nation to an audience.

This is the history of the new senior editor of the *Reader's Digest*.

Reader's Digest Fascism

Nothing as crude as the labor-baiting campaigns of the Scripps-Howard chain papers, as violent as the red-baiting in the Hearst chain papers, as defeatist as the McCormick-Patterson chain papers or as viciously anti-Semitic as Coughlin's *Social Justice* and the vermin press of the 28 persons indicted for sedition, has ever appeared in the *Reader's Digest,* nevertheless labor-baiting, red-baiting, defeatism and anti-Semitism do appear in the world's biggest magazine. They appear because the owner has a fascist mind, and these are some of the main traits of Fascism.

Incidentally, Mr. Wallace, in addition to a fascist mind and a dictatorial editorial viewpoint, is also one of the "sweetest" men who ever lived. The girl employees think he is a "honey." At the drop of a sneeze he sends around a dozen American Beauty roses, and it is nothing for him to pay for an appendix operation or to hand $71,400 to the staff of 348 as a bonus on Christmas eve. But let an editor take issue with him on one of his pet fascist articles and Mr. Wallace will revenge himself with cruel subtlety: he won't fire the upper-bracket editor but he'll put him to work clipping snippets for filler.

On the other hand a journalist like the Rev. Dr. Stanley High may sometimes say to Mr. Wallace that his suggestion for a story is vicious, or "it stinks" or that he could not possibly do it; and then Mr. Wallace ups the price $500 and Stanley High does the article the reactionary way Mr. Wallace first suggested.

The Stanley High smear on consumers is one instance of the policy of reaction (which is Fascism) of the *Reader's Digest.* By consumers of course we mean the entire American people; and while it is the purpose of a democracy to aid the people, to aid all consumers, it is the purpose of a Big Business dictatorship (Germany, Italy, Japan, Spain, Portugal, Mannerheim-Finland, etc.) to aid only the industrialists who subsidize the fascist party and the top party leaders at the expense of the entire nation. This is what Fascism in every nation was founded for.

We the people—the consumer, labor, the majority—never get a square deal in the newspapers or in the magazines which take advertising for two reasons: (1) the advertiser does not want us to know the facts and (2) the advertiser is part of the Big Business setup which is the enemy of labor and of the consumer, the majority. Enlightened America therefore has always prayed for newspapers and magazines which will not be prostituted by advertising and which will therefore be in a position to tell the truth. Most publications which refuse advertising are more honest than most publications which live by advertising, but in recent history two horrible exceptions to the rule almost ruined it. They are *Social Justice,* which spread more actual falsehood and more maliciousness than any publication in the country; and *Reader's Digest,* which was in the position to lead the Henry Wallace Crusade for the Century of the Common Man, but which preferred instead to lead the DeWitt Wallace retreat into the economic and social barbarism of Fascism.

The Stanley High smear on consumers' organizations is a good example because it betrays the fact that the typical Fascist is a hypocrite as well as an enemy of the people.

Taking no advertising, *Reader's Digest* would have no fear of writing honestly about the cooperatives, the cooperative commonwealth of the future, liberal and radical minority parties or movements, fraudulent medicines, the corrupt press, the treason of Big Business in wartime. But whereas the newspaper publisher is afraid of the advertiser, the little man who started out with a pastepot and scissors 22 years ago is today scared to death of losing some of his accumulated millions. Mr. DeWitt Wallace believes that he can take it with him.

And so even consumers' cooperatives and non-profitmaking public welfare organizations are smeared, and the leading brass-checker of upper-bracket journalism, Stanley High, does the smearing.

The smear, entitled *Guinea Pigs, Left March,* was planted by Wallace in the *Forum* magazine, October, 1939. According to a revelation later made by *New Republic* (January 1, 1940) the original order for High's smear came from the offices of Hearst's *Good Housekeeping,* which had been charged with fraud by the U. S. Government in the operation of its Seal of Approval and other enterprises in conjunction with the advertisers of patent medicines, Miracle Whip, which was later found to have killed four children, and other products. It is also a fact that Hearst's Good Housekeeping Club Service sent the *Forum-Reader's Digest* piece throughout the country with a foreword saying that the cooperatives and consumers' protection organizations were "radical elements . . . bent on foisting their revolutionary views on an unsuspecting public." Here is an instance of Mr. Wallace, aided by the bootlicking writer High, doing a job for America's No. 1 Fascist, William Randolph Hearst. But this is not the first or last time the *Digest* followed the Hearst line.

As originally published in the *Forum,* non-profitmaking cooperatives and public service organizations were attacked. Listed alike were Consumers Research and Consumers Union, both of which test products and issue reports. But when Mr. Wallace, who had ordered and planted the High article in the *Forum,* reprinted it in the *Reader's Digest*, he made one change: he censored out the name of Consumers Research.

Here is the explanation: Consumers Union was formed as a non-profitmaking organization by employees of Consumers Research after a strike against Consumers Research owners, including J. B. Matthews, who were making fine money and paying workers as little as $13.13 a week. Liberal publications and liberal-labor organizations denounced Matthews, and pledged their support to the new organization, Consumers Union. Matthews in revenge went over to the Dies Committee and became its chief smearer of labor-liberal organizations. Matthews cooperated with the maker of Listerine (Lund, once head of NAM); Hearst and Sokolsky joined in the Dies smear against cooperatives and consumers' organizations shortly afterwards. But so far as Wallace, High and the *Reader's Digest* were concerned, both consumers' organizations did the same work, and both had been smeared in the original *Forum* article, but because Matthews had already aligned himself with the fascist forces of the country, Wallace cut the name of his organization out of the *Reader's Digest* reprint of the smear. This is not only venal censorship, it is a high water mark of hypocrisy. (We still insist the Pulitzer journalism committee should issue hypocrisy prizes annually.)

Again, in the High article the author, who attacks everything benefiting the consumer as "'subversive," also deplores the bulletin of the Idaho State Department of Education which says: "Advertising has assisted in bringing about a fake scale of value in our civilization." Hearst and other Fascists who live on the millions from advertising, and the Pacific Coast ad organizations, declared such statements subversive, but what explanation is there for a similar viewpoint in the only big publication in the world which takes no advertising? Obviously Wallace's interests and Hearst's interests are identical as are the interests of most millionaires.

Digest Publishes Nazi Agent

Being one of the richest publications in the world, and dominating American magazine journalism, *Reader's Digest* is in a position to choose whatever it likes. Its choice, therefore, is evidence of its policies. (None but a moron would deny that there is a policy behind the selections, and Mr. Wallace would not care to deny that there have been numerous, but discreet, quarrels in the editorial office when junior editors protested selections of reactionary or fascist articles.)

There are of course many entertaining articles and book condensations, and once in a while something which is literature and really honest, but too frequently there is the usual catering to the moron taste which prevails in every publication which has to satisfy many millions, and there is the obvious choice of the stuff of the native (and foreign) Fascisti.

Surely Mr. Wallace cannot deny he is a knave or a fool when he chooses the work of George E. Sokolsky frequently. Mr. Sokolsky was exposed by the La Follette Committee as being secretly in the pay of the National Association of Manufacturers. He was a paid anti-labor writer and lecturer. The NAM was accused officially of working in secrecy and deceit. The fact Mr. Sokolsky was appearing as a columnist at the time he was secretly in the pay of the worst native fascist outfit in America resulted in one of the greatest scandals in the history of American journalism—a scandal so great that even *Editor & Publisher*, and its editor, Arthur Robb, could for once find no brasscheck excuse. But Sokolsky is still a labor-baiter and Mr. Wallace, having the choice of the whole world of columnists, chose Sokolsky for one and only one reason: because Sokolsky expresses Mr. Wallace's own bias and prejudice and reactionary mind.

In its March, 1941, issue *Reader's Digest* published a hoax by a Nazi agent.

Here is the evidence: In an order for the arrest of Richard Krebs published in all newspapers the evening of November 24, 1942, the Board of Immigration Appeal declared:

> "His life has been so marked with violence, intrigue and treachery that it would be difficult, if not wholly unwarranted, to conclude that his present reliability and good character have been established. . . . Within the past five years [i.e., from 1937, when he entered America, to date] the subject has been considered an agent of Nazi Germany."

The *New York Mirror* (for which same publisher this Nazi agent wrote many anti-Russian and generally red-baiting articles for big money) said November 25: "In effect, the decision means he perpetrated a huge literary hoax."

Thus ends the story of Jan Valtin (Richard Krebs) and his fabulous *Out of the Night,* the hoax which the *Reader's Digest* palmed off on its readers because it was willing to use a Nazi agent's frauds in order to smear Russia.

Mr. DeWitt Wallace, in his introduction to his condensation of the so-called non-fictional book *Out of the Night* (published by Alliance Book Corp., distributed by Book-of-the-Month Club), said: "*Out of the Night* will be one of the most-discussed books of 1941. . . . Carefully authenticated by the publishers."

Mr. Wallace, the publishers, and the Book-of-the-Month, for as little as the cost of a letter addressed to the Los Angeles police department, could have had all the evidence necessary to prove that Valtin-Krebs was a liar, an anti-Semite, a thief, and hoodlum, a Fascist and a Nazi. In New York and Connecticut, the novelist Wellington Roe had made an investigation of General Krivitsky and Jan Valtin and found that both were Fascists and frauds, and that "there is no doubt the State Department and the F.B.I. have been protecting Valtin, a criminal alien." But here is the evidence the Los Angeles police were giving out to the newspapers for the asking—the evidence which Mr. Wallace could have had weeks before he reprinted Valtin, evidence already printed in the anti-fascist press:

"He [Richard Krebs, said the judge in the Los Angeles assault case] went into a clothing store and after purchasing certain articles got into a controversy with the proprietor. He thereupon pulled a revolver and threatened the proprietor and started to beat him over the head with the revolver. He then took the articles of purchase and left the store and was apprehended."

This same episode appears in *Out of the Night* as an order from the O.G.P.U. in Moscow to murder an enemy of the Soviets in America.

But this is not all. The reason Valtin-Krebs so brutally beat up the shopkeeper was because his name was Morris Goldstein and he was a Jew. Here is the evidence:

Assistant District Attorney Kenneth Thomas at the preliminary hearing, August 19, 1926: "Defendant (Valtin-Krebs) took the stand and testified that he struck the victim because 'The Jew made me mad.'" (Full court record: Los Angeles Superior Court, Case No. 28625.)

Also, in January, 1938, Valtin-Krebs was openly charged with still being a Nazi spy in America by *Paa Torn* (Stand Watch), the Scandinavian Seamen's Club paper.

It is true, however, that the Book-of-the-Month Club did get an approval from Assistant Secretary of State A. A. Berle, the so-called "liberal" in our State Department, to publish the book, but Berle is one of the many officials of our State Department frequently on the Fascist-appeasement side.

Said Kenneth Stewart, an editor of *PM,* in that paper (March 3, 1941, p. 15):

"It [*Out of the Night*] is being crammed down the public's throat whole—no questions asked. . . . The Book-of-the-Month Club's promotion and publicity, *Life* magazine, and the *Reader's Digest* seem more interested in discrediting our enemies than in being reasonably skeptical. [Note: enemies then meant Russia first, Germany second.]

"I am convinced that at least some representatives of the U. S. Government have played active roles. Harry Scherman is not the kind of fellow to go out on a limb. Everybody agrees that he got his go-ahead from Adolf Berle in the State Department."

As for Mr. Scherman, he is the same Scherman who put over a National Association of Manufacturers anti-labor so-called anti-inflation piece, had it printed in *Reader's Digest,* then tried to get every member of the same Book-of-the-Month Club, which he controls, to spread his reactionary propaganda.

Reader's Digest Labor Baiting

In America every native Fascist, from the DuPonts to Pegler and Kaltenborn to DeWitt Wallace of *Reader's Digest* and Hearst, Howard, McCormick and Patterson and the rest of the defeatist, native-fascist press, does the next best thing to destroying labor: all these native Fascists fight labor with propaganda and falsehood. Ninety-two per cent of the American press, according to a poll taken by Federated Press, is anti-labor.

Any fair person can spot anti-labor bias in almost any issue of *Reader's Digest*. But here is a case where Wallace was called on his propaganda. It concerns the Federation of Architects, Engineers, Chemists and Technicians (F.A.E.C.T.), a C.I.O. union which together with 19 other C.I.O. unions was once smeared by Chairman Dies of the Un-American Commitee—this was before Vice-President Wallace declared that Dies was acting as if he is in the pay of the Nazi propaganda head, Goebbels.

Following the typical collections of falsehoods and half-truths which the pro-Dies newspapers frontpaged, the F.A.E.C.T. had inserted in the Congressional Record (April 30, 1941) a statement showing the Dies charges were falsehoods and that Dies, in violation of accepted rules, refused to permit persons and organizations slandered to appear before his committee. One of Martin Dies' many lies concerned the technical school where F.A.E.C.T. was teaching men to build ships. F.A.E.C.T. started this school when the Navy failed to listen to its plea for the future defense of the nation in a probable war. F.A.E.C.T. joined the C.I.O. in 1937 and its constitution declares no one shall be barred because of "race, color, creed, nationality, sex, religious or political belief." Naturally the poll-taxer and Negro-baiter Dies smeared the C.I.O. union as red.

This was no excuse, however, for Mr. Wallace of *Reader's Digest* to do the same. Nevertheless, in the July, 1941, issue there is a piece called "We Are Already Invaded" by Stanley High which is a more yellow, sensational and wild-eyed piece than Hearst ever printed, and smears the unions as Moscow agents who have already captured the country. Among the unions smeared is the F.A.E.C.T.

I have the entire correspondence between the Navy Yard Civil Service Association, F.A.E.C.T., and *Reader's Digest*. On August 26 Wallace was asked to take notice of errors in the High article. On September 3 a letter signed "The Editors" says they have read the statement in the Congressional Record "and feel it offers comforting assurance of the patriotic purposes of the F.A.E.C.T. . . . We welcome your denial. . . . Upon Mr. High's return your letter and the reprint from the Congressional Record will be referred to him."

On September 27 the Navy Yard Civil Service Association wrote "Your reply is far from satisfactory. Your article has done our organization incalculable harm." On the basis of the article 23 employees had been dismissed without a hearing by the U. S. Navy. *Reader's Digest* was informed it was libel, and asked to retract.

On December 8, having no reply, the association wrote again. On December 24 it repeated its request for a retraction of the libels, which the first *Reader's Digest* letter indicated. On January 12, 1942—a month after Pearl Harbor—*Reader's Digest* sent the following letter:

"Our failure to reply to your letters was due to the fact that after further investigation we found no basis for any affirmative action on our part in connection with the article which you criticized. Hence there seemed no point in protracting the discussion.

"There seems to us less point in so doing now. In the present emergency, with the American people forgetting bygone political and social dissensions, for spontaneous and unified action . . . this struggle for national survival regardless of any political theories . . . December 7th. . . ."

Under American law it is legal to libel groups, minorities, "races," religions, Negroes, Jews, Catholics, political parties. It is doubtful if the union could have sued *Reader's Digest* for libel, no matter how big the falsehoods. But the code of ethics of all branches of publishing provides for a fair hearing. The union could not get it. Its final letter to Kenneth Payne, executive editor, said:

"This is the fifth [letter]. . . . Your last letter wraps up the American flag in the libel you committed against our organization. Today, more than ever, it is necessary that the truth be told and the facts which were misrepresented by Stanley High be given. Today more than in the recent past, the F.B.I. is watching all employees in defense industries, and by redbaiting and libeling us you have furnished an excuse for the F.B.I. to regard the entire membership of the . . . Association . . . with suspicion. I have presented you with the facts. The facts are that you did not tell the truth. The facts are that you harmed us. . . . You have hurt individuals and the organization. I have asked you on four previous occasions to be decent about this and publish an honest retraction of a serious slander, if not a criminal libel against us, and you have stalled us for half a year, and now try a cheap flag-waving trick."

Mr. Wallace has not replied.

Another victim of *Reader's Digest* labor-smearing—and falsehood, according to Senator Sheridan Downey of California—is the Railroad Brotherhoods, a conservative association of many organizations totaling a million and a quarter men.

Mr. Wallace joined America's No. 1 Nazi, Hearst, and numerous other labor-baiters, notably Pegler and the Scripps-Howard press, in publishing an attack on what they term "featherbedding" in the railroad unions. This is a smear which is repeated many times in each generation, but is of particular use in wartime when the corporations, and notably the railroads, are attempting to destroy the unions and the Wagner Act, and all the gains labor has made. Mr. Wallace went to the aid of the corporations by reprinting the propaganda which appeared under the names of John Patric and Frank J. Taylor, two brasscheck polishers of Big Business, in *Barron's,* a commercial anti-labor publication. The *Reader's Digest-Barron's* smear was so raw that Downey protested in the Senate. He said:

"Lately, certain newspapers and magazines have been carrying derogatory and false articles concerning the number of hours being worked by railroad men. Someone is trying to popularize and propagandize the expression 'featherbedding' in an attempt to make the public believe that large numbers of railroad workers are working very short hours, and that due to arbitrary rules there has been a large waste of railroad workers. I desire to brand such statements and articles as wholly false.

"The *Reader's Digest,* in its last issue, has a most unfair and misleading article on that very subject. It is true that in the U. S. there are approximately 500 railroad engineers and firemen who have what we call a fast blue-chip run. The article in the *Reader's Digest* discussed that particular group of 500 men as though its members worked under conditions typical of those of hundreds of thousands of other railroad workers. . . . In the State of California, to which the *Reader's Digest* refers . . . there are probably only 30. . . . To cite conditions surrounding less than 500 workers in an endeavor to make the American people believe it is typical of the railroad workers, cannot be condemned in too vigorous language. I do not intend to engage in a discussion of that particular group. What I am castigating are the propagandizing articles printed in magazines and broadcast over the nation to make the American people think that railroad workers at the present time are not working long hours a week." [At this point Senator Downey placed statistics into the Record.]

"Any magazine, any newspaper, any speaker who takes isolated statements and then attempts to prove from such statements the truth about the whole group is committing, in my opinion, a treasonable offense. Why do I say 'treasonable'? I say it in the broad meaning of the word, it is true, but I say it because when magazines and newspapers give out data wholly misleading and unfair to the railroad workers, it not only creates a false impression in the mind of the public as to such workers, but it causes bitterness and resentment among the railroad workers against the propagandizing instruments that issue the figures.

"Likewise, I might say, that the same thing is true of the figures with respect to absenteeism."

Senator Downey placed in the Record reports from London which show that investigations prove that only 2% of absenteeism is due to malicious intent. No less than 66 2/3% of absenteeism is due to sickness. Fatigue due to long hours of work is another factor. Labour Minister Bevin is quoted as saying "The majority of the absentees stay away occasionally because of exhaustion."

In its March, 1943, issue *Reader's Digest* committed another fascist sin: it reprinted a piece of propaganda from the propaganda clip sheets sent out by an outfit whose chairman had already been denounced as one of the worst Fascists in the United States.

Under this item Mr. Wallace wrote: "Condensed from a publication of the New York State Economic Council." This sounds just fine. It sounds as if it was an official agency of the state of New York, and that it was an economic council, whereas in truth it is nothing more or less than a pro-Big Money, anti-labor, pro-Fascist outfit run by Merwin K. Hart. Every editor in America who is not a Fascist places the propaganda sheets of the N.Y.S.E.C. in the wastebasket, but it remained for Mr. Wallace, who will call you a liar if you label him a Fascist, to reprint a piece of this propaganda and spread it before 50,000,000 persons.

Mr. Wallace reprints Mr. Hart. Mr. Hart is also one of the leading propagandists for Franco and Spanish Fascism; he was closely associated with the Rev. Charles E. Coughlin of *Social Justice* fame. Mr. Hart contributed to this publication—which escaped a charge of sedition by folding up after Pearl Harbor. Mr. Hart was associated with one Allen Zoll, now in jail facing a criminal charge of common extortion and another charge of being actively pro-Nazi. Mr. Hart was the associate of John B. Trevor, John B. Snow and a dozen other Bundists, Fascists, and anti-Semites.

Fascists of a feather flock together. The Mr. Hart who runs the New York Economic Council is the same Mr. Hart who originated the school textbook witch hunt and who succeeded in banning Professor Rugg's works from several upper New York public schools before the NAM took up the matter, with Professor Robey doing the Goebbels act.

Sokolsky, paid agent of the NAM, wrote a defense of Hart and an excuse for his being a Franco-Fascist, in his *New York Sun* column (April 15, 1941), which Senator Nye obligingly placed in the Congressional Record (May 23, 1941, p. A2631). This piece smears the friends of Republican Spain, supports Franco, and also smears Congressman Joseph Clark Baldwin because Baldwin had declared that he had been informed "that certain sponsors of the N.Y.S.E.C. hold views on our American democracy completely at variance with mine. . . . Those who attempt to divide our nation today . . . those who place race or party prejudice above patriotism; those who refuse to recognize the vital importance of national unity . . . are wittingly or unwittingly preparing the downfall of our nation, just as the same elements prepared the downfall of France. . . ."

Mr. DeWitt Wallace has seen fit to present to fifty million readers the propaganda of Hart's N.Y.S.E.C. Nevertheless, Mr. Justice Jackson of the Supreme Court included Hart and his organization in a denunciation of the leading enemies of American democracy; Justice Jackson also called them underminers of morale and economic exploiters. These are the native Fascists Mr. Justice Jackson named:

1. **H. W. Prentis, Jr. (then)** President National Association of Manufacturers, head of Armstrong Cork Co., friend of Fascist Franco.

2. Charles A. Lindbergh, Jr.

3. The *Saturday Evening Post,* published by Walter D. Fuller, one time president of the NAM, and still a director.

4. League for Constitutional Government. This is the outfit run by ex-Congressman Samuel Pettengill, now G.O.P. director, the Rev. Norman Vincent Peale, S. S. McClure the Fascist, Dr. Rumely, the former German agent, and Frank Gannett, the chain newspaper publisher.

5. Major General Van Horn Mosely, U. S. Army, retired, who wanted to lead a fascist march to take over the government.

6. Merwin K. Hart.

Said Mr. Justice Jackson:

". . . Merwin K. Hart, president of the so-called New York State Economic Council, which is closely allied with the manufacturers' associations. Merwin Hart is well-known for pro-fascist leanings. In 1936 it was his proposal that every person who accepted any form of government help should be denied the right to vote. And now . . . Mr. Hart says that 'it is time to brush aside this word "democracy" with its connotations.' That was the theme of his speech [at the Union League Club], that democracy is a danger to this country."

In an address at Columbia University December 17, 1940, on "The Threat of Fascism" Secretary of the Interior Harold L. Ickes denounced "native fascist-minded Nazi sympathizers, profit-seeking business men, appeasers," etc. He named: Lawrence Dennis, the only overt American propagandist for Fascism; Lindbergh, Charles E. Coughlin and Merwin K. Hart.

In an address to the Protestant Digest Associates February 25, 1941, Mr. Ickes denounced five "Quislings" and named them as: Colonel Lindbergh, the Rev. Charles E. Coughlin, Major Alford J. Williams, Lawrence Dennis and Merwin K. Hart, adding that these are men "who would sacrifice democratic ideals and Christian civilization to alien economic and social predispositions. These men are supported by others who play upon the prejudices of the anti-Semite, the anti-Negro and the anti-sharecropper. These are the Quislings who, in pretended patriotism, would cravenly spike our guns and ground our planes in order that Hitlerism might more easily overcome us." (In August, 1942, Hart sued the Friends of Democracy for $1,000,000, saying it was a libel to call him a Quisling; this was a year and a half after this Quisling charge was published in the *New York Times.*)

And in March, 1943, the Non-Sectarian Anti-Nazi League published its Bulletin charging Hart with attending a secret meeting in Chicago with anti-Semites, native Fascists, America Firsters, etc. Named are Harry A. Jung, notorious peddler of anti-Semitic propaganda, aid to Mrs. Dilling and advisor on radicalism to Col. McCormick of the *Chicago Tribune;* Earl Southard, Illinois chairman of the America First Party, now being run by Gerald L. K. Smith.

Mr. Hart frequently has denied that he is an anti-Semite. In his speeches—he was one of the promoters of a Christian Front rally in honor of Franco, along with John Eoghan Kelly, who is now under indictment as a Fascist agent—Hart did not use

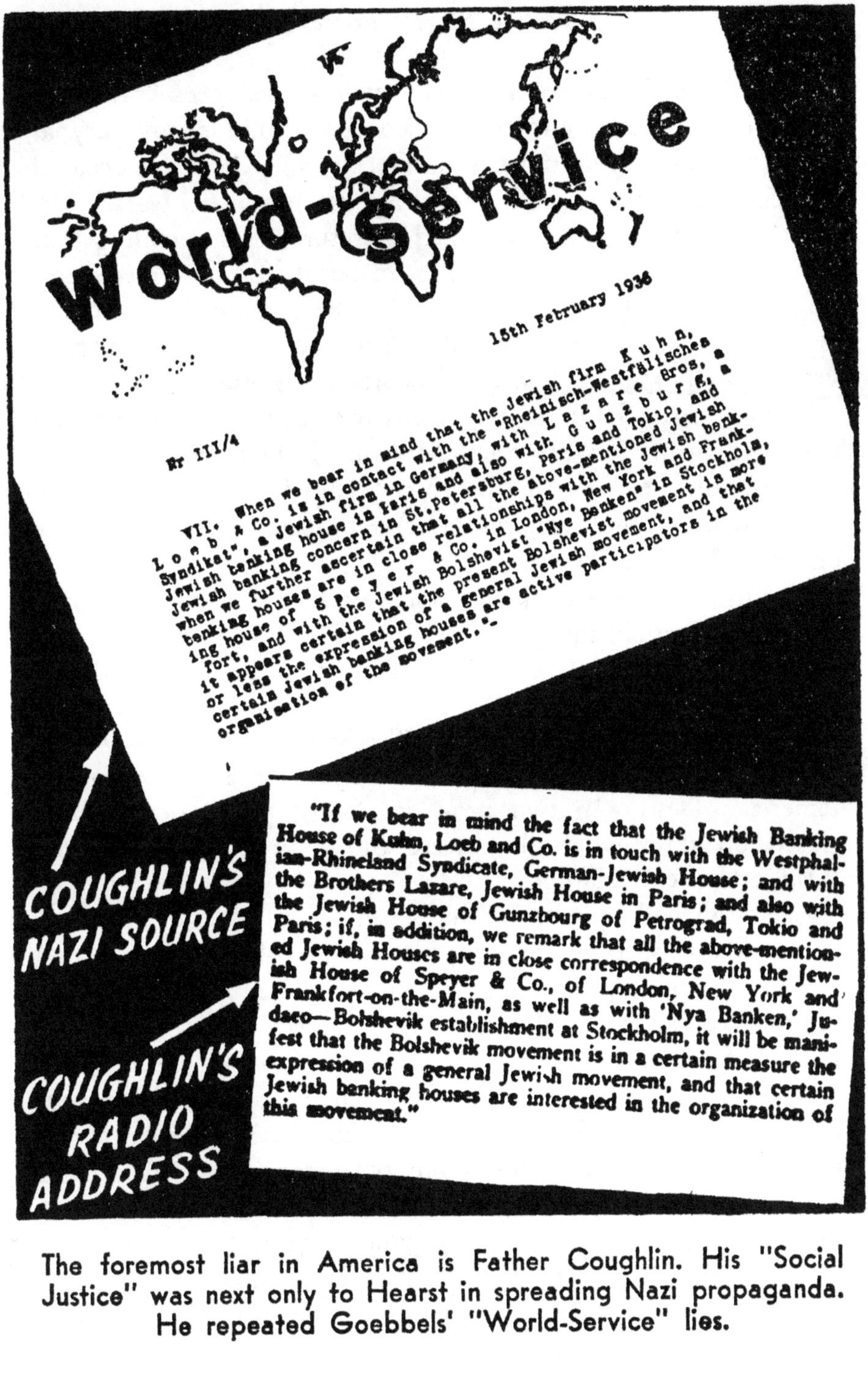

World-Service
15th February 1936
Nr III/4
VII. When we bear in mind that the Jewish firm K u h n, L o e b & Co. is in contact with the "Rheinisch-Westfälisches Syndikat", a Jewish firm in Germany, with L a z a r e Bros, a Jewish banking house in Paris and also with G u n z b u r g, a Jewish banking concern in St.Petersburg, Paris and Tokio, and when we further ascertain that all the above-mentioned Jewish banking houses are in close relationships with the Jewish banking house of S p e y e r & Co. in London, New York and Frankfort, and with the Jewish Bolshevist "Nye Banken" in Stockholm, it appears certain that the present Bolshevist movement is more or less the expression of a general Jewish movement, and that certain Jewish banking houses are active participators in the organisation of the movement."-
COUGHLIN'S NAZI SOURCE
"If we bear in mind the fact that the Jewish Banking House of Kuhn, Loeb and Co. is in touch with the Westphalian-Rhineland Syndicate, German-Jewish House; and with the Brothers Lazare, Jewish House in Paris; and also with the Jewish House of Gunzbourg of Petrograd, Tokio and Paris; if, in addition, we remark that all the above-mentioned Jewish Houses are in close correspondence with the Jewish House of Speyer & Co., of London, New York and Frankfort-on-the-Main, as well as with 'Nya Banken,' Judaeo—Bolshevik establishment at Stockholm, it will be manifest that the Bolshevik movement is in a certain measure the expression of a general Jewish movement, and that certain Jewish banking houses are interested in the organization of this movement."
COUGHLIN'S RADIO ADDRESS

The foremost liar in America is Father Coughlin. His "Social Justice" was next only to Hearst in spreading Nazi propaganda. He repeated Goebbels' "World-Service" lies.

the word "Jew" but phony words such as "refugees," "international liberals," etc., and denounced those "blinded by fury at the persecution of minorities in Germany," whom he accused of being those who want "to drag us into their wars." Mr. Hart's Council has also published literature recommending that its members read Mrs. Dilling's material (now termed seditious) and buy literature put out by the notorious anti-Semite and labor-spy, Harry Jung. A preface to a pamphlet urging use of this propaganda material is signed by Hart.

In May, 1943, John Eoghan Kelly was found guilty of being a Fascist agent. His associate, Merwin K. Hart, who was just as pro-Franco as Kelly, although not paid for it, as Kelly was, is the man whose economic fascist propaganda Mr. Wallace prints in *Reader's Digest.*

In July, 1943, the columnist Charles Fisher of the *Philadelphia Record* established the fact that Mr. DeWitt Wallace had been employing one George T. Eggleston to do some work for the *Reader's Digest.*

Eggleston had been editor of *Scribner's Commentator* and *The Herald* ("The National Newspaper for an Independent American Destiny"), two pro-Nazi fascist publications which closed up shop when they were under investigation by the F.B.I. after Pearl Harbor.

Eggleston had been with Lindbergh when he made his most vile pro-Nazi speech—the race, blood and color oration at Des Moines; Eggleston had collaborated with Henry Ford in making a propaganda list of fascist sympathizers, and according to Editor Morris Watson (in his newsletter *Release*) the German Library of Information, Nazi propaganda agency in America, had also collaborated. Finally, Eggleston had as associate editor Ralph Townsend, who wrote pro-Japanese propaganda in both *Scribner's Commentator* and *The Herald* and who is at present in the penitentiary as a Japanese agent.

We now have Mr. DeWitt Wallace employing as senior editor Paul Palmer, the first fascist editor in America, the man who used the *American Mercury* for Lawrence Dennis's and other frankly fascist propaganda; publishing the pro-Franco article of Ellery Sedgwick, employing as editor one Max Eastman, a Trotsky propagandist and Russia-smearer; publishing the articles of numerous labor-baiters and labor-liars; employing as editors and writers every "liberal" and "radical" who sold out for money; publishing articles in favor of the Nazis ("What's Good in Germany"); publishing the falsehoods of Lindbergh and other "racists"; and finally, employing Mr. Eggleston, editor of the first fascist publication to disappear in the roar of the guns of Pearl Harbor and an associate of an American Japanese agent.

Mr. Wallace denies he is a Fascist.

DOCUMENTATION AND REFERENCES:

Mr. Justice Jackson (as Attorney General of the United States) exposed the leading Fascists at Boston City Club, October 16, 1940. *The United Press* and *Associated Press* suppressed all the names but one. The full text is in *Law Society Journal,* Boston, November, 1940.

CHAPTER V

NAM MOUTH ORGAN: FULTON LEWIS, JR.

NOT ALL the American type of reactionary propaganda (or fascist propaganda as Mussolini would have labeled it) is confined to the newspaper and magazine press, notably the big circulation publications such as the McCormick-Patterson and Hearst newspapers, and the *Reader's Digest.* Considerable native Fascism comes over the radio. This is easily explained. The national hookups are paid for by the biggest corporations, and with the exception of Ford, they are all subsidizers, backers, directors and members of the National Association of Manufacturers, and members of its propaganda subsidiary, known as the National Industrial Information Committee.

With only three or four exceptions all the big newspaper columnists and radio commentators who form American public opinion are reactionaries. Pegler, Kaltenborn, Paul Mallon, Sokolsky, Mark Sullivan, Boake Carter, Frank Kent, David Lawrence reach from three to eight million persons each. On the liberal side there are a few writers and speakers who do not have a tenth this vast audience.

Fulton Lewis, Jr., reaches between 2,500,000 and 3,000,000 persons daily over more than 150 stations of the Mutual Network. He is sponsored by nationally known manufacturers such as Old Gold cigarettes and in some towns by local merchants. Today Lewis is the chief spokesman for Reaction. He was formerly employed by the National Association of Manufacturers and right now he is echoing the propaganda line laid down at the secret meeting of the resolutions committee of the NAM.

Mr. Lewis is not now employed by the NAM. Mr. Lewis denies that he has any connection with the NAM. Mr. Lewis is working for some 60 corporations and if he wants to say it is purely a coincidence that the propaganda he is putting out today and that which the NAM is putting out are alike, his word should be taken at face value. We present herewith certain facts about Mr. Lewis, the DuPont campaign for "Free Enterprise" originated less than a year ago, Mr. Lewis's former connection with the NAM, and Mr. Lewis's present "Free Enterprise" campaign which tallies with the Hearst-Howard-NAM and American fascist campaign of Free Enterprise.

Fulton Lewis, Jr., was in the pay of the NAM, broadcasting Big Business propaganda (up to June 19, 1942) at a time many of his colleagues, notably Kaltenborn and Pegler, were working the other end of the NAM street by smearing labor.

In defense of his position, Mr. Lewis wrote me on August 10, 1942:

"Your little publication has tremendous influence and a tremendous and loyal following. You have built up what I have tried to build up over the air—a feeling among your readers that you are telling them the truth, the whole truth, and nothing but the truth—and I think you do that within the usual human qualifications of all of us. This letter is not written as a complaint nor as a request for any correction. It rather is written to show you what tremendous power you have. . . . I have never heard of the subsidiary of the NAM (Industrial Information Committee). . . ."

My reply said in part:

"The only matter worth serious discussion is that line in your letter (re N.I.I.C. being part of NAM). Before I take up the matter . . . I would like to ask you some questions:

"1. Do you know what Fascism is?

"2. Are you aware that there is Fascism in America?

"3. Do you know that Hitler's Naziism and Mussolini's Fascism are to a great extent the armed forces of the special big interests, such as the German cartels?

"4. Are you aware that Mussolini was subsidized by the Associazione fra Industriali Metallurgici Meccani and the Confederazione Generale dell'Industria . . . which corresponds exactly to our U. S. Chamber of Commerce and our NAM?

"5. Are you aware, as Thyssen showed, that the Nazi equivalent of the NAM and N.I.I.C. taxed themselves so much per ton, so much per piece of goods manufactured, to subsidize Hitler and put him in power . . .?

"6. Are you or are you not aware that Pew of Sunoco, E. T. Weir, Bell of Cyanamid . . . Fuller, Lammot DuPont . . . A. P. Sloan of General Motors . . . all of them officers of the N.I.I.C., are the equivalent of the subsidizers of Fascism abroad, and subsidizers of the various fascist organizations exposed in the Lobby Investigation run by Senator (now Justice) Black?

"If you are not aware of these facts, then there is an excuse for your ever having been in the employ of the N.I.I.C.

"But it must be an excuse based on ignorance only. You know very well that when the La Follette Committee exposed the notorious George Sokolsky as being secretly in the pay of the NAM it was a first-rate scandal. It seems to me it was the most notorious scandal in the recent history of American journalism, and the fact the *New York Herald Tribune* and now the *New York Sun* publish the writings of this NAM hireling is still a greater scandal. The NAM was exposed three times in recent history. It actually resorted to corruption and bribery of Congressmen. It did about 90% of all the hiring in America of thugs, gunmen, racketeers, murderers and spies. Finally, it sought by a great corruption fund to change the thinking of American people by hiring professors and introducing text books in the public schools.

"I am sure that you know these facts about the NAM. I think therefore it is advisable for you to make a public statement saying that when you did the job for the N.I.I.C. you were not aware that it was formed by the NAM out of its more pro-fascist elements, and that its present plan is to invade the public schools with its anti-social propaganda. . . ."

Mr. Lewis replied again emphasizing that he had been in the employ of the NAM, not the N.I.I.C. "I have never been in the pay of the Industrial Information Committee of the NAM; in fact, I never heard of the damned thing until a former issue of your paper mentioned it in connection with me," he wrote. Of the NAM, he added: "I am totally dissympathetic and completely opposed to their labor policies. . . . I fought them tooth and toenail . . . on the 40-hour-week issue." And on August 31 Lewis said in a long letter that:

"1. I know very well what Fascism is, and I disapprove of it 100%.

"2. I am not aware that there is Fascism in America at this moment. . . .

"3. I am, of course, well aware that Hitler's Naziism [was subsidized].

"4. I did not know specifically that Mussolini was subsidized by the particular organizations. . . [Here Mr. Lewis declares that comparing these to the Chamber of Commerce and the NAM constitutes no proof].

"5. I am quite well aware that German industrialists own and control Naziism, Hitler, and whatever profits accrue from the war.

"6. I am not aware that Pew, Weir, Bell, Fuller, DuPont and A. P. Sloan are all officers of the N.I.I.C. . . . not aware that they are the 'equivalent of the subsidizers of Fascism abroad' although your charge is very interesting. . . . I was not aware that they were exposed as subsidizers of 'the various fascist organizations' by the Lobby investigation of Senator (now Justice) Black."

Mr. Lewis then declares that he never heard of the three Congressional investigations of the NAM, and he declares that if proof can be found the NAMzies employed 90% of all the thugs and murderers and spies—("that statement seems fantastic, extreme, and too much to swallow")—he will be "glad to help publicize it the nation over."

The facts are: the La Follette Committee held public hearings and issued official reports showing that 90% or more of all the spies, thugs, murderers employed by Big Industry were employed by General Motors (controlled by DuPonts, bossed by Knudsen and Sloan) and other like members of the NAM. Of course Mr. Fulton Lewis, Jr., will not even breathe a word of these facts over the radio stations when he is paid by many of these same men and corporations.

But Mr. Lewis says he knows best what is "in my mind and heart," and that he reaches "many millions of people, the rank-and-file, middle-of-the-road people" and that "the greatest need of the labor movement is to have the support and confidence of those people, to have them told the truth, to have them debunked of anti-labor propaganda and lies and insinuations, and I have done that consistently and repeatedly."

Finally, Mr. Lewis, still not asking for any correction of any news items about him, suggests that the following reply be published. Here it is in full:

"I have never heard of the N.I.I.C. before you stated in your newsletter that I was employed by it. That statement was absolutely false, regardless of what the N.I.I.C. or anyone else in Heaven or Earth says to the contrary. I not only had never heard of it, but to this day I have never met any of the individuals whom you list as officers of it. I know nothing about it and care less. I did a series of broadcasts for the NAM, once a week, from war production plants all over the nation for slightly more than a year. I defy you or anyone else to point to a single word, phrase, or innuendo in any broadcast that was remotely or by the slightest indirection anti-labor. On the contrary, a large part of every broadcast was devoted to showing the tremendous and constructive part that labor was playing in that particular plant. My assistant who went to the plants in advance and helped gather material for each broadcast was a fanatical pro-laborite. We had numerous union leaders on the program.

"My contract with the NAM specifically provided that I was to have absolute final discretion and power as to what was said in every broadcast, and I exercised that power on all occasions. I had no conferences, instructions, or hints about any NAM policies on labor or anything else either before or during my connection; in fact, all I know of NAM policies is what I have read in the newspapers.

"I heartily disapprove of anti-labor propaganda, whether it be by the NAM or any other organization, and I strongly resent and challenge anyone to cite any statement that I have ever made that has been anti-labor. I have stated that I had no connection with the N.I.I.C., and even my connection with the NAM as here set forth was terminated June 18, 1942, and, therefore, your statement printed

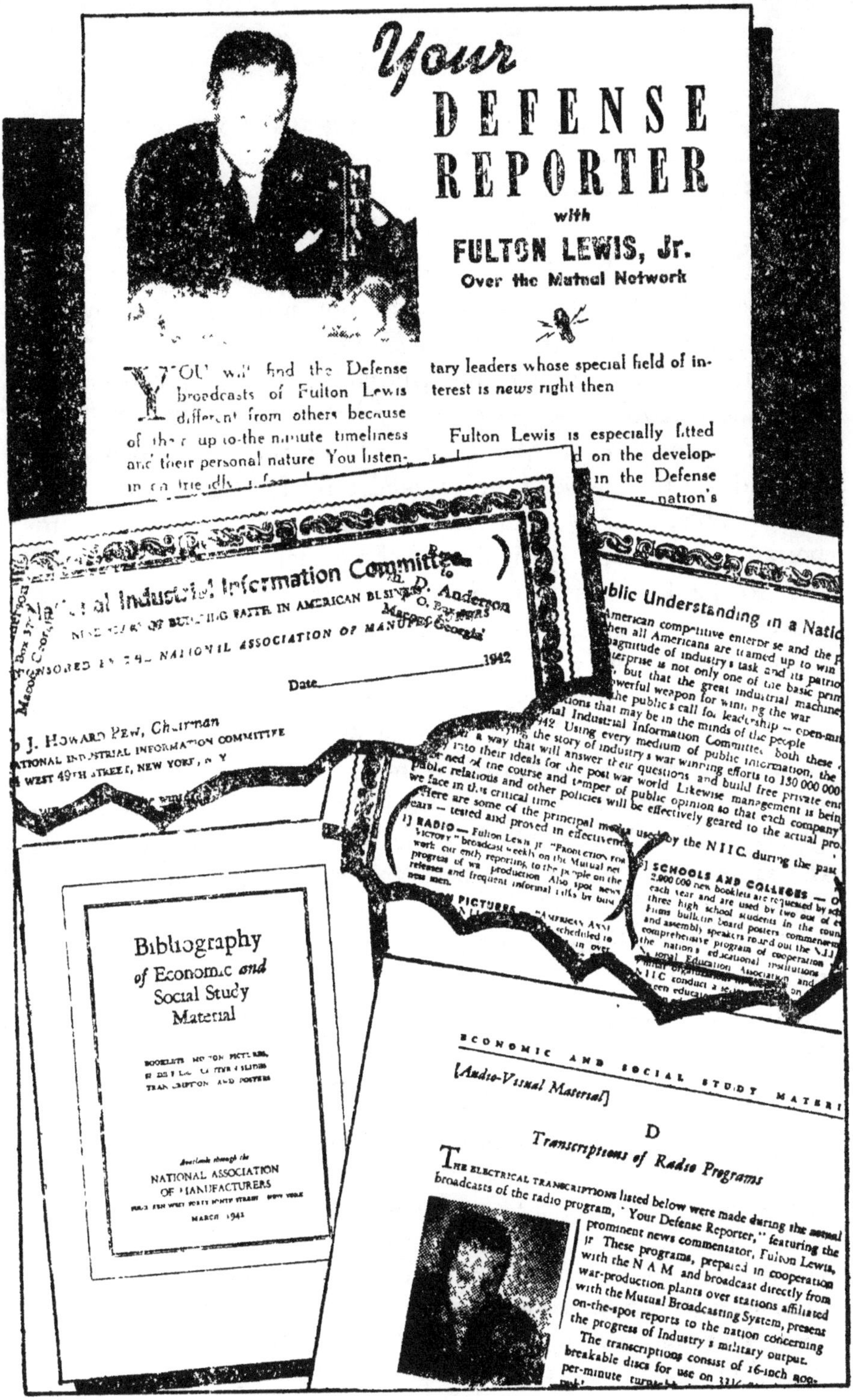

Here is the evidence the NAM and NIIC are one, and that Fulton Lewis, Jr., spread their propaganda over the radio.

in *In Fact* in the July and August issues that I was at that time connected with the N.I.I.C. was untrue, not only for the N.I.I.C. but for the NAM as well.

"(signed) Fulton Lewis, Jr."

Furthermore, Mr. Lewis suggests that he is not "the 1942 George Sokolsky" because he was not hired secretly by the NAM; every broadcast closed with this announcement: "This program is presented by the Mutual Network in cooperation with the NAM."

The main part of Mr. Lewis's statement is his denial he worked for the N.I.I.C.; he worked only for the NAM. This is a quibble, a straw man set up to demolish. It is of no importance whatever. All it does is show that Mr. Lewis in addition to not knowing what Fascism really is, not knowing that there is Fascism in America, and not knowing that the men who paid him are also the paymasters of every fascist organization, past, present and future—the past being officially on Congressional records—also did not know that as far back as 1936 it was officially admitted to the La Follette Committee that the N.I.I.C. was a branch of the NAM. In fact, most propaganda work of the NAM is done by the N.I.I.C., and exactly the same men own, run, control and subsidize the two organizations.

One whole volume of the La Follette report is devoted to exposing the NAM—it is Report No. 6, part 6: Part III, the NAM, published in 1939, giving testimony from 1938 on. On page 154 Mr. Lewis will find this statement about his paymasters:

"The NAM had opposed the principal legislative measures sponsored by the national administration during the congressional session of 1935. It had opposed the National Labor Relations Act [the Wagner Act, Magna Carta of Labor, which Mr. Lewis's NAM is still fighting], the Social Security Act, the Banking Act, the Utility Holding Company Act, and the President's tax program. In spite of the Association's opposition, all these measures became law. This was a great blow to the Association; but its officers remained undaunted and they redoubled their propaganda efforts. . . .

(Page 155) "After the crushing defeat of the NAM's lobby during the 1935 congressional session, its officers decided to intensify its effort in local 'education.' . . . The Association set up the National Industrial Information Committee under the chairmanship of E. T. Weir. . . . The 1935 annual report of the Association referred to the organization of these committees: 'In furtherance of this better understanding of industry by the public the N.I.I.C. was organized. Under the chairmanship of Mr. E. T. Weir, committees have been formed in the 20 major industrial states to facilitate development of the NAM program for the dissemination of sound American doctrine to the public. . . .'

"The N.I.I.C. appealed to leaders of industry for financial support of the public information program . . . to 'sell' industry to the public. . . . [In the letter of appeal for funds signed by W. B. Warner, editor of *McCall's Magazine,* he said the N.I.I.C.-NAM propaganda campaign would 'save the whole of the industrial system.']

(Page 6) "The NAM has blanketed the country with a propaganda which in technique has relied upon indirection of meaning, and in presentation upon secrecy and deception."

Pages 8 and 9 of the Digest of Report, Committee on Education and Labor, 76th Congress, 1st Session, states:

"The activities of the NAM became so bold and sometimes indiscreet that a scandal occurred in 1913 when public charges were made that agents of the Association had given 'financial rewards' to Congressmen to promote its legislative program. . . . Investigations disclosed that the Association had placed an employee of the House of Representatives on its payrolls in order to obtain information not available to the public; the Association's agents had contributed large sums of money to Congressional candidates in their campaigns for re-election and had opposed candidates friendly to labor—[Note: this has been done in every election, will be done in 1944, etc.]—the Association had carried on a disguised propaganda campaign through newspaper syndicates . . . placing publicists on its payroll. . . . Responsible officials of the NAM did not renounce any part of their activities revealed before the Senate and House Committees of 1913. On the contrary, they reasserted the necessity of pursuing the course they had followed previously in order to counteract the 'operations of organized labor.' . . . After 1920 it became what it always had been, a candid open-shop drive which was the spearhead for the anti-union movement then sweeping the country. . . .

"While opposing union organization under the cover of 'patriotism and freedom,' the Association's representatives maintain their unyielding attitude on social legislation . . . opposition to modification of the anti-trust laws to exempt labor unions from the application . . . regulation of child labor . . . establishment of collective bargaining . . . many other legislative proposals designed to correct some of the basic dislocations which gave rise to social unrest."

In other words the NAM, for which Mr. Lewis admits doing a public relations job, is an outfit which is devoted to fighting the general welfare and social progress of America, so that the 270 corporations which subsidize the NAM may profit.

If Mr. Lewis will also read the Digest of Senate Report No. 6, part 3, 76th Congress, 1st Session, he will find the names of the men and corporations who employed strikebreaking espionage, private police systems, guns and poison gas—"the four chief instrumentalities of anti-unionism." Some sample names are: Republic Steel, U. S. Steel, Bethlehem, General Motors, National Steel of Weirton, Mr. Knudsen. Let him look up the NAM and N.I.I.C. list of officers and directors and find how many are named in the report.

If Mr. Lewis will obtain mimeographed report No. 24, La Follette Statement, he will learn:

"Those few but powerful employers who utilize such practices [spies, gas warfare, etc.] wield great influence throughout industry. . . . The powerful minority of employers who utilize oppressive labor practices is well organized. . . . Their influence is exerted through highly paid propagandists to conceal their own offenses and to raise a public clamor against collective bargaining and bona fide unions. . . . In the name of industrial harmony they have incited the most dangerous forms of class conflicts. . . . I do not exaggerate when I say that these belligerent employers already exercise an influence in the affairs of employers' associations which is out of proportion to their numbers and their economic significance. Some 45 companies making the largest contributions to, or exerting great influence in the NAM, purchased over 55% of the tear gas and tear gas equipment sold to the industry. . . . E. T. Weir, whose National Steel Corporation is another outstanding purchaser of industrial arms, has assumed leadership of the efforts of the NAM to disseminate propaganda on a lavish scale. . . . Civil liberties are under attack. . . . There are forces within the country which openly clamor for the destruction of civil liberties through the perversion of governmental power. These forces are encouraged by the existence of private tyrannies maintained by private armed forces and by private gestapos."

Will Mr. Fulton Lewis, Jr., broadcast the fact a mere 45 companies or less than 5% of the NAM bought 55% of the tear gas, and other official proofs that NAM members bought 90% of all guns and gas and hired 90% or more of all spies, murderers and racketeers in fighting labor? It'll be a big day over Mutual, C.B.S., N.B.C. and the Blue Network when Mr. Lewis Jr. mentions DuPont, General Motors, Girdler, Weir and all the other American Fascists.

The Documentary Evidence

The documentary evidence shows:

1. That the NAM and the N.I.I.C. are one and the same.

2. That the NAM was exposed as criminally corrupt by one Congressional investigation, and more recently exposed by the La Follette investigation as at present working "in secrecy" and "in deceit."

3. That both the NAM and the N.I.I.C. claim Fulton Lewis, Jr., as their chief radio spokesman.

Exhibit A. First of all, here is the complete catalogue of propaganda materials which the NAM is using right now to corrupt the American people to its way of thinking. It is called "Bibliography of Economic and Social Study Material. Booklets, motion pictures, slide films, lantern slides, transcriptions and posters. Available through NAM. March, 1942." Millions of dollars are spent a year telling the American people to believe certain views which are the views of the multi-millionaires who own the NAM. This propaganda works for the dollar and cents profit of these men and corporations. It is directed against the general welfare of the American people. All this propaganda material is given out free.

Page 25 of this catalogue says:

"The audio-visual materials produced as a part of the National Industrial Information Program by the NAM and the National Industrial Council include sound and silent motion picture films, slide films, lantern slides, etc." [Note the names of the outfits. They now admit they are part of the same set-up.]

Page 36 states:

"The electrical transcriptions listed below were made during the actual broadcasts of the radio program, 'Your Defense Reporter,' featuring the prominent news commentator, Fulton Lewis, Jr. These programs, prepared in cooperation with the NAM and broadcast directly from war-production plants over stations affiliated with the Mutual Broadcasting System, present on-the-spot reports to the nation concerning the progress of Industry's military output. . . . Transcriptions are lent one at a time and without charge."

There follows a list of eight broadcasts glorifying Big Business in iron and steel, jeep making, naval craft production, radio, drugs, textiles, torpedo boats and planes.

The purpose of the broadcasts was to answer the charges, made by Senator Truman, Assistant Attorney General Thurman Arnold, the Bone, Tolan, and other Congressional investigations which proved conclusively that the only traitor to the war effort was Big Business. It had refused to convert even 50% to war production before Pearl Harbor, and maintained business-as-usual for months thereafter. The Aluminum Trust, Standard Oil, the Auto industry (with the exception of a few small firms), General Electric, Standard Drugs and others having cartel contracts with Hitler's I. G. Farbenindustrie, and practically all the big corporations—and main subsidizers of the NAM—were proven guilty of sit-downs, sabotage, lack of patriotism and even treasonable delays. Of course, the newspapers suppressed as much of this great story as possible and ran great campaigns of whitewash for Alcoa and Esso simultaneously with great advertising campaigns by these very corporations, but somehow the truth did get about, and the NAM put on a new $1,000,000 propaganda campaign, and Lewis Jr. was one of its hired mouths.

Exhibit B. This is a folder called "Industry—The Arsenal of Democracy. Defense on the Radio." On the inside page it announces

"from coast to coast, two major broadcasting systems in cooperation with the NAM—regularly report on the progress of Industry's Defense output. You and millions of other radio listeners can learn the inside story (Sic!) of what is being done, and what remains to be done, to make our country invulnerable. Through the blessings of uncensored radio broadcasting, we free Americans can follow the course of the greatest demonstration of industrial efficiency the world has ever known—a performance that only free enterprise can give."

Page 3 pictures Graham McNamee, "over the Red Network of the N.B.C." Page 6 pictures "Your Defense Reporter with Fulton Lewis, Jr., over the Mutual."

In small type, page 2, is this notice: "This booklet is prepared and distributed without charge in the interests of National Defense by the NAM." Under the McNamee announcement appears: "Don't fail to see the thrilling film: 'Defense for America' . . . Produced by Paramount in cooperation with the NAM." Otherwise there is no indication that this is part of the NAM's million dollar propaganda campaign.

Exhibit C. In 1942 the National Industrial Information Committee sent every big business man of the country a package of its new propaganda and a request for funds. It states: "We agree that the winning of the war and the preservation of freedom require that the American people have a complete understanding of the job industry is doing to win the battle of production, of the basic characteristics of the private competitive enterprise system, and of the sincere motives of American management." Firms capitalized at $100,000 are told to send in $25; firms worth a million, $225, and all over six million are asked to send $1,000 to $25,000. More than $1,000,000 has been raised and spent to date.

On page 2 of the subscription sheet is "Your program for Public Understanding in a Nation at War," and under it are listed radio, movies, posters, car cards, newspapers, schools and colleges, churches, women's clubs and other activities, all of which have already been exposed by the La Follette Committee as a campaign to corrupt the minds of the American people. This is what the N.I.I.C. says:

"The relationship between American competitive enterprise and the people is exceedingly important today. . . . The people must understand the magnitude of industry's task and its patriotism. They must know that freedom of enterprise is not only one of the basic principles that America is fighting to preserve. . . ."

Note that it was the NAM-N.I.I.C. propaganda machine which originated the slogan "Free Enterprise" which all the stooges of Big Business repeat. First on the N.I.I.C.'s list of activities is:

"1. RADIO—Fulton Lewis, Jr., 'Production for Victory,' broadcast weekly on the Mutual network, currently reporting to the people on the progress of war production. Also spot news releases and frequently informal talks by business men."

Note that in appealing for the million dollar propaganda fund to put over the "free enterprise" line, at a time Congressional investigations were showing the corruption of the "free enterprise" corporations, the N.I.I.C. listed Fulton Lewis, Jr., first as its hired man, asked for money to sustain its radio program.

When the NAM resolutions committee met in New York, in September, 1942, to prepare its December convention program, only three members voted in favor of making the winning of the war the main subject for the convention, the majority decided to fight the New Deal, labor and social legislation and to plan a post-war program in which Freedom of Enterprise would be paramount. F. C. Crawford, president of Tapco, J. H. Rand, Jr., of Remington Rand and Lammot DuPont dominated the session.

Labor-management committees were denounced. The committee also favored the end of restrictions on Wall Street speculation, more taxes on labor and less on corporations and the rich, the end of the New Deal. Everyone declared Free Enterprise was the NAM program.

That indeed was the slogan of the December, 1942, convention of the NAM.

Mr. Fulton Lewis made it his policy June 2, 1943.

First he gave himself a terrific build-up June 1, He intimated that tomorrow he would make the most important broadcast of our time. He was about to tell millions of Americans the greatest truth of all. It was super-colossal.

Came tomorrow. Mr. Lewis again built himself up and spilled over. He denounced the New Deal for selling the people a "gold brick" when it launched the Four Freedoms idea.

He approved freedom of speech and freedom of religion, but "freedom from fear and the freedom from want, the last two to finish up this trick phrase, are just so much humbug." (*Daily Commercial News,* San Francisco, headlined the story: "Four Freedoms Called New Deal Humbug.")

The Four Freedoms, Mr. Lewis continued, are not the philosophy of the United States, do not mean America, are not what the boys are fighting for. No government can guarantee to supply them. "It is like selling gold bricks, and if any individual were to crack out with anything of this nature, he would be thrown into jail at once." Mr. Lewis praised the pioneers, adding:

> "The smart boys in Washington have left out the most important freedom of all—and that is Freedom No. 5—freedom of individual enterprise—freedom of initiative; freedom to rise in the world....
>
> "We have heard Vice President Wallace's ideas of a quart of milk on every doorstep and other Utopian schemes. Actually the things our boys are fighting for is to have a doorstep of their own and the right to have on that doorstep anything they can earn and put there. . . .
>
> "This is the greatest freedom of them all—the freedom that is America—the Freedom of Individual Enterprise."

As for freedom from want and freedom from fear, Mr. Lewis said they were "luxuries, if you can afford them." The usual sneer at "college economists," the usual hoodlum-minded anti-cultural slurs against "do-gooders."

As for Freedom of Enterprise, the great blinding new idea, the Fifth Freedom for which he had worked up his broadcast, "without it there can be no tomorrow for America." It was the "real America, the most important, the most vital freedom of all."

June 11 Mr. Lewis said that in response to public clamor he was repeating his great oration, and "according to my philosophy" (which is nothing more than the propaganda dope of the NAM) he was going to tell about the foundation stone of America, the most important thing worth fighting for throughout the world (Free Enterprise, of course). "It was fear and want which made this country," said Mr. Lewis. A sneer at "government by college economists." Freedom from want and freedom from fear he called "vote getting" items. "No government can give the people freedom from want."

The facts are: the two countries where Freedom of Enterprise have reached the ultimate state are Germany and Italy. In these and other totalitarian Big Business countries the corporations have not only been allowed the complete free enterprise of trusts and monopolies but they have been allowed to swallow little business, enslave labor, and finally to take over the political government itself. In Germany and Italy, Japan and Spain —as documented in this book—the equivalents of the NAM and the U. S. Chamber of Commerce, Associated Farmers and Associated Industries own and control the government, the banks, the wealth of the land and the land itself. This is the real aim of Free Enterprise, and it is 100% at work in fascist countries only.

The second fact which Lewis denies is the possibility of abolishing want and fear due to want. Any system providing for full production—preferably production for use and not for profits, but full production and no unemployment—such as was advocated by the Bishops of the Church of England in their

Malvern Declarations (the report smeared by the NAM's hired professors), provides the essential needs of humanity: food, clothing and shelter—ample, even abundant, for every human being. It could be done overnight in the United States, which has natural resources; it is even possible throughout the world if the profits were taken from the few, and the wealth of the world given to the many. Mr. Lewis and the NAM both know this but neither dare mention it, and both are working against it. They prefer profits.

DOCUMENTATION AND REFERENCES:

One entire volume of the La Follette reports exposes the NAM: Committee on Education and Labor, 76th Congress, 1st Session; Report No. 6, part 6; III The National Association of Manufacturers.

Digest of Report, Committee on Education and Labor, 76th Congress, 1st Session.

T.N.E.C. Monograph 26.

Part 3

Our Press as a Fascist Force

CHAPTER I

THE PRESS IN CHAINS

THERE are traitors among the owners, publishers and editors of the big American newspapers.

This charge was made before the American Society of Newspaper Editors on April 17, 1942, by Archibald MacLeish, Librarian of Congress and then head of the Office of Facts and Figures, predecessor of the Office of War Information. It was broadcast at 1:30 P.M. over Station WOR and others.

Unfortunately, Mr. MacLeish could not and therefore did not name any names, but all the editors present knew to whom he referred when he mentioned the publication of one of the secret military plans of the War Department.

Interesting also is the fact that although Mr. MacLeish used the word "treason" twice in his address, the paragraphs containing it were suppressed by many newspapers, including the Olympian *New York Times*. Mr. MacLeish had said that he knew of one publisher who actually told his staff that he intended to come "as close to treason as I dare," and that "the defeatists and divisionists who strike from that ambiguous and doubtful shadow where freedom of expression darkens into treason" should be policed out of journalism by their fellow publishers themselves.

Another charge of treason was made by no less an authority than the head of the Department of Justice, Attorney General Biddle. At the time the question of censorship was uppermost, Mr. Biddle appeared before the Senate Judiciary Committee and, speaking in favor of a military censorship, disclosed the fact that certain newspapers and magazines had committed acts "approaching" treason. "The most closely guarded military secrets of the government have come into the possession of newspapers and magazines and ultimately into the hands of agents of enemy governments." This story was of course suppressed in all newspapers, guilty and innocent, but *Labor* reported from Washington:

"Biddle was testifying on an administration measure making it unlawful for unauthorized persons to divulge the contents of any confidential government document. The measure is under heavy fire. The newspapers are attacking it as a blow at 'freedom of the press,' and liberals in and out of Congress are fearful it may invade the citizen's constitutional guarantees. . . .

"Biddle . . . cited many instances where vital information has 'leaked,' some to newspapers willing to pay the price. . . . Maps of Midway Island and its naval installations, copies of army codes, communications between the Navy Department and commanders at sea, and photographs of army camps and airfields, Biddle asserted, had been made available to newspapers and enemy agents. . . . A newspaper whose identity was not disclosed was declared to have purchased secret aircraft data from employees of the Wright airplane plant at Paterson, N. J. A technical journal . . . was declared to have printed 'detailed data' on planes under construction at the North American Aviation factory. This information, Biddle said, is now being studied by German experts in Berlin. . . . Biddle (asked Senators) to keep in mind the main objective—the protection of the government from unscrupulous newspapers and enemy intelligence agents."

Again, no names were mentioned.

Another indication of the worry over un-American acts on the part of big publishers was given by the *New York Daily News'* Washington columnist, John O'Donnell, who wrote (March 30, 1942):

"Last night members of the Cabinet and Supreme Court were guests at the Willard of the Overseas Writers Association and heard some bloodthirsty appeals, with much talk of concentration camps and treason, from ex-reporters now turned starry-eyed crusaders at so much per month or per lecture.

"The American press which had opposed this nation's intervention into the war before the Pearl Harbor attack was hammered lustily, with the anvil chorus led by three former reporters of the *Chicago Tribune*. . . .

"Roosevelt advisers . . . applauded lustily such declarations as: 'The American Senate must be taught the facts of life. . . . The important thing is to put an end (to criticism of the Roosevelt Administration) by whatever means may be necessary—be as ruthless as the enemy. . . Get him on his income tax or the Mann Act. . . . Hang him, shoot him or lock him up in a concentration camp.' "

Readers will note that O'Donnell put his own phrase in parentheses about "criticism of the Roosevelt Administration" whereas the speakers talked about treason, sabotage of the war effort, etc., and not about criticism.

O'Donnell also failed to state (or his newspapers suppressed the fact) that the former *Chicago Tribune* correspondents named the *Chicago Tribune* and its owners, Col. McCormick and Capt. Patterson, as candidates for hanging, shooting or the concentration camp. Moreover, the attack was not made on papers which opposed intervention before Pearl Harbor but on those papers which since Pearl Harbor have continued to publish news, editorials and cartoons which must please Hitler.

Also mentioned as a Hitlerite publisher who should be tried for treason or put in jail was Charles E. Coughlin. It was suggested that the income tax law under which Al Capone and M. L. Annenberg were retired from circulation could be invoked in an investigation of Coughlin's financing.

But despite the fact that some of their members had been accused of everything from treason to following the Axis propaganda line (Divide and Conquer) the American Newspaper Publishers Associations (the Lords of the Press) held their usual convention in 1942 and devoted the major part of their week to discussing more profits despite the war.

They got together on helping the Associated Press maintain

that it is not a monopoly, because it is registered under the hunting and fishing law of New York as a cooperative—it is, in truth, the only "cooperative" in the world which refuses to accept members, and therefore a fake as well as a hypocrite and a monopolist. The publishers also discussed the newsprint situation of Canada; they were eager to keep curtailment at 10%, but no one suggested that the manufacture of newsprint instead of aluminum by the Canadian pulp mills (many owned by Americans) had curtailed the metals needed by MacArthur at Bataan and Guadalcanal. They also held secret sessions, at which no reporters were allowed, when they discussed the work of their strikebreaking committee (called Standing Committee) and their union-busting committee (called Open Shop Committee). They also brought in the Global War in this way: they argued whether or not to ask money from Uncle Sam for publicizing the bonds the nation was selling to wage a victorious war.

The eyes and ears of America's great publishers were as usual on their pocketbooks. In a special A.N.P.A. issue their mouth organ, *Editor & Publisher,* reported the convention would: "... examine problems created by the war," which, it explained, were: rising costs of operation, decreased revenue ... shortage of supplies, and censorship ... most important A.N.P.A. convention to be held in the past two decades. ... Among the outstanding questions of 60 scheduled for Tuesday discussion are the following:

"What is going to happen to both local and national advertising during the war? What can a newspaper do to promote new sources of advertising in a period of war emergency?

"What are newspapers under 50,000 circulation doing to offset lineage losses . . .?

"What is the general attitude of publishers toward advertising by the government?"

Treason? Freedom of the Press? Ethics? Corruption? The anti-labor bias of 75% or more of the press? Aid given to the Axis by the *Chicago Tribune* and *New York Daily News* and other reactionary papers? There was no mention of anything but business in any of the points *Editor & Publisher* listed except one: "Should headlines over war news 'slant' optimistically or pessimistically?"

During the convention the press devoted more columns to its discussion of whether or not to ask the government for war advertising money than to the war itself. The special convention number of *Editor & Publisher* carried eight big stories, of which six dealt with money and profits, one with the A.P. monopoly which makes it almost impossible for new papers to break into the present combine, and only one dealt with patriotism. Where was MacLeish's sensational charge that there is treason among America's leading newspaper publishers? *Editor & Publisher* did not suppress that story, the biggest story of the convention, one of the biggest stories since the Global War began. But it buried it on page 94, column 3.

The A.N.P.A. convention followed the American Society of Newspaper Editors Convention and was held simultaneously with the Associated Press convention and other editor-publisher meetings. Director of Office of Facts and Figures Archibald MacLeish spoke to the A.N.P.A. as he had to the A.S.N.E., before whom he had made the charge that there is treason among a minority of American publishers.

Reporter William Wiener asked questions. William Allen White, *Emporia Gazette,* replied that "MacLeish made a good speech. But I wish he had named names—Coughlin, McCormick, Patterson, Pelley, et al, ad lib." Houston Harte, *Standard Times,* said "Sure there are papers that are doing that [undermining public confidence]. . . . What MacLeish said is true." Palmer Hoyt, *Portland Oregonian,* said "What MacLeish said is true." A. W. Norton, *Christian Science Monitor,* was in favor of convicting certain papers of their wrongdoing. Senator Capper, *Topeka Capital,* said "I endorse what MacLeish said. We can well take notice of his suggestions"; Herbert Bayard Swope, once editor of America's leading liberal paper, the defunct *New York World,* said "MacLeish is right." John S. Knight, *Detroit Free*

Press, Akron Beacon-Journal and *Miami Herald,* said "I don't think it ethical for one paper to attack another."

However, the persons who favored driving America's traitors out of America's journalism are with two exceptions small town editors, whereas the owners of the powerful city press refused to agree, or sneered, or threatened. Here is *PM's* poll:

Col. McCormick (*Chicago Tribune*): "MacLeish is a Communist. Russia goes on the other side—MacLeish goes on the other side."

William Randolph Hearst, Jr. (*New York Journal-American*): "I didn't read MacLeish's speech fully enough to comment on it."

Roy Howard (Scripps-Howard chain): "I know of many daily newspaper publishers with whose editorial attitude toward the war I heartily disagree. I know of none whose loyalty I question."

Eleanor Patterson (*Washington Times-Herald*): "*PM* will get nothing from me. I'm going to sue you. You don't print the truth."

Frank E. Gannett (Gannett chain; sponsor of the native fascist strikebreaking organization called Committee to Uphold the Constitution): "I consider it most unfair for anyone to say that even a minority of our press are trying to undermine our Government."

J. H. Torbett, Gannett chain newspapers: "It was the type of speech to be expected from the director of the O. F. F."

L. W. Gracey, *Geneva Daily Times*: "Don't know the facts. I must have been lighting a cigaret while he was talking."

The foregoing also give a clue to the editorial mind of America —both smalltown and metropolitan.

Nothing was done about the defeatists, the divisionists and the traitors in the ranks.

In fact, there was a suspicion current at the convention that this group—the friends of Fascism and enemies of the welfare of the American people—actually owned the majority of powerful newspapers of big circulation and could easily control the convention if a patriot were to propose action against a traitor.

The nearest the President has come to indicating a large part

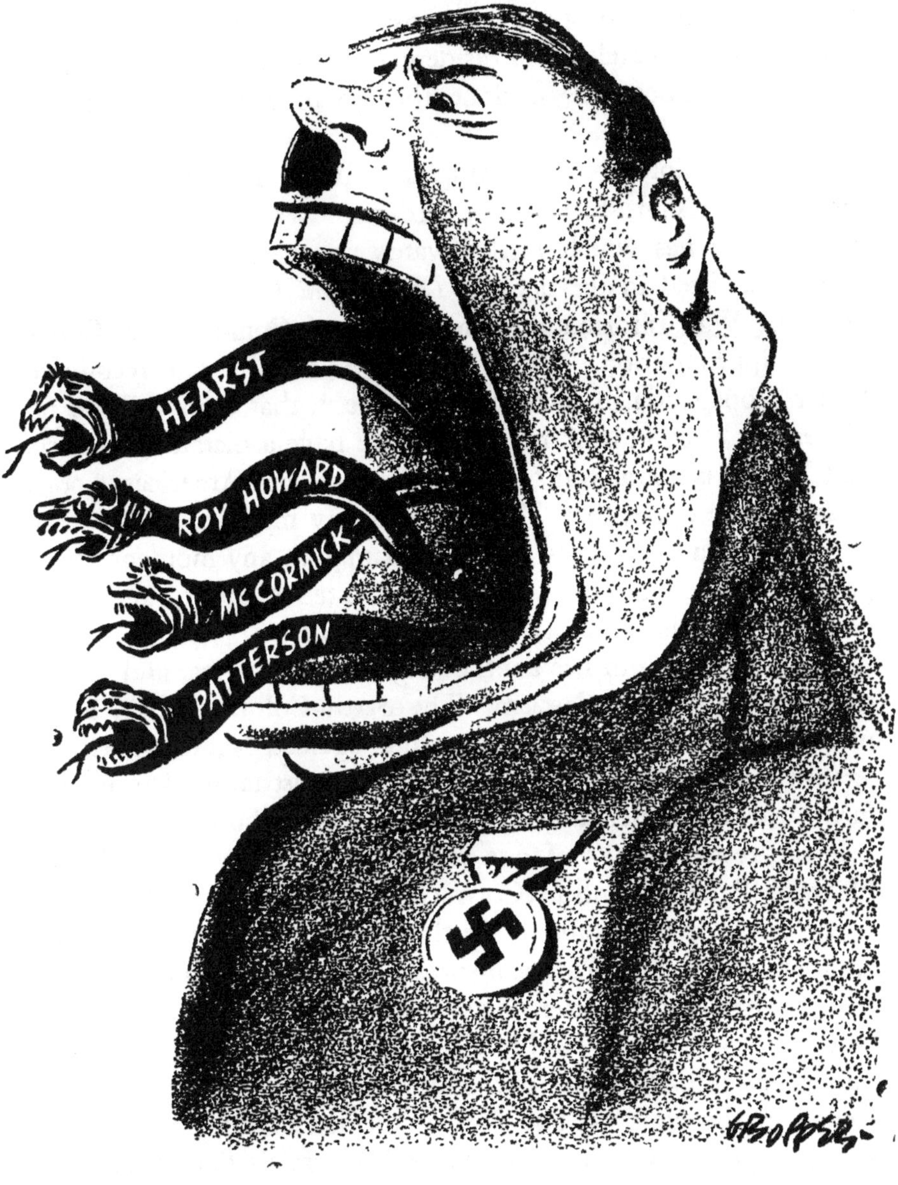

of our press as the main enemy of American democracy and the chief agent of foreign Fascism was his indictment in March, 1942, of what he termed the "Sixth Column" which was using the means of communication—most powerful of which is the daily newspaper—to spread dissension, disunity, fear and suspicion. Unfortunately the President is not in a position to name names, and unless this is done the job of fighting Fascism is hampered.

The Sixth Column is working for Hitler. Hitler said: "Confusion, indecision, fear; these are my weapons." There are fifteen main lies which Hitler wants you to believe. You will find them listed in the booklet *Divide and Conquer* which the Office of War Information sent free until Congress cut Elmer Davis' appropriation. Those who have read it can recognize Hitler propaganda in such stories as these: that there will be no November election in America, that we have a dictatorship here, that Britain is not at war but using Russian and American troops to save her empire, that China may at any moment make peace with Japan and betray us, that Russia may at any moment make peace with Germany and betray the United Nations, and scores of other defeatist and divisionist statements.

The Sixth Column has another big job in America, and that is to spread American Fascism. The Sixth Column today, as in peacetime, is active in setting white against Negro, Christian against Jew, Protestant against Catholic, industrial worker against farm worker, American-born against foreign-born.

If the reader thinks of our chain newspaper owners, Hearst, Howard, Patterson and McCormick, as merely four of America's 15,000 publishers, he fails to see the danger to America from an anti-democratic, anti-American press. These four publishers put out one fourth of all the newspapers sold daily on our streets, they own forty of the 200 big city papers which make American public opinion, they run not only the three biggest newspaper chains in the country, but two of the three big news services which supply news to a majority of America's dailies, and because they have always been anti-labor, anti-liberal, and anti-democratic even when not openly following the Mussolini and Hitler lines, they constitute what I believe is the greatest force hostile to the general welfare of the common people of America.

These publishers are all native Fascists. Two of them stand

accused of treason, all of them of following the fascist line. In order that there may be no question of the power and influence of this fascist group, and so that Americans throughout the country may know who spreads defeatism, divisionism and fascist propaganda in their cities, I have compiled the facts on these three newspaper chains. (See Appendix 5.)

Colonel McCormick, Capt. Patterson and Eleanor (Cissy) Patterson are the multi-millionaire enemies of the people today. E. W. ("Lusty") Scripps founded the Scripps-Howard empire but after his death Roy Howard forgot the liberalism of the founder, devoted himself to tax-dodging and amassing millions. Everyone knows who William Randolph Hearst is. Of this whole journalistic lot (Hearst, Howard, McCormick, Patterson) it may be said that there is not a spark of social conscience left in them, that it soured to Fascism in the one who was once a Socialist (Patterson) and that the five powerful persons well represent native Fascism. Although they own forty papers and great news agencies, they are all socially and economically illiterate; and all of them are socially irresponsible. They are animated by nothing above their pocketbooks. They are doing nothing to make America a better nation, nothing to advance the welfare of the American people, although they are powerful enough to create a public opinion which could bring about an almost ideal state.

In peace time they are the enemies of American democracy. In war time they are our Sixth Column. Hitler, Mussolini, Hirohito represent the enemies we have to fight with guns; Hearst, Howard, McCormick and Patterson represent the enemy within.

CHAPTER II

BERLIN-CHICAGO-NEW YORK AXIS

DESPITE the amazing *Fortune* poll which showed 26½% of the American people doubting the honesty of our daily newspapers and despite the universal feeling that the press is subsidized and therefore betrays the reader, it is a fact that millions who could do something about this situation are not enough aware of the danger to take any action. All know how powerful the press is and many realize that inasmuch as it is the main force creating public opinion it is, ipso facto, the force which largely directs Congress, the making of laws, taxation, the standard of living, the style of our clothes and our thinking about waging war on Fascism. Nevertheless millions do little or nothing either to fight the harmful influence of a corrupt press or to establish an honest and therefore free press.

The majority of Americans are wage and salary workers. They number 52,000,000 in normal times. Nevertheless it is impossible to name half a dozen newspapers which are at least neutral and impartial in handling the news for these fifty-two millions, and even less which protect and defend them. A vote of labor editors has shown that 92% of them think the entire press is unfair to labor, and other opinion polls taken of labor leaders and writers and editors have declared some 98% of the big city press—the opinion-forming press—unfair. And yet labor reads the press which betrays it.

There are many reasons for this, too many and too long to be entered into here, but the point to emphasize is that the facts of the situation are no reason for despair and defeatism. On the contrary, there is such a fast and vast awakening that one is warranted in predicting great and good changes in the near future.

It is important that the labor unions of America are taking the leadership in exposing our commercial corrupt press and laying the foundation for a free press—the first since colonial times, when any man with a hundred dollars and a pioneer spirit could become a publisher. Here are some bright labor straws in the foul American journalistic winds.

1. The 1942 convention of the C.I.O. in Boston went on record, first for winning the war (as contrasted with the 1942 convention of the National Association of Manufacturers which went all out for Free Enterprise and the 1942 convention of the American Newspaper Publishers Association which went all out for profits); it voted for a "Second Front Now," following the victory in North Africa, "to complete destruction of the Nazi forces on the European continent"; it denounced the fascist appeasement forces still at large in America, and it named the vermin press which follows the "disruptive and appeaser line" as the McCormick-Patterson *Chicago Tribune, New York Daily News, Washington Times-Herald* and the nineteen Hearst newspapers. It accused the American press of anti-labor reporting, suppressing Vice President Wallace's great declaration known as "The Century of the Common Man," suppressing important statements on labor by the President, and "slanting the news to fit the publishers' prejudice." The entire press and publicity committee's report on our venal and corrupt anti-labor press was adopted.

2. The national convention of the International Longshoremen's & Warehousemen's Union at its June, 1943, convention in San Francisco went on record on the foremost and dominant subject: winning the war and the part this union can do to speed victory. The commercial press which attacks labor was generally denounced and the columnist Westbrook Pegler and newspaper owner William Randolph Hearst were both denounced as Fifth Columnists who were hindering rather than helping win the war. (May I be permitted to include the following resolution

unanimously adopted by the convention: "*In Fact,* a weekly publication edited by George Seldes, is particularly effective in exposing the suppression and distortions of the appeaser and reactionary press. For this reason it is important that it be given the widest possible circulation.")

3. The American Newspaper Guild, which consists of more than 20,000 men and women who work for the press, the majority in the editorial department, at their 1943 national convention in Boston also made victory the order of the day and decided to watch those newspapers which are hindering rather than aiding in the war against Fascism. The Newspaper Guild resolution pledged it to "expose actions of the press which are disruptive of the war effort" and the Guild will "provide to the *Guild Reporter* and all other publications in which it can obtain space, material to publish and comment upon the activities of the free press during wartime."

There have always been two parties among the organized newspaper men of the country, one which believed it was wrong to criticize the press—although fighting it for wage increases and other union rights was right; the other which had a larger outlook and followed in the footsteps of Heywood Broun in relentless criticism of the publishers, editors, owners and corrupters of the newspapers. The Boston convention heard members denounce their own *Guild Reporter,* official organ, for "slanting the news headlines, inaccuracies of statement, misquotations, injection of editorial opinion and redbaiting" and a resolution instructed the editor to further unity within the Guild, rather than continue his past practices.

The Guild action can make it one of the greatest forces in the nation in a fight for a free press. Its twenty thousand members can supply it with all the evidence in the world to expose the corruption of the newspapers, and a great campaign of exposure must result in at least a little reform, a little less hypocrisy, a little more decency, if not a big step towards fairness.

4. William Green, president of the A. F. of L., made this declaration (published in his *American Federationist*):

"Recently a bitter campaign of malicious propaganda to poison the public's mind against organized labor has been carried on by the subsidized press which is composed of reactionary daily newspapers controlled, through ownership and advertising, by exploiting profiteers and union-haters. Together with the bourbon politicians, idle rich and anti-labor columnists, they are the real parasites of our country. . . . By peddling falsehoods about labor, the subsidized press is creating factionalism, disunity and class hatred. If Hitler were not so busy running away from a victorious Russian army he would take time to pin medals on the editors and columnists who are misleading the public.

"The reactionary editors of the newspapers are doing just what Hitler predicted he could accomplish here through his agents."

5. The most consistent fighter of the corrupt press among the powerful labor papers has been *Labor,* edited by Edward Keating, and representing the Railroad Brotherhoods.

The facts therefore are that organized labor, 13,000,000 persons, have through their leaders and their unions gone on record as aware that the American press is corrupt, their enemy and betrayer, and that something must be done about it.

How much of an enemy is the press? How deep in Fascism is our press? Let us look at one of the great newspaper chains mentioned in the last chapter, the powerful McCormick-Patterson chain, to see how one family betrays the welfare of many million people.

The McCormick-Patterson-Berlin Axis

Declaring war on the United States, Adolf Hitler screamed his hatred and his fascist reasons, arriving at this climax:

"A plan prepared by President Roosevelt has been revealed in the United States, according to which his intention was to attack Germany by 1943 with all the resources at the disposal of the United States.

"Thus our patience has come to the breaking point. . . ."

One week earlier, three days before the outrageous Japanese attack at Pearl Harbor, the *Chicago Tribune* spread across its front page in the largest type it has ever used, the following story:

"F. D. R.'S WAR PLANS!
"GOAL IS 10 MILLION ARMED MEN;
HALF TO FIGHT IN A.E.F.
"PROPOSES LAND DRIVE BY JULY 1, 1943, TO SMASH NAZIS;
PRESIDENT TOLD OF EQUIPMENT SHORTAGE
"*By* CHESLY MANLY
"(Copyright 1941 by the *Chicago Tribune.*)

"Washington, D. C., Dec. 3—A confidential report prepared by the joint Army and Navy high command by direction of President Roosevelt calls for American Expeditionary Forces aggregating 5,000,000 men for a final land offensive against Germany and her satellites. It contemplates total armed forces of 10,045,658 men.

"One of the few existing copies of this astounding document, which represents decisions and commitments affecting the destinies of peoples throughout the civilized world, became available to *The Tribune* today.

"It is a blueprint for total war on a scale unprecedented in at least two oceans and three continents, Europe, Africa, and Asia. . . .

"July 1, 1943, is fixed as the date for the beginning of the final supreme effort by American land forces to defeat the mighty German army in Europe.

"In the meantime . . . gradual encirclement of Germany by the establishment of military bases. . . .

"The war prospectus is dated Sept. 11, 1941, and was prepared by the Army and Navy Joint Board, which is the supreme command of the United States, in response to a letter addressed to Secretary of War Stimson by President Roosevelt. . . ."

This is the document to which Hitler referred when he declared war. The document was furnished to Herr Hitler and to 5,000,000 people in twelve midwestern states who read the million copies the *Chicago Tribune* prints daily, by Colonel McCormick.

Technically this was not an act of treason.

However, McCormick, being an army man, knows better than any layman that the publication of the secret war plans of any nation is right next to treason, if not treason itself.

Colonel McCormick, however, was too interested in fighting

2 CENTS PAY NO MORE!

Chicago Daily Tribune

THE WORLD'S GREATEST NEWSPAPER

FINAL

VOLUME C—NO. 290 C (REG. U. S. PAT. OFFICE COPYRIGHT 1941 BY THE CHICAGO TRIBUNE.) THURSDAY, DECEMBER 4, 1941.—46 PAGES THIS PAPER CONSISTS OF THREE SECTIONS—SECTION ONE PRICE TWO CENTS IN CHICAGO AND SUBURBS ELSEWHERE THREE CENTS

F.D.R.'S WAR PLANS!

REDS BEGIN NEW DRIVE TO BREAK VISE ON MOSCOW

Strike at Nazi Line South of Leningrad.

BULLETIN

BERNE, Switzerland, Dec. 4 (Thursday) — A special bulletin from Moscow early today announced soviet forces had launched a heavy attack along the entire northern line from Kalinin to Leningrad in a terrific effort to crush the German threat against Moscow. The main fighting [illegible]

LEIBER TRADED TO GIANTS; CUBS GET BOWMAN

The Chicago Cubs early this morning traded Outfielder Hank Leiber to the New York Giants for Pitcher Bob Bowman and an unannounced sum of cash. The deal was completed at the minor league baseball convention in Jacksonville, Fla. Leiber was one of three Giants sent to the Cubs after the 1938 season in exchange for Bill Jurges, Frank Demaree, and Ken O'Dea.

(Details on sports pages.)

NEWS SUMMARY of The Tribune

And Historical Scrap Book

Thursday, December 4, 1941

HOUSE ADOPTS DRASTIC BILL TO BLOCK STRIKES

Goes to Senate on 252-136 Vote.

BY WILLIAM STRAND

(Chicago Tribune Press Service.)

Washington, D. C., Dec. 3.—The house of representatives by a vote of 252 to 136 today passed sweeping antistrike legislation designed to prevent work stoppages [illegible]

THE STRONGHOLD OF PEACE.

GOAL IS 10 MILLION ARMED MEN; HALF TO FIGHT IN AEF

Proposes Land Drive by July 1, 1943, to Smash Nazis; President Told of Equipment Shortage.

BY CHESLY MANLY

(Copyright 1941 By The Chicago Tribune.)

Washington, D. C., Dec. 3.—A confidential report prepared by the joint army and navy high command by direction of President Roosevelt calls for American expeditionary forces aggregating 5,000,000 men for a final land offensive against Germany and her satellites. It contemplates total armed forces of 10,045,658 men [illegible]

Three days before Pearl Harbor the Chicago Tribune published the confidential U. S. Army plan, but the owner escaped trial for treason.

the New Deal and working with fascist appeasers to care whether or not he betrayed his country. He published one of the many war plans which his country had made to protect itself. (McCormick knew only too well that every nation, ours included, has plans made years or months in advance for every sort of invasion of every country in the world; it would be criminal folly for a general staff not to have them; and that this plan which he betrayed was one of many prepared to deal with any future situation and not a plot to enter the war and attack Germany.) Said Secretary Stimson:

"What would you think of an American General Staff which in the present condition of the world did not investigate and study every conceivable type of emergency which may confront this country and every possible method of meeting the emergency?

"What do you think of the patriotism of a man or a newspaper that would take those confidential studies and make them public to the enemies of this country?

"While their publication doubtless will be a gratification to our potential enemies as a possible source of impairment and embarrassment to our national defense, the chief evil of their publication is the revelation that there should be among us any group of persons so lacking in appreciation of the danger that confronts the country and so wanting in loyalty and patriotism to their government, that they would be willing to publish such papers."

This, however, does not explain why the government failed to take any action whatever. Obviously someone had betrayed America. Obviously if someone had sold this document to a Nazi agent he would have been arrested for treason. But Colonel McCormick, who supplied Hitler and Hirohito with one of our war plans, went scot free.

In August, 1942, the *Chicago Tribune, New York Daily News,* and *Washington Times-Herald*—the three McCormick family newspapers—were on trial for betraying secrets to Japan in their reports of the Coral Sea battle. They were found not guilty. They had published a list of ships participating, they quoted as a source for their information some officials of the U. S. Navy,

The Chicago Tribune AND THE DAILY NEWS NEW YORK

Société Anonyme Française au Capital de Frs 100 000

R. C. Seine 10' 256

5, RUE LAMARTINE, PARIS

Paris Information Office
1, Rue Scribe.
Telephone . Gutenberg 51-22
Theater Tickets : Gutenberg 09-31

rib-Paris

& 50-92
udaine 88)
415

April 22nd 1925

Mr. G. SELDES
Galleria Colonna
(Scala A)
ROME

[redacted]

Dear George: [redacted]

If I were you, I would attempt to have reinstated the free telegraph service to America as well as to Paris, because in the first place if the Government grants us this privilege now but later decides because of the nature of the news sent by you, to discontinue the service, then and not now would be the time to give the matter consideration and adopt other means of transportation.

[redacted]

Sincerely,

J.H. HUMMEL

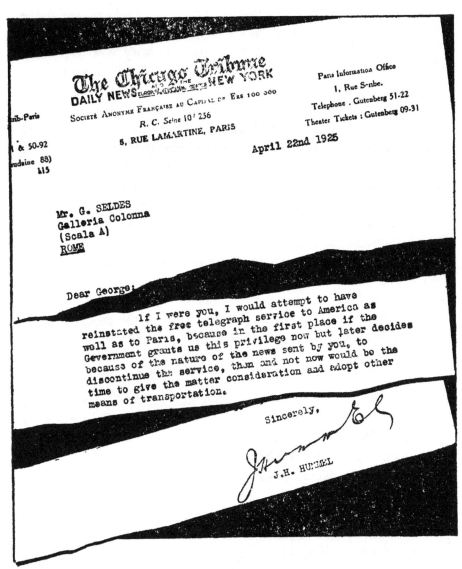

The American press was bribed with free cable and radio service by Mussolini. The Chicago Tribune asked for the bribe. Here is the documentary evidence.

and they published the news under a Washington dateline.

In pleading not guilty to aiding the enemy the *Tribune* made the confession that it had faked at least parts of the story: the Washington dateline was false because the story was written in Chicago; the list of battleships which participated was just made up out of a book on ships; and the statement that the information came from U. S. Navy officials was just 100 per cent a lie.

Congressman Elmer Holland of Pennsylvania said to the House of Representatives that Joseph Medill Patterson (*News*) and Eleanor Patterson (*Times-Herald*) were "America's No. 1 and No. 2 exponents of the Nazi propaganda line . . . doing their best to bring about a fascist victory." When Joe Patterson replied with an editorial headed "Congressman Holland: You Are a Liar," Holland made a list of all the defeatest fascist news items, editorials and cartoons in the McCormick-Patterson press and concluded: "Daily these publishers rub at the morale of the American people. Daily they sow suspicion. Daily they preach that we are in a hopeless struggle. Daily they wear at the moral fiber of the people, softening it, rotting it, preparing us for defeat."

A Hundred Years of Falsehood

In addition to following the Nazi line, the *Chicago Tribune* has a line of its own, and has followed it for almost a hundred years. It is the policy of using falsehood for its own editorial purposes—and it started on this career three-quarters of a century before Hitler in *Mein Kampf* wrote his amazing paragraphs on the value of the colossal lie.

No matter which side the *Tribune* has been on, it has not hesitated to fake the news to favor its viewpoint. It has been on the side of general welfare—but that was long ago. In 1858 it was for Lincoln. It fought slavery. In the Lincoln-Douglas debates it was so partisan to Lincoln that it garbled and distorted Douglas' speeches, and printed Lincoln's honestly. (Source: Edgar Lee Masters, *Tale of Chicago,* page 132.)

In 1864, after Joseph Medill had helped elect Lincoln, he headed a delegation protesting the draft. Lincoln was very angry with the *Tribune* owner. He said to him: "You, Medill, you are acting like a coward. You and your *Tribune* have had more influence than any paper in the Northwest in making this war. You can influence great masses, and yet you cry to be spared, at a moment when your cause is suffering." (Source: Ida M. Tarbell, *Life of Abraham Lincoln,* Vol. II, p. 149.)

And although Medill fought human slavery, he did his best to encourage wage slavery. He fought the labor movement, the eight-hour day, unions, and every attempt to better the life of the common man. When hard times came Joseph Medill published an editorial favoring the poisoning of the unemployed. That was his idea of solving the crisis of 1877.

From 1873 through the panic years unemployment increased, thousands of men began to roam the country, looking for work. The wealthy were scared. Chicago passed a Vagrant Law, making all unemployed subject to arrest. A reader asked the *Chicago Tribune* what to do with the barefooted and ragged who came begging for food. The reader called the unemployed tramps and also accused them of theft. The *Tribune* editor replied (July 12, 1877):

> "The [Vagrant] Law, while an improvement on the old one, is not of much use for suburban districts, where officers are scarce and Justices of Peace hard to find. The simplest plan, probably, where one is not a member of the Humane Society, is to put a little strychnine or arsenic in the meat and other supplies furnished the tramps. This produces death within a comparatively short period of time, is a warning to other tramps to keep out of the neighborhood. . . ."

The faking of news to harm labor, which began in the 1850's, is continued by McCormick to the present day. The *Tribune* has fought organized labor, from the Knights of Labor to the A. F. of L. to the C. I. O.

The greatest proof in modern history that the press publishes tremendous lies for the purpose of smashing labor was the treatment of the Memorial Day massacre in Chicago in 1937. It is true that when the Paramount news reel—which the *St. Louis*

Post-Dispatch forced into the open after attempts at suppression —showed that labor was entirely innocent, the police entirely to blame for the coldblooded murder of ten peaceful strikers, many newspapers did print this fact. But not the *Chicago Tribune.*

The *Tribune* stuck to its lies after the proof was given to the world. It stuck to its lies after the newspapermen who were present at the massacre testified before a Congressional investigating commission that the police were murderers, the strikers blameless. The *Tribune* ran an editorial saying the massacre was justified because property must be protected. Although the victims of the police were shot in the back, although the newsreel shows the police starting the shooting without reason, and murdering men who were doing nothing but watching, the *Tribune* editorial yelled "reds."

The Ku Klux Klan was in its second childhood in 1921. It had millions of members—its peak was about 6,000,000 before its decline began three or four years later. The *Chicago Tribune* was one of the few big papers which openly favored the Klan.

In 1921 Bernard Shaw canceled a visit to America. He wrote:

> "I have no intention of going to prison with Debs or taking my wife to Texas, where Ku Klux Klan mobs snatch white women from out of hotel verandas and tar and feather them."

The *Chicago Tribune* suppressed the name of the Ku Klux Klan. Its version read just "mobs."

This was on April 19. On April 16 the *Tribune* had carried a full page ad (netting the owners thousands of dollars) signed by Imperial Wizard Simmons of the K. K. K. and saying:

> "The Knights of the K. K. K. is a lawabiding, legally chartered, standard, fraternal order, designed to teach and inculcate the purest ideals of American citizenship, with malice towards none and justice to every citizen regardless of race, color or creed."

When readers protested that the ad was a lie, that the Klan attacked Catholics, Jews and Negroes, and was barred to them, the *Tribune* replied (Aug. 27) that the old K. K. K. had been created because of intolerable conditions and "danger of Negro domination," and although evils were committed in its name, it served an important end, while "contributing one of the romantic episodes of our history." The new K. K. K., continued the *Tribune,* was virtually the old. "All the great fraternal orders," it added, "which accomplish so much quiet good . . . make use of this natural liking for mysterious rites and secret ties, and the new Klan will hardly be denied the right to adopt the same policy." At this time the K. K. K. had already been accused of murders, and much terrorism. "The head of the order repudiates them," concluded the *Tribune.*

On occasions the *Chicago Times,* the *Madison Capital-Times* and La Follette's *Progressive* have offered rewards of $1,000 and $5,000 to anyone who could prove that certain items in the *Tribune* were not lies. The rewards were not claimed, the *Tribune* did not sue for libel. On the other hand the *Tribune*, caught lying, did not attempt to explain or apologize.

The *Times,* Aug. 28, 1936, offered $5,000 "if the *Tribune* or any other newspaper can prove to the satisfaction of the American Society of Newspaper Editors and the A. N. P. A. that the *Tribune* dispatch from Donald Day datelined Riga, Latvia, August 8, with its heading, is true." The fake story said that "Moscow has ordered 'reds' in the United States to back Roosevelt against Landon." Four years later Col. McCormick, in a nationwide radio speech, again repeated the Donald Day story. (WOR, February 15, 1940, 10 P. M.)

On October 29, 1938, the *Progressive* offered $1,000 to anyone who could prove that Washington correspondent Chesly Manly's story headlined "New Deal Hit in Red Inquiry" was not false. In that story the *Tribune* said "La Follette's so-called inquiry [into denial of civil liberties and rights of labor] was conceived by John L. Lewis, dictator of the C.I.O. and political ally of Mr. Roosevelt." The *Tribune* heading using the word "red" was a smear; the story, the *Progressive* said, was a lie, and it would donate $1,000 to the *Tribune* charity fund if it was proven not to be a lie. The *Tribune* did not reply.

It is not often that a President of the United States calls a paper or a news service a liar, but it has happened more frequently of late. President Roosevelt has denounced Hearst, Roy Howard's United Press and the *Chicago Tribune* for their lies used for political purposes against him and his party.

On August 26, 1941, the President at his press conference denounced several stories "as examples of the vicious rumors, distortions of facts, or just plain dirty falsehoods." The cause of the outburst was a *Chicago Tribune* story signed Walter Trohan appearing in the *Washington Times-Herald*. This story was in line with the *Tribune* policy on Lend-Lease.

No American newspaper outside the Hearst and Howard chains has fought labor so viciously as the *Tribune*. Not satisfied with smearing the C. I. O., distorting the news, using headlines, editorials, bias, perversion against labor, the *Tribune* also resorted to falsehood. On November 27, 1938, the *Tribune* had the following sensational headline:

"C. I. O. Strangles San Francisco, Industries Die"

This, one of the many sensational stories blaming everything on labor, appeared on the front page, continuing to page 4. The main "fact" revealed, after the usual buncombe and propaganda and wild false generalities, was that the situation created by the C. I. O. auto workers was so bad that the Chevrolet plant moved away to Los Angeles.

A. L. Kennedy, manager, industrial department, Oakland Chamber of Commerce, protested this *Tribune* lie. He wrote:

> "In the first place, the Chevrolet automobile assembly plant is not located in San Francisco; it is located in Oakland. In the second place and most important, it did not move to Los Angeles; it is still here. Furthermore, it has never had to operate under strike conditions. . . . In fairness to this community a retraction is in order."

After lying on pages 1 and 4, the *Tribune* printed exactly 2¼ inches of Kennedy's protest as a letter to the editor! (January 4, 1939.)

Another favorite subject on which not only the *Tribune* but many more respected papers lied frequently, is W.P.A. Every reactionary pro-fascist anti-labor paper, and notably Hearst fought civilian aid. The *Tribune* naturally was not content with posed pictures of workmen leaning on shovels. It came out with two weeks of falsehood of which the following is a typical heading:

"GRAFT, FRAUDS, THEFT;
"W. P. A. REEKS WITH CORRUPTION"

Howard O. Hunter, assistant W. P. A. administrator, invited nineteen Chicago newspapermen to his office and handed them a twenty-five-page statement proving all fourteen stories in the *Tribune* false. He said the *Tribune* engaged in "deliberate, vicious, and wholesale lying." The pictures showing lazy men were taken at a private sewer-digging job. One picture had been changed between editions because its background showed many men at work. The *Tribune* writer had been discharged from W. P. A. for drunkenness. But Hunter did not blame the reporter or Managing Editor Robert M. Lee. He called Publisher McCormick "vicious," and "irrational." Said Hunter:

"Every statement published by the *Tribune* was found to be false. Ordinarily we would not dignify such accusations made by the *Chicago Tribune* by going to the trouble of answering them, because any intelligent person in Chicago knows that such charges have been faked and trumped up by the *Tribune* for years.

"But when column after column is pawned off on the public as news, none of which has any foundation, when columns are used to falsely attack individual unemployed citizens and to misrepresent to the public the work they are doing, it is time that the public is acquainted with the truth surrounding the publication of these articles."

The *Tribune,* of course, printed not a word about the Hunter documentation, but its brasscheck polisher, the cartoonist Carey Orr, continued to draw pictures slandering W. P. A.

It is significant that in the newspaper profession everyone knows that the *Chicago Tribune* is the most unfair and least reliable paper in the country, and many trustworthy journalists have openly accused the *Tribune* of lying.

The Washington press corps is the elite of the profession. Most of its members are highly paid. Some of them have the same financial interests as their employers; some lead a double life, writing the propaganda to suit their owners but retaining a free and liberal mind. The latter are certainly not brasscheck polishers of the Pegler variety; they are not prostitutes. Proof of this was given when Leo Rosten took numerous polls in which these journalists told the truth.

Rosten asked America's leading press corps to vote for the "least fair and reliable" papers in the country, and here is the result in the order of their badness:

1. The Hearst papers: *New York Journal-American, Mirror; Albany Times-Union; Boston Record, American, Advertiser; Baltimore News-Post, American; Pittsburgh Sun-Telegraph, Chicago Herald-American, Milwaukee News-Sentinel, Detroit Times, San Francisco Examiner, Call-Bulletin; Oakland Post-Enquirer, Los Angeles Examiner, Herald-Express; San Antonio Light, Seattle Post-Intelligencer.*

2. *Chicago Tribune.*

3. *Los Angeles Times.*

4. Scripps-Howard chain: *New York World-Telegram, Cleveland Press, Pittsburgh Press, San Francisco News, Indianapolis Times, Columbus Citizen, Cincinnati Post, Kentucky Post, Knoxville News-Sentinel, Denver News, Birmingham Post, Memphis Press-Scimitar, Memphis Commercial-Appeal, Washington News, Houston Press, Ft. Worth Press, Albuquerque Tribune, El Paso Herald-Post, Evansville Press.*

It is to be noted that, of the three big and powerful chains, two are listed (first and fourth worst) and the third, the McCormick-Patterson chain, has its leading paper listed as the worst single paper in America.

Of the ninety-three Washington correspondents who were in this poll, eighty-seven voted the Hearst papers the worst, seventy-one voted against the *Chicago Tribune;* next were *Los Angeles*

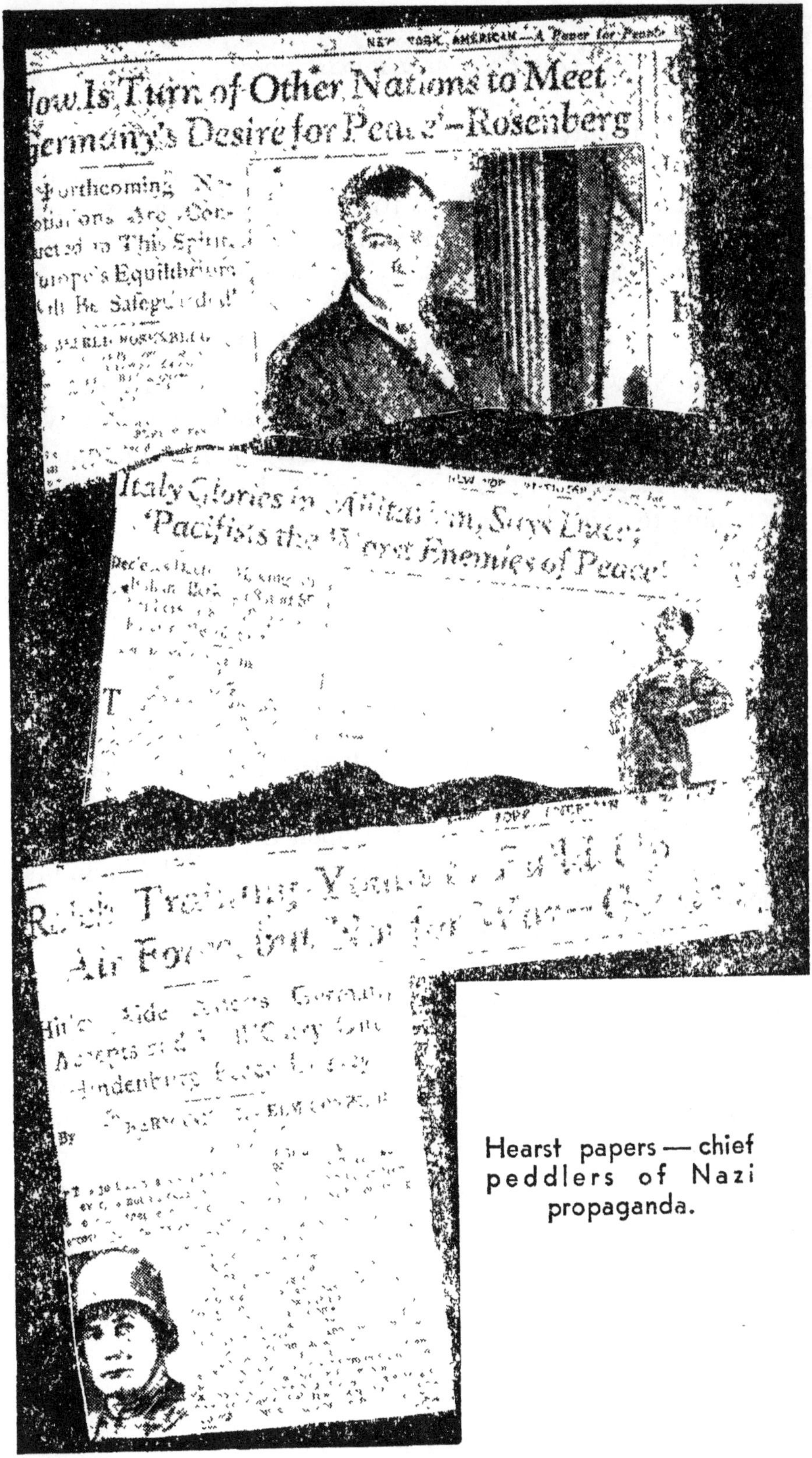

Hearst papers — chief peddlers of Nazi propaganda.

Times with twenty-five votes and the Howard chain with thirteen. The Scripps-Howard papers had once been the leading liberals of the country, and it is true that Roy Howard still permits certain among them to remain so. Not all Howard papers are as filthy (under daily orders) as the papers of the Hearst chain.

Rosten also took a vote on what is the best newspaper in America. Ninety-nine Washington journalists took part and the *Chicago Tribune* received only one vote. In other words, it was last. But inasmuch as the *Tribune* has a large staff, and inasmuch as several *Tribune* writers participated in the vote, it is indeed heartening to note that the *Tribune's* own men have no illusions about it being a decent newspaper.

The situation was similar with votes affecting the Hearst news services. Although several Hearst men voted, the total which believed the agency was best, more liberal, or more reliable was less than the total of Hearst men participating.

The voting is significant. When the day comes for chains of free newspapers—a press which will deal fairly with labor, a press which will not be afraid to fight Fascism at home as well as abroad—they will be able to call upon the newspaper workers, the reporters and, in many instances, the noted columnists who work for the corrupt press but who are not corrupted by either the money they make or the company they have to keep. For every Benjamin De Casseres, Paul Mallon, Westbrook Pegler, Frederic Woltman, William Philip Simms, James O'Donnell, Chesly Manly, whose mouth is black with the polish off the shoes of Hearst and Howard and McCormick and Patterson (as Heywood Broun so often said), there are many better men who may be working for the same corrupters of our free press but who have not been polishing the fast disappearing brass check of the ancient profession.

CHAPTER III

POISON PEN PEGLER

It is the *opinion* of many persons and organizations that one of the most widely known and read newspaper columnists, Westbrook Pegler, is aiding the Axis rather than the United States in this war; it is a *fact* that the New York Newspaper Guild, the organization of thousands of Pegler's colleagues, so stated when it sent President Roosevelt a documentation of twelve instances out of Pegler's writings.

It is a fact that newspapers, columnists, radio orators and others who form public opinion have served the Axis propaganda. It is also true that too frequently those who know and who make these charges do not name names. They, therefore, emasculate their own words.

For example, here is the director of the U. S. Conciliation Service, Dr. John S. Steelman, who states:

"Careless recital of the dramatic side of strikes in the press and on the screen and over the radio has given too many people the impression that our war efforts are being held up in a serious way because of willful strife in a major part of American industry. This is a dangerous lie that serves the purpose of the Axis, but serves no good end among us." Dr. Steelman knows the culprits, but he is not in a position to name them. He is aware that Kaltenborn on the radio, Pegler in the newspapers, the entire Hearst and Howard press are those guilty of careless recitals about strikes.

On the other hand here is the statement issued by the conference directors of C. I. O. editors (Washington, April 11, 1942):

"Labor has been subjected to an infamous campaign of misrepresentation, for the purpose of cutting wages, destroying union organization, and in advancing the profits of special interest groups. Most of the daily press has joined in this campaign, together with such radio commentators as H. V. Kaltenborn and others of his type. This anti-labor propaganda campaign, if not directly inspired by Axis agents and American appeasers, at any rate plays their game by striking at national unity and undermining labor morale."

Again, the official organ of the National Maritime Union, *The Pilot,* states that "Pegler's sales talk has the made-in-Berlin label."

Again, the National Maritime Union, holding its 1943 convention and confirming its pledge to place the winning of the war above everything else, passed a resolution naming the leading fascist organization in the country and the twelve leading fascists, namely: The National Association of Manufacturers, Senators Nye, Wheeler and Tom Connally, the Texas polltaxer of anti-labor bill fame; Representatives Martin Dies, Hamilton Fish and Howard Smith, the notorious Virginia polltaxer of anti-labor bill fame; the great chain publishers Hearst, Howard, Patterson and McCormick; and the clerical fascist leaders, Father Coughlin and the Rev. Gerald L. K. Smith, and the elements of the Christian Front and Ku Klux Klan which follow them.

No better list could be written. The most powerful force on it is the NAM; the most powerful individuals are the four publishers who in turn employ a hundred brasscheck columnists to spread their American fascist ideologies.

The columnists have risen to great power. The editorial page of the newspapers has fallen into disrepute as the American people have realized more and more that it represents not honest opinion but the prostitute views of the paymasters of the editors and publishers—advertisers, the special interests, the Big Money, the well-known ruling families of the nation. Somehow or other the view spread that there was a certain amount of independence and integrity among the newspaper columnists. This view, of course, is based on the fact that there is a percentage of honest columnists, perhaps a higher percentage than among editorial

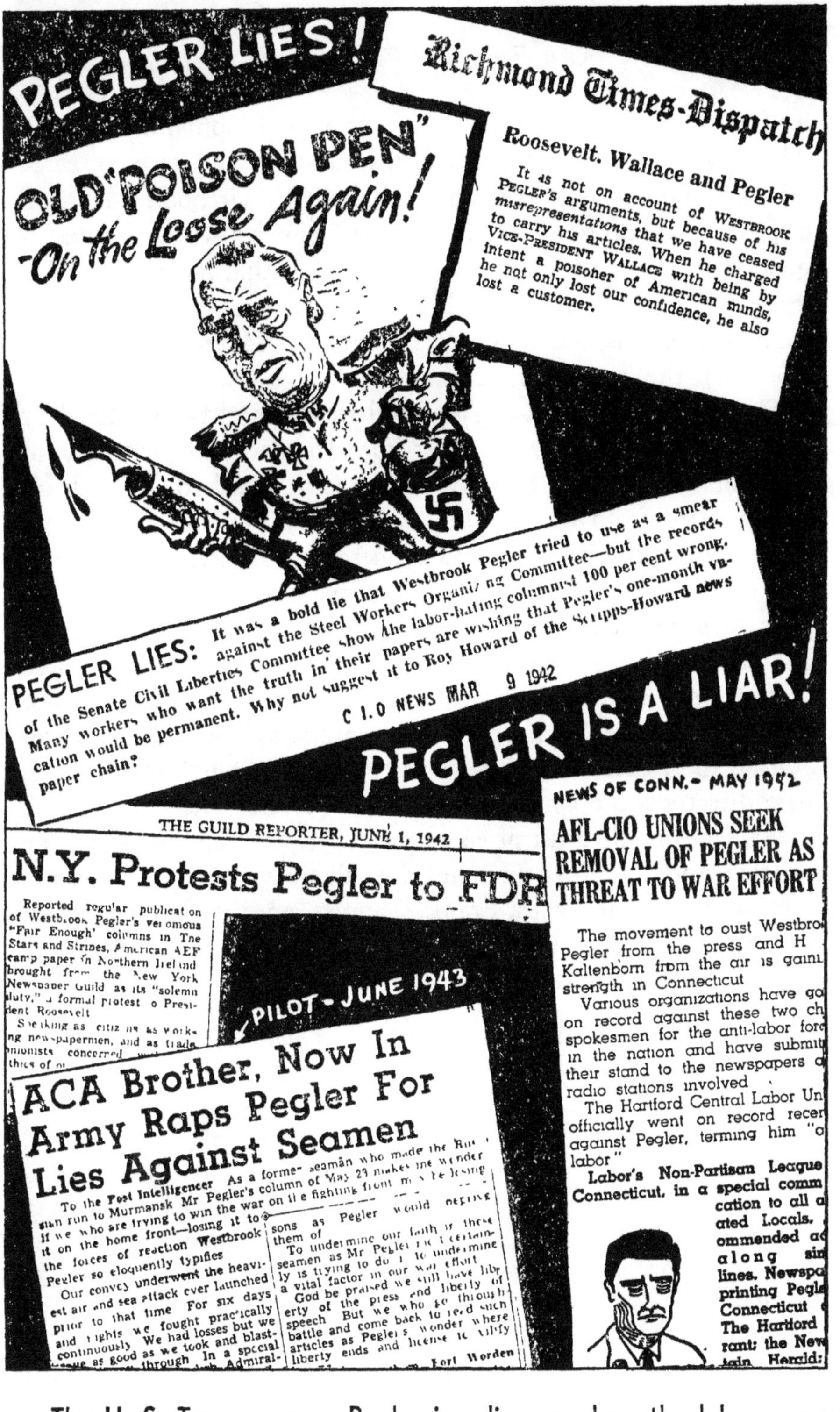

PEGLER LIES!

Richmond Times-Dispatch

Roosevelt, Wallace and Pegler

It is not on account of WESTBROOK PEGLER'S arguments, but because of his misrepresentations that we have ceased to carry his articles. When he charged VICE-PRESIDENT WALLACE with being by intent a poisoner of American minds, he not only lost our confidence, he also lost a customer.

OLD "POISON PEN" -On the Loose Again!

PEGLER LIES: It was a bold lie that Westbrook Pegler tried to use as a smear against the Steel Workers Organizing Committee—but the records of the Senate Civil Liberties Committee show the labor-hating columnist 100 per cent wrong. Many workers who want the truth in their papers are wishing that Pegler's one-month vacation would be permanent. Why not suggest it to Roy Howard of the Scripps-Howard news paper chain?

C I.O NEWS MAR 9 1942

PEGLER IS A LIAR!

NEWS OF CONN. - MAY 1942

AFL-CIO UNIONS SEEK REMOVAL OF PEGLER AS THREAT TO WAR EFFORT

The movement to oust Westbro[ok] Pegler from the press and H[.] Kaltenborn from the air is gain[ing] strength in Connecticut

Various organizations have go[ne] on record against these two ch[ief] spokesmen for the anti-labor forc[es] in the nation and have submit[ted] their stand to the newspapers a[nd] radio stations involved

The Hartford Central Labor Un[ion] officially went on record recen[tly] against Pegler, terming him "a[...] labor"

Labor's Non-Partisan League [of] Connecticut, in a special comm[uni]cation to all a[ffili]ated Locals, [rec]ommended ac[tion] along sim[ilar] lines. Newspa[pers] printing Pegle[r in] Connecticut [are] The Hartford [Cou]rant; the New [Bri]tain Herald;

THE GUILD REPORTER, JUNE 1, 1942

N.Y. Protests Pegler to FDR

Reported regular publication of Westbrook Pegler's venomous "Fair Enough" columns in The Stars and Stripes, American AEF camp paper in Northern Ireland brought from the New York Newspaper Guild as its "solemn duty," a formal protest to President Roosevelt

Speaking as citizens, as working newspapermen, and as trade unionists concerned ... ethics of ou...

PILOT - JUNE 1943

ACA Brother, Now In Army Raps Pegler For Lies Against Seamen

To the Post Intelligencer As a former seaman who made the Russian run to Murmansk Mr Pegler's column of May 23 makes me wonder if we who are trying to win the war on the fighting front may be losing it on the home front—losing it to the forces of reaction Westbrook Pegler so eloquently typifies

Our convoy underwent the heaviest air and sea attack ever launched prior to that time For six days and nights we fought practically continuously We had losses but we gave as good as we took and blasted through In a special ... Admiral-

... sons as Pegler would negrine them of

To undermine our faith in these seamen as Mr Pegler ... undermine ly is trying to do ... to undermine a vital factor in our war effort

God be praised we still have liberty of the press and liberty of speech But we who go through battle and come back to read such articles as Pegler's wonder where liberty ends and license to vilify ...

... Fort Worden

The U. S. Treasury says Pegler is a liar; so does the labor press; but 8,000,000 Americans read his daily poison.

writers. One may not agree with Walter Lippmann, Dorothy Thompson, Johannes Steel, Samuel Grafton and two or three others, but there is no reason to challenge their bona fides, and a few outstanding names have given columnists in general a good reputation for reliability. The truth is that most columnists inhabit the same gilt-edged bordellos and counting rooms and country clubs as the newspaper owners, and are no better or worse—in the history of harlotry.

The best columnist was Heywood Broun, and he was fired by the *New York World*, the most liberal paper in the country, at the time he defended Sacco and Vanzetti. Just before his death he was fired from the *World-Telegram* by Roy Howard for no other reason than that he was a liberal columnist, and Howard had swung far towards the true international reaction which in Italy Mussolini named Fascism. Secretary of the Interior Ickes, an old newspaper man himself, quotes Broun saying: "Three or four well-known syndicated columnists wield more influence than the average lawmaker in Washington," and, Ickes adds: "Of all the columnists, Sokolsky is probably the only one who is paid directly and openly by Big Business to act as its spokesman."

Mr. Ickes made a list of columnists, their circulation, and their salaries, and in return for the journalistic material I furnished him in his debate with Frank Gannett on the freedom (and integrity) of the press, I am helping myself to his table (from his book, *America's House of Lords,* page 96):

Name	*No. of Newspapers*	*Total Circulation*	*Salary*
Broun, Heywood	41	2,924,000	$36,260
Carter, Boake	83	7,187,000	
Clapper, Raymond	49	3,653,385	
Johnson, Hugh S.	76	5,323,000	15,600
Kent, Frank R.	112	7,000,000	33,243
Lawrence, David	133	6,000,000	
Lippmann, Walter	184	7,147,000	62,476
Mallon, Paul	200		17,600
Pearson and Allen	313	12,000,000	
Pegler, Westbrook	117	6,186,000	46,263

Name	*No. of Newspapers*	*Total Circulation*	*Salary*
Sokolsky, George E.	25		
Sullivan, Mark	46	2,881,000	24,426
Thompson, Dorothy	196	7,555,000	

Broun and Johnson have died since this list was made out. Pegler has gotten into 120 newspapers with 8,000,000 circulation and his salary from Howard, $25,000, is augmented by half of the proceeds of syndication rights, giving him a total of $65,000.

In this list the only great liberal was Broun. Miss Thompson and Mr. Lippmann are fair weather liberals, neither having the courage to break a lance or lose an eye in the war against American reaction although both are ardent fighters against Faraway Fascism. Pearson takes no part in politics—Allen is in the army. Walter Winchell is the most syndicated of all columnists but Mr. Ickes chose to exclude him, not realizing perhaps that Winchell does devote a part of his gossip columns to political, social and other matters, which makes him a power in this country.

The list then shows: Carter, a notorious labor-baiter who was put off the air for years on the protest of unions and who, after promising to behave, still smears organized labor frequently; Clapper, who was probably too scared of his job with Roy Howard to be the liberal his friends say he was personally; Kent, a typical servant of the special interests; Lawrence, one of the worst of reactionaries; Paul Mallon, who has been denounced as a liar by Mr. Ickes (See *Time,* April 24, 1939) and who is a typical Hearstling; Sokolsky, exposed by the La Follette Committee as an NAM agent; Mark Sullivan, another spokesman for Big Money; Lippmann and Miss Thompson and Westbrook Pegler.

It can fairly be said that the two columnists who have the most influence in the country are Lippmann and Pegler: Lippmann influences all men of intelligence, Pegler is the monitor of the morons. Lippmann has one of the best minds in America, Pegler is a mental hoodlum. He has absolutely no education, no culture, no literary quality, no intelligence, no knowledge of economics, no knowledge of most of the things he writes about outside sports and plain news sensations; he is, in short, a sort of glorified moron himself and, therefore, so successful in finding an audience of eight million who believe in not only his daily propaganda but in the numerous lies which he tells without any apparent knowledge that he is lying.

U. S. Treasury Exposes a Pegler Lie

The use of the colossal lie has been acclaimed by Hitler as a fascist method. Apparently the Peglerian mind, which was capable of advocating lynching years ago, must now employ a Nazi trick in the campaign against the welfare of the American people. Everything the Roosevelt administration has done has been attacked by Pegler for the simple reason (as Broun disclosed) that "he was bitten by an income tax return," and in January, 1943, Pegler engaged in falsehood in order to smear the government.

Exhibit A: In his papers of January 2 Pegler wrote a column beginning: "Mr. Morgenthau, the Secretary of the Treasury, is sensitive to aspersions on the ethics and fairness of his income tax reviewers, who are, as has been observed before, masters of a repertoire of sly and shady shyster tricks of interpretation, having the color if not the odor, of legality." This statement, like some 90 per cent of all Pegler statements, is not a matter of fact, nor a matter of opinion, but a matter of prejudice and bias, unfair enough to violate the code of ethics of journalism, under which all Pegler papers are supposed to operate.

The Pegler column then continues: "We have before us a plain case of larceny from millions of citizens of all income brackets committed by the Treasury, apparently with the knowledge and approval of Secretary Morgenthau and certainly on his responsibility."

If this statement is true, those accused of larceny should be in jail. If this statement is untrue, then the person who makes it is spreading a falsehood. However, since the statement is directed against a government official, the maker cannot apparently be sued for libel.

The Pegler statement continues: "In passing the 5 per cent victory tax, Congress said unmistakably that it was to be a tax on 1943 income. Yet, the Treasury Department, in violation of the will and intent of Congress, and of the law, has usurped the Congressional legislative power and decided that all pay checks . . . delivered after midnight Thursday, shall be taxable at 5 per cent even though most or all of the money was earned before the first of the year.

"In simple words, the Treasury decided to steal this money from the people and to make the employers parties to the theft by compelling them to withhold the tax and turn it in.

"Theft is the only word for it. It is a bold and cynical defiance of law and morality. . . ." Next paragraphs contain phrases: "amount . . . stolen," "victims of larceny," "swipe the dough," and "not taxation but larceny."

Exhibit B: Pegler column, January 19, began: "Apparently more in sorrowful patience with a miserable sinner than in mighty anger, the Treasury Department sends me Press Service Bulletin No. 34-80, which purports to put me in error in accusing the department of plain larceny in its plan to collect the 5 per cent tax on individual income earned in 1942.

"Taking something that belongs to someone else . . . is stealing, and in violation of a well known commandment, and as done by the Treasury Department of the U.S.A. is a bad example to the people who might reasonably decide to take up stealing as a regular line of work and get into serious trouble, in all innocence. . . ."

It is the general rule of departments of the U. S. Government to ignore misstatements and falsehood. However, this was a matter affecting millions of people, an urgent matter, and a correction was necessary. Therefore the Treasury had to expose Pegler as a liar. It sent the following letter to Pegler's syndicate:

"TREASURY DEPARTMENT
"Washington

"January 26, 1943

"Mr. George V. Carlin, Manager,
"United Feature Syndicate, Inc.,
"220 East 42nd St., New York.
"Dear Mr. Carlin:

"I have just read Westbrook Pegler's column in today's *Washington Daily News,* the second in which he has given circulation to serious misinformation with respect to the Victory Tax and has made grave charges against the Treasury Department.

"Whatever Mr. Pegler's motives may be, his repetition of erroneous assertions is likely to spread confusion in the minds of taxpayers and may seriously interfere with the collection of wartime taxes.

"Because the facts in this connection have been brought to Mr. Pegler's attention by telephone and letter following the publication of his first column on the subject in the News *of Jan. 1, I am writing to demand, in behalf of the Treasury Department, that a copy of this letter be made available to all of your subscribers who receive the Pegler column.*

"Mr. Pegler in both instances accuses the Treasury Department of 'theft' and 'larceny' because the withholding tax out of which the Victory tax will be paid was applied to some wages earned at the end of 1942 but paid early this year. He argued that withholding should have been applied only against wages earned in 1943.

"I feel warranted, therefore, in asking those newspapers which print this column to present their readers the simple facts which he has insisted on distorting.

"The second paragraph of today's column, discussing the authority under which the tax is collected, contains a complete misstatement of fact in the sentence, 'It does not say that this tax shall be collected on any income occurring before December 31.' On the contrary, the section of the statute covering the withholding sets forth very clearly, 'The provisions of this section shall take effect on January 1, 1943, and shall be applicable to all wages . . . paid on or after such date.' The law makes the time of payment the test—not the time during which the wage was earned.

"Any inspection of this portion of the Revenue Act, or any attempt to have checked its application with the Bureau of Internal Revenue, would have shown Mr. Pegler that the total amounts collected through the withholding tax will be completely credited against such individual's Victory tax liability at the end of this year. As a result, there cannot possibly be any question of 'theft' from any taxpayer of a portion of income not intended to be covered by Congress.

"In spite of explanations, Mr. Pegler also has persisted in presenting as synonymous a tax and a method of tax collection. Twice in today's column he refers to the 'withholding or Victory tax.' The fact is that the Victory tax will be due on March 15, 1944, on all income other than capital gains and interest from tax-exempt securities, much of that income not now being subjected to the withholding provisions of the law.

"I hope that by the distribution of this letter you will be able to undo some of the harm that has undoubtedly been done by Mr. Pegler's persistent misrepresentation.

"(Signed) CHARLES SCHWARZ,
"Director of Public Relations,
"Treasury Department, Washington, D. C."

There is not a newspaper man in America who does not know that Pegler wilfully and persistently misrepresents. But no newspaper likes to have itself and its most cherished columnist called a liar in public, and the 120 newspapers which were asked by the U. S. Treasury to publish its condemnation of Pegler either suppressed the letter, killed parts of it, or buried parts of it in that graveyard of journalistic skulduggery and hypocrisy, the "Letters to the Editor" department.

In the document above the three paragraphs to which attention is especially called are those suppressed by the *Los Angeles Times,* the most notorious anti-labor paper in the country.

A few newspapers are deserving of some credit: the Treasury informs the present writer that it has received a few letters from editors saying that upon reading Pegler's columns on the Victory Tax they realized he was lying and they did not run the stuff those two days. But not one newspaper threw Pegler out because of his persistent misrepresentations.

So long as Pegler makes it his main business to attack labor, liberals, the New Deal, he remains the leading columnist of our press, whose editors are not morons or hoodlums but who are on the contrary very smart gentlemen who know how to use a panderer to that sort of mind.

Pegler as a Fascist Stooge

Pegler answers every description of a perfect fascist journalist. In 1933, when he went from sports to columning, the first piece he wrote was in favor of lynching. There followed a consultation with Roy Howard, and it was decided to hold the pro-lynching column up. However, it was run within the week, and the blame must be shared equally by the two hoodlum-minded journalists.

Incidentally, the lynching in question was of white men in San Jose, California. However, since then Pegler has come out against the Anti-Lynching Bill and he has repeatedly attacked the Negro people.

September 15, 1940, the *Guild Reporter,* official organ of newspapermen, reported that James P. Kirby, *Cleveland Press* unit, "has hurled the lie back at Westbrook Pegler . . . giving documentary proof of his charges." Said Kirby: "To Mr. Pegler's denial that he defended lynching I quote from his column of December 13, 1933, in which he said: 'As one of the rabble, I will admit that I said fine, that is swell, when the papers came up that recent day telling of the lynching of two men who killed the young fellow in California, and I haven't changed my mind yet.'"

Pegler topped his pro-lynching column with a pro-murder column March 31, 1942. Referring to a dirty smear of Interior Secretary Ickes by a Bridgeport (Conn.) paper, Pegler wrote: "I don't blame Ickes for resenting the editorial but I do insist that he should have gone right up to Bridgeport, sought out the editor and shot him dead. Or he might have knocked his head off with a ball-bat. I say this seriously. . . . Had Ickes killed the editor he would have performed a valuable service for the community in general and for the press in particular. . . ."

For years Pegler has smeared Mr. Ickes in revenge for Mr. Ickes' statement that "Pegler is less discriminating than [Hugh]

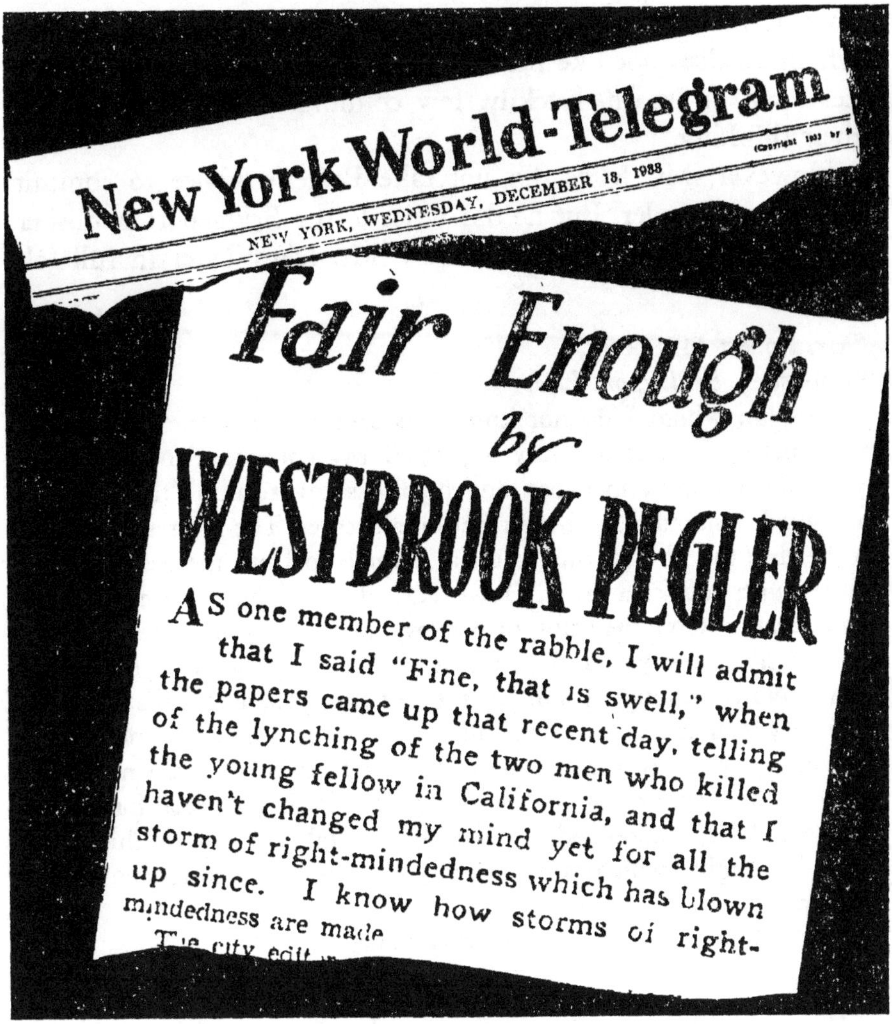

New York World-Telegram

NEW YORK, WEDNESDAY, DECEMBER 13, 1933

Fair Enough

by

WESTBROOK PEGLER

AS one member of the rabble, I will admit that I said "Fine, that is swell," when the papers came up that recent day, telling of the lynching of the two men who killed the young fellow in California, and that I haven't changed my mind yet for all the storm of right-mindedness which has blown up since. I know how storms of right-mindedness are made

The city edit [illegible]

Pegler likes lynching, too.

Johnson, and much more irresponsible." Mr. Ickes had also said that Pegler "jumps from false premises to falser conclusions." Also, that "Pegler . . . is the Mrs. Dilling of columnists. When invective and vituperation fail him, he flatteringly imitates Colonel McCormick by calling the object of his diatribes a 'communist.' . . . According to Pegler's code that man is a 'communist' whom he does not like personally or with whose political views he is not in accord. Luckily, few columnists are as unstable in their thinking."

However, Mr. Ickes did not take Pegler's advice to commit a common murder. But he did write to the Bridgeport publisher (instead of suing him for slander). Mr. Ickes' letter in full follows:

"Mr. Robert M. Sperry,
"Publisher, *Bridgeport Life.*

"A man whom I do not know has sent to me a tear sheet from your issue of Saturday, July 26, 1941. My correspondent speaks of your 'filthy mind and paper' and he also seems to think that you are a coward. Undoubtedly, he is right on all scores. The impression seems to be that the filth in this editorial surged up from the cesspool that passes with you for a mind. However, it doesn't much matter whether you actually wrote the thing or not; as a publisher you are responsible.

"I don't know you and I had never heard of you until this letter came. Now, although I still have never met you, I feel that I know you very well as a cowardly, skulking cur. I can see you in my mind's eye eating your own vomit with relish but enjoying even more the savor of the excrement in the pigsty in which you root for choice morsels. It is, undoubtedly, perfectly natural for you to think the putrid thoughts which you naturally express in the language of the gutter.

"Very truly yours,
"HAROLD L. ICKES."

The Sperry editorial which caused this reply from Ickes is unprintable.

Much more important, however, than Pegler's lie about the Victory Tax, or Pegler's endorsement of lynching, or even the reprint of Pegler anti-labor propaganda by notorious fascist organizations, such as the Associated Industries of Cleveland, is the Pegler line of war thinking which caused the New York Newspaper Guild to protest.

Between June, 1941, and December 7, 1942, Pegler expressed

the hope that Germany and Russia would exterminate each other. It is true that when Pegler covered the Olympic Games in Germany in 1936 he wrote several columns against Hitler, but as between Germany and Russia, Pegler did not hide his preference for the former. However, America was not in the war when Pegler wrote he feared the liberal New Deal and the few gains labor had made under it more than he feared Hitler. But since December 7, Pegler has followed the line which Director of Facts and Figures MacLeish denounced before the publishers' convention as defeatism and divisionism. In attacking America's Allies, in attacking labor, in attacking the Negroes, Pegler has done what Hitler predicted would aid his propaganda in America.

The New York Newspaper Guild, which upholds the Broun tradition, on May 21, 1942, acting on information that Pegler was appearing in the official Army publication, *Stars and Stripes,* protested to the Commander-in-Chief, President Roosevelt. The Guild statement said:

"The Newspaper Guild of New York membership on May 13 urged discontinuance of publication of a column by Westbrook Pegler . . . in *Stars and Stripes.* . . .

"Calling the attention of President Roosevelt to a report that Pegler was among the contributors to this soldier paper, the Guild charged that this columnist had since December 7 cast doubt on the wisdom of a United Nations victory, and by his writings in domestic newspapers had served the cause of disunity. Copies of the resolutions were directed to Chief of Staff General George C. Marshall, Mr. Philip Murray and Mr. William Green."

The Guild resolution said in part:

"As citizens, as working newspapermen, and as trade unionists concerned with the ethics of our profession, with the patriotic duty to support the war effort, and conscious of the obligation of a union of newspapermen to keep up morale, the Newspaper Guild of New York's membership lodges this protest against continued publication of Mr. Pegler's articles intended for American soldiers facing Hitler across the English Channel.

"Mr. Pegler has actually raised a question as to whether a victory of the United Nations against the Fascist Axis would be worthwhile. . . . Mr. Pegler by his written word since December 7 has given circulation to opinions, views and distortions of fact which would result in setting one group of people against other groups instead of knitting all the people more firmly together for the united war effort essential to the conduct of the war.

"In support of this appeal, and in justification of the assertions involving Mr. Pegler, the Guild appends sample exhibitions of his written words since December 7:

"December 8, 1941. Pegler . . . warns: 'We all know that most of the arguments that American boys would not be sent to a foreign war were campaign trickery.'

"December 11. Pegler accuses the government of treachery: 'Dealing off the bottom of the deck, the national government betrayed every worker in the country in the decision of the packed arbitration board to grant Lewis the closed shop in the so-called captive mines. . . . The whole transaction reeked of treachery.'

"December 17. Casts doubts on the aims of our Allies: 'Our people are not going to believe that our gallant Allies of Russia are fighting for the four freedoms. . . .'

"January 6, 1942. Casts doubt on our own aims and discourages cooperation between capital and labor: 'The [automotive] industry is sure to be socialized now and God only knows who will get it when the war is over, but the odds are that it will never be turned back to the stockholders. . . .'

"January 22. Unity . . . disastrous: 'A unified or combined organization of the C. I. O. and the A. F. of L. under the present laws and under the leadership of any of the men now prominent in union politics would be disastrous to every American worker.'

"January 29. Charges President is moving toward totalitarian state: 'The President is using the bosses of the A. F. of L. and C. I. O. for his own political purposes which plainly and irresistibly tend toward a totalitarian state. . . .'

'February 18. He tends to tear down our support of an ally: 'They [the Russians] are the most practical patriots of all, fighting for Russia only, and it is inconceivable that they would prolong the war a single hour beyond some point at which they decided that a truce or peace would best serve the interests of Soviet Russia.'

"[March. Pegler on vacation.]

"April 4. He again attempts to divide our own people: 'The bitter fact is that the whole American people . . . are never allowed to forget that they are being used to create a new internal force, governed by a few personalities who are contributing nothing to the war, which plans to inherit the government after the war is won.'

"May 1. Divisionist attempt: 'If our side wins the war, Russia will plan the peace of the European continent, and on the basis of all Russia's past performances we can confidently assume that in Germany it will be a peace not much different from that which Hitler has imposed on Poland. . . .'

"May 5. Doubts own war efforts: 'The obliteration of Germany . . . would be a drastic way of preserving civilization, but the only question is whether the real war aim of the U. S. justifies the only positive means of securing that aim.'

"May 13. Cynicism toward our own democratic institutions: 'The Senate is our Reichstag. . . . The Senate is protecting a gigantic political racket. . . . The Senate is a very arrogant organization, blown up with pomposity and indifferent to the will and interest of the people.' "

Ever since this protest was filed Mr. Pegler concentrated on baiting labor. In this way he continues to be of service to the divisionists.

CHAPTER IV

WALLACE'S SUPPRESSED SPEECH

"The press is the hired agent of a monied system, and set up for no other purpose than to tell lies, where its interests are involved. One can trust nobody and nothing."—*The Letters of Henry Adams,* Vol. II, p. 99.

If the American press were at least frank about its being a commercial institution, as many of its leaders and owners, notably William Allen White, have admitted, then one of the main indictments against it would fall flat on the ground: the indictment of hypocrisy. When Mr. White said that journalism was once a profession, "a noble calling; now it is an 8 per cent investment and an industry," none of the hundreds of commercialized publishers would agree with him. If, however, the American Newspaper Publishers Association (the Lords of the Press) were to come out openly with a statement that it was in business for profits and that the code of ethics (adopted by the editors, not owners) in 1923 was a dead letter, since it has never been honored, the atmosphere would at least be cleared of the greatest piece of hypocrisy in the American panorama.

Of all the hypocrisies of American journalism the greatest is the claim of a free press, coupled with a barrage of editorials, news stories, cartoons and orations deriding the dictator countries for the manner in which their newspapers follow the orders, wishes, and whims of the ruling party. But it is a fact that about 95 per cent—perhaps it is 98 per cent or even 99 per cent—of the

American press is also dictated to, and also follows the wishes of a superior power, which Henry Adams has named the "monied system."

The commercial press, in another of its brazen hypocritical proclamations, points with pride to the fact that it is free because it upholds a free system in which there are two political parties. But there is probably not one member of the A.N.P.A. who does not know that the Republican and Democratic parties both feed out of the same bag provided by the monied system, and that the same persons frequently subscribe funds to both major parties, and that where the list frequently differs the same interests are represented. They know this very well, and they also know very well that the press has never given honest news coverage to the formation, platform and campaign of any third party which was independent enough not to feed on the same money.

Furthermore, the A.N.P.A. knows that where there is a choice between the two parties, when one is more liberal than the other, when one gives the majority of the American people (labor) a new deal or a square deal or a better deal, the press turns against that party to the extent of 85 to 95 per cent. If one leaves out of the accounting certain rock bound papers, such as the rock ribbed southern Democrats and the granite ribbed Vermonters, then the tally for the various Roosevelt campaigns has shown that he was attacked, abused, unsupported by 85 to 95 per cent of the press, and that he was even suppressed in certain big papers including the *Chicago Tribune*. Moreover, all this was done without an official order from a fascist dictator. It was not quite 100 per cent; and so we might say that although we have no press dictator as in fascist countries, the American press is already about 85 to 95 per cent totalitarian on certain issues.

In my opinion this is a fair estimate. There are various polls and reliable estimates and weekly and monthly surveys on the editorial viewpoints of the American press. They show divided opinion on many things. But when the issue is the general welfare of the many against the increased profits of the few, when it is liberty and democracy versus special privilege, the American press is so unanimously on the side of the latter that it can be said that without being dictated to by a fascist dictator it follows the line of native American Fascism.

There is no doubt but that the most important fascist force in the nation is the National Association of Manufacturers, since this organization of the 9,000 biggest businesses is in the control of only 207 powerful men who use it for anti-social purposes. In the year 1935 the La Follette Committee's report said, "the NAM had opposed the principal legislative measures sponsored by the national administration . . . National Labor Relations Act [the Wagner Act, the Magna Carta of labor, which the NAM is still trying to have repealed or emasculated], Social Security Act, the Banking Act, the Utility Holding Company Act. . . ." This fact alone does not show the fascist ideology of the NAM, but it does show that this most powerful lobby in Washington worked against every piece of legislation aiding and protecting the people of the country, and worked for special privilege and profits.

Any test of the alignment on these same measures will show that the press was more than 50 per cent for the program of the NAM, in some cases 98 per cent. Between 1935 and 1939, when the Global War broke out, the *New York Times* ran an average of 12 editorials a year in favor of the NAM policy of repealing or amending and hamstringing the Wagner Act, and more venal papers were even worse. Of course, no one wrote or phoned Sulzberger of the *Times*, McCormick of the *Chicago Tribune*, Mr. Hearst and Mr. Howard and the other imposing reactionaries and gave them instructions to attack the Wagner Act, or the Social Security Act or, indeed, any piece of legislation of the Roosevelt administration which disinterested persons favored and which favored the general welfare. Neither an American Mussolini nor the publicity department of the NAM took any action, and yet the great newspaper chains which enslave the American mind all rattled with the uniform sound which Mussolini once described as so pleasing to his journalistic-dictatorial ears.

Let us consider some examples of the behavior of the American press in handling and suppressing big news stories. They will show that it is not necessary to have a fascist dictator in our country to get totalitarianism—or at least 85 to 95 per cent of it —in the press. Here are a few instances.

It would be the greatest crime in the history of civilization to ask our men to give their arms and their legs, their eyes, their health and their lives for a cause that did not justify it. There is today a cause which justifies the risk and the sacrifice: it is the cause of destroying Fascism, which is the enemy of the good life. Vice President Henry Wallace realized this, and in the great days of confusion of May, 1942, he delivered his now famous speech on The Century of the Common Man.

Mr. Wallace said that this was a war between a free world and a slave world. This war is part of the "march of freedom of the past 150 years." This war is "a people's revolution" taking up where the "American Revolution of 1775, the French Revolution of 1792, the Latin American revolutions of the Bolivarian era, the German Revolution of 1848 and the Russian Revolution of 1917" left off.

"Everywhere the common people are on the march," proclaimed Mr. Wallace.

The Vice President is also aware of the profits in Fascism for the few. He said: "The demagogue is the curse of the modern world, and of all the demagogues the worst are those financed by well-meaning wealthy men who sincerely believe that their wealth is likely to be safer if they can hire men with political 'it' to change the sign posts and lure the people back into slavery of the most degraded kind."

Mr. Wallace also advocated the Four Freedoms, the last two being Freedom from Fear and Freedom from Want. These are of course the economic freedoms, and since they imply a better world for the many they have scared the living pocketbooks out of the few.

The most important fact of all about the Wallace speech is that it was the big declaration of the war program of the nation, and as such was entitled to most of the front page of every honest newspaper from coast to coast.

Actually it was about 95 per cent suppressed and distorted. A dozen liberal newspapers ran the speech in full, some a week or two late when public pressure demanded it. In the nation's capital the speech was so badly reported that an industrial concern (Latex Corp.) paid to have it inserted as an ad. (We have said much about the evils of advertising; this is a rare instance of its social value.) In the metropolis where the speech was heard over the radio, only one paper, *PM,* ran the text. Only *PM* headlined the great statement on the war—the war between a slave world and a free world; the war as a continuation of the American and other revolutions for the rights of all people. This is how the metropolitan press handled the story:

Howard's *World-Telegram;* one-third column; *"Wallace Sees Possibility of Raid on Alaska."*

Hearst's *Mirror;* one-half column; *"Axis May Soon Hit at Alaska, Says Wallace."*

Hearst's *Journal-American;* one-quarter column; *"Attack on Alaska Seen by Wallace."*

Patterson's *News;* two-thirds of a column; *"Wallace Sees Alaska Target of Jap Attack."*

These are four papers owned by men who favored appeasing Japan and who published Nazi and Italian fascist propaganda in their papers ever since 1922; they are three of the four publishers (the other is McCormick of the *Chicago Tribune*) named as suspects following the MacLeish speech before the publishers' New York Convention in which he charged treason and near-treason in the press.

The anti-fascist press did little better. The *Post* ran one-third of a column, mostly on Alaska; The *Times* ran four-fifths of a column, with Alaska in the head and lead; the *Herald Tribune* ran one and one-half columns with an Alaska lead but mentioned the free world theme; the *Brooklyn Eagle* ran one-half column on Alaska.

An apologist for the press is Raymond Clapper, Howard columnist, who while praising Wallace suggested that the speech "was lost in the shuffle of the news desks of the country, like Lincoln's Gettysburg Address. . . . Every newspaper office and press association desk muffs a play now and then. Instead of there having been a plot to suppress this most significant address, I suspect that most newspapermen who handled it are kicking themselves for having missed the story. I go into this because there are people who can't see anything around newspaper offices but dark suppression plots. They mistake a muffed play for sinister intent."

This is nonsense, if not worse. The Vice-President's office sent out "hold-for-release" copies days earlier. If Clapper were not always a paid apologist for Roy Howard and his venal papers his present apology might sound better.

The suppression of the speech (and publication of the Alaska paragraph cannot support a claim the story was reported) was followed immediately by a series of apologies by the brasscheck writers of the Clapper type, and from June, 1942, to date by a series of attacks on Wallace and his ideas which reached a high point in the National Association of Manufacturers' convention of December, 1942. The attack still continues. It must be noted that the very newspapers which suppressed the news are the leaders in attacking the views.

It can be said factually that the vast majority of our newspapers have sought to poison the public mind against the Wallace declarations. In doing so they have also degraded our war aims.

All our native fascist, near-fascist, anti-labor and reactionary columnists, headed by Westbrook Pegler, joined all the corrupt editorial writers and radio speakers who until this day continue the NAM propaganda campaign against the Century of the Common Man. Here are some samples of the attack:

WESTBROOK PEGLER (a fair sample of the illiterate writings of a hoodlum mentality):

"This nonsense about the war aims of the United States is beginning to get out of control, so, before we become a lot of confirmed political hopheads walking around in a dream of international and interracial fellowship and love, it should be stated with such force as to snap us out of our daze that the fighters and people of the

United States are at war for the sole purpose of defending this country from a combination of enemies who touched off the fight by a treacherous attack under cover of protestations of friendship."

Paul Mallon (Hearst service): used his May 26 column to sneer at Wallace.

"Heptisax" (Rodney Gilbert) in his *New York Herald Tribune* column said Wallace's speech suggested "asinine world improvement"; he called it "this perambulating Iowa pipe dream." The peace of the common man, Heptisax said, was propaganda. Finally the writer for the $50,000,000 paper showed his disgust for both ideas of education and milk for the common people.

Frank R. Kent (*Baltimore Sun*) wrote:

"The strenuous effort to make Vice President Wallace into a superman has been pushed just a little too far. . . . The overpraise brought the inevitable reaction. Some of his associates in the Senate have begun to laugh. . . . The radicals also went into hysterics about it [the Wallace speech]. . . . The whole thing has become ridiculous. . . ."

New Orleans Item (editorial) said it favored education and milk for all but declared this is visionary and impossible.

"Who," it asked, "would pay the bills for educating, feeding and making democrats of all these mixed and myriad breeds . . . if we conformed to the Wallace dream?"

New York Daily News (editorial) decided that Wallace was "vague," that his idea was "a lovely thing to talk about and to dream about," but "we can assure the talkers and the dreamers, however, that when and if they try to bring these dreams into cold, solid reality after the war, they will fan up a fight in this country which will make the recent isolationist-interventionist fight look like a mere warm-up."

Chicago Tribune suppressed the Wallace speech, ignored it editorially, but referred to Wallace once as "mystic—engaged in dreams."

Arizona Daily Star, Tucson:

"Will such a plan embracing racial equality and removal of our tariff and immigration barriers work out? Will the people of America support a people's revolution? But even more than that Mr. Wallace and his followers will probably find out that such a plan will lead to a 'people's revolution' all right, but not the kind he has in mind."

LYNN LANDRUM, *The Dallas News'* own Pegler:

"You supposed you were really fighting to keep things the way they are in the United States instead of proposing any bloody crusade to ram freedom down the throats of the rest of the world."

San Diego Union-Tribune: "Wallace's speech sounds wonderful but, insofar as its being practical is concerned, it is so much oratorical flapdoodle."

"DING" (J. N. Darling, cartoonist; *New York Herald Tribune, Des Moines Register*) drew a vicious cartoon making fun of Wallace. So many readers protested that Darling had to write a letter of apology (*Register,* July 1). Darling spends most of his time doing anti-labor cartoons.

HARRY M. BEARDSLEY, *Chicago Daily News,* wrote a three-column attack on the Wallace speech (June 5).

THOMAS F. WOODLOCK, clerico-fascist columnist, and RAYMOND MOLEY, New Deal renegade, both wrote their columns in the *Wall Street Journal* in opposition to Wallace, Welles, Milo Perkins, and others who have expressed idealism for the coming peace, rather than hope for big business triumphs. Editorially the *Wall Street Journal* said (June 6) that whereas it approved the Atlantic Charter, it opposed "additional promises so far reaching as to be either meaningless or dangerous." These included "demanding higher social and economic standards." Then Wall Street's speaker came across with a brand new idea: "There are not four but five freedoms for which the war must be fought. The fifth is the freedom of any people to reject the first four." (In other words, freedom not to have freedom, which equals Fascism.)

CHAPTER V

THE PRESS AND WAR PROFITEERS

No PRESS and propaganda department of a fascist regime could be more successful than is the American self-styled free press in doing the double job of attacking labor while suppressing the news of the real traitors and saboteurs of the great Global War production effort.

The profit system, Free Enterprise, are the great golden calves and sacred bulls of the American press. It is now certain that the editorials it published after the Munitions Committee disclosed corruption for profit in the World War and the support it gave Mr. Bernard M. Baruch who published his program entitled "Take the Profits out of War" were also items for the dossier of journalistic hypocrisy. Even if all the lies and biased reports against labor in this war were fair and true they would not have a fraction of the importance that the treason has which was committed by certain corporations and industries before and after Pearl Harbor—treason for profits protected by the press. Yet the history of our wartime journalism shows clearly two trends: one of slander, libel and daily attack on labor; the other defense and whitewash of the elements which have committed treason for money: the war profit makers.

The documentary evidence of this treason can be found in the reports made either to government departments and agencies or by Congressional committees. Notable are the reports of Thurman Arnold, assistant attorney general, the Tolan Committee, the Bone patents investigation, the several and most important Truman Committee reports. Together they indict General

Motors, the DuPonts, Chrysler, Ford, Aluminum Corporation, the Mellons, Standard Oil and in short the elite of big business of what may be termed industrial treason. In fact it was Senator Truman who said "This is treason" when testimony before him showed that the synthetic rubber cartel agreements between Standard Oil and I. G. Farben had prevented the manufacture of rubber in our country.

Only two important newspapers headlined the treason charge. The January, 1942, report of the Special Senate Committee Investigating National Defense named names, notably Bethlehem Steel and Aluminum Corporation, but in Chicago the *Tribune* and the Hearst *Herald-American* suppressed them. The report was official and could not be ignored. Nevertheless the most important paper in the country, the *New York Times,* suppressed the names of General Motors, Chrysler, Ford, Alcoa, Bethlehem Steel, these being among its advertisers.

The Tolan House Committee report, also suppressed or played down or buried, said:

"The testimony before the committee was almost universal that production to date has been a failure, measured against the available facilities and the visible needs for military purposes.

"The largest and most efficient manufacturing facilities are not being used in the armament effort. At the same time, the system of contract awards in effect excludes from production the facilities of tens of thousands of small producers. As a result, the mass production of critical military materials is awaiting, to a considerable extent, the completion of new plants. Thus, when speed in production is vital to the nation, the potentially greatest arsenals stand unused and their unemployed workers are waiting for new plants to open. The battles of today cannot be waged with deliveries from the plants of tomorrow."

Assistant Attorney General Thurman Arnold's report to Congress said in part:

"Looking back over 10 months of defense effort we can now see how much it has been hampered by the attitude of powerful private groups dominating basic industries who have feared to expand their production because expansion would endanger their future control of industry. These groups have been afraid to develop new production themselves. They have been afraid to let others come into the field."

The worst criminal of all was the auto industry. It simply had insisted on pleasure cars as usual; it had promised conversion of some plants but even after Pearl Harbor it was found that 80% of the industry was still manufacturing civilian cars. In mid-January, 1942, I asked leaders of the industry and leading members of Congress: "Can the present management of the automobile industry be relied on to convert the industry to a full war effort? Do you think the government should take over? What limit would you set before demanding that the government step in?" Among the replies, all favoring government operation, was the following from George Addes, international secretary-treasurer of United Automobile Workers and member of the seven-man board set up under Knudsen's Office of Production Management to "advise" on conversion of auto plants:

"From the attitude conveyed in the recent conferences held in Washington between labor, industry and government, industry cannot be relied upon to convert its facilities to full war effort unless government or the President of the United States issues an executive order to that effect.

"On that matter of government taking over industries, it is my thought that government should harness or conscript industry as it has harnessed or conscripted labor, if management refuses to have its facilities converted and under way within the next thirty or sixty days. It is quite evident that labor has sacrificed far more than industry and will no doubt continue to make those sacrifices for the duration."

The fact remains that the auto industry, the oil industry, the aluminum industry, the steel industry and many great corporations sabotaged America before and after Pearl Harbor, and that crime continued up to the moment of writing. Here are some of the highlights of what profiteering, also known as Free Enterprise, did to undermine the war against Fascism:

Scandal in Aviation

Before Pearl Harbor the biggest scandal was in aviation. The government in 1940 had awarded $85,000,000 for 4,000 planes, but Secretary Stimson said only thirty-three planes had been produced by Aug. 9, 1940. Knudsen, to the contrary, said that 45% of the Army and 75% of the Navy plane funds had been awarded. What was the truth? The truth was there were no planes. The "awards" had been made, but the aviation firms, many dominated by Knudsen's General Motors, refused to take the contracts. There were awards, but no planes. "Only a thin verbal partition separated him [Knudsen] from falsehood," concluded I. F. Stone in his book, *Business As Usual.*

Why were almost no planes built in 1940? Because Big Business staged the greatest financial sit-down in American history and the newspapers, busy shouting against labor, suppressed all mention of it. For six months, from May to October, 1940, there was a sit-down of money and industry, aviation being used as a "front" by Big Business to break the President's plan (even at the cost of national safety) and get special tax privileges on defense contracts. "Unlike the strike of labor," says Stone, "the sit-down strike of capital in the summer of 1940 had the support of the nation's great newspapers, of the War and Navy Departments, and of the new Defense Commission." The notorious merchants of death, the DuPonts, are a major factor in aviation; DuPonts control General Motors; General Motors' Knudsen refused to break the aviation sit-down, but fooled the American people with a tricky statement about "awards" for planes.

Curiously enough, in World War I the industry which came closest to committing treason was the auto industry. Auto companies actually refused in the last half of 1918 to cut production to 25% of 1917. Bernard Baruch's war industries board threatened to seize their coal and iron but the war ended before the showdown.

According to Stone, Knudsen's General Motors in this war has again sabotaged defense. In 1940 its defense production was only

3½%; in the first quarter of 1941 only 8%. Why the failure? Because producing defense goods—and General Motors had then the second largest order in America, next to Bethlehem—meant building new plants, and General Motors preferred instead to hog the orders and produce civilian autos. At the same time it put a full page ad in the papers saying it would not produce new models in 1943. But it went ahead with new models for 1942.

Curtiss-Wright and Hitler. At the moment of writing Senator Truman's latest report against the Curtiss-Wright company is a national sensation. But among the little known facts is the Munitions Investigation report showing that Curtiss-Wright is the actual originator of the Stuka bombing idea and that when Hitler came into power Curtiss-Wright joined the DuPonts, Pratt & Whitney, and others in secretly arming Naziism for world conquest. The evidence includes a letter sent in January, 1934, by the president of Curtiss-Wright to his salesmen in foreign lands. It says:

"We have been nosing around in the bureau in Washington and find that they hold as most strictly confidential their divebombing tactics, and procedure, and they frown upon our even mentioning dive-bombing in connection with the Hawks, or any other airplanes to any foreign powers.

"It is also unwise and unethical at this time, and probably for some time to come, for us to indicate that we know anything about the technique and tactics of dive-bombing.

"It may be all right . . . to put on a dive-bombing show, to show the strength of the airplanes—but to refer in contracts to dive-bombing or endeavor to teach dive-bombing is what I am cautioning against doing."

This was an open order to the salesmen of Curtiss-Wright planes to put on shows of dive-bombing and let foreign nations, including Hitler-Germany, learn the secrets which were being guarded by the Navy Department, which had invented the technique before Hitler came into power. The Curtiss-Wright Company committed the equivalent of an act of treason in order to sell its airplanes abroad. It helped make Hitler.

"It is apparent," reads the Senate report, "that American aviation companies did their part to assist Germany's air armament. It seems apparent also that there was not an adequate check on the foreign shipments by . . . the War and Navy Departments."

The first six months in 1933 the sales figure took a tremendous jump to $1,445,000. Pratt & Whitney was exposed as one of the largest smugglers of planes to Hitler. The Nye report then states that by May, 1934, a year after Hitler took over, he had bought parts for making 2,500 modern bombing and fighting planes chiefly from Pratt & Whitney, Curtiss-Wright and Douglas Aircraft. He also got planes from Vickers and from Armstrong-Sidley, in England, and was already rated "superior in the air to France, Russia, England or any other European power."

Anaconda. One of the worst cases in American history of a corporation "defrauding the government and endangering the lives of American soldiers," was exposed in Attorney General Biddle's indictment of Anaconda Wire & Cable Co., whose Marion, Indiana, branch had sold the United States $6,000,000 worth of telephone wire and cable for war purposes, and had previously sold the Russian government wire which was 50% defective and which no doubt resulted in the death of many soldiers.

One newspaper (the *Milwaukee Journal*) suggested that the death penalty for corporation heads responsible for sabotaging the war should be instituted. The newspapers, generally speaking, did their best to bury the Anaconda scandal. It broke about New Year's Day, and it is the custom of the newspapers—one of their most corrupt customs—to hold up Big Business for good-will advertisements for a special supplement (known in the trade as a racketeering job) to celebrate the passing of a commercial year. There were no indignant editorials in the big New York papers—the *Times,* the *Herald Tribune,* the Hearst *Journal-American*—but their annual business supplements each had a full page advertisement signed by Anaconda of Montana and listing all affiliates, including Anaconda Wire & Cable, Andes Copper, Chile Copper, Greene Cananea, American Brass and International

Smelting & Refining Co. The ad contained this phrase: "The Army-Navy 'E' pennant for excellence in production flies over eight plants." And wooden crosses surmount the graves of soldiers murdered by Anaconda for profit.

The press, of course, is equaled by the radio in venality. December 21, 1942, the date of the Anaconda scandal, several nonsponsored news broadcasts had the Anaconda indictment as the biggest news of the day. Not so Lowell Thomas. His broadcast (for the Pews of Sunoco) had no mention of the copper firm. Both Sunoco and Anaconda are members and subsidizers of the NAM, and Mr. Thomas had done jobs of work both for the NAM and for General Motors, the DuPont controlled auto firm which is one of the main pillars of NAM Free Enterprise.

Treason in Rubber

It was March 26, 1942, that Senator Truman applied the word "treason" to the Standard Oil, after listening to Mr. Arnold's testimony. Immediately afterward Standard Oil began a nationwide advertising and propaganda campaign, asking every editorial writer, publisher, columnist, radio commentator and other maker of public opinion to whitewash it. Many who received money did so.

An excellent example of usual newspaper and magazine venality was shown in the indecent rush of our leading paper, the *New York Times,* and leading newsweekly, *Time,* to defend Standard Oil from the treason charge.

Time, April 6, said Standard Oil had been smeared, said its treason "turned out to be strictly of the dinnertable variety," poked fun at Thurman Arnold's "horrific" charges, and tried to answer every one of them. This was on page 16. On page 89 *Time* carried a $5,000 Standard Oil ad.

The *New York Times,* April 2, main editorial whitewashed Standard Oil. Reading it one can conclude either that the entire press which does not take advertising lied, or that the *New York Times* and *Time,* which live on the money which Standard

Oil and other corporations give to them, are lying today.

The day after the *Times* whitewash Assistant Secretary of State A. A. Berle testified Standard Oil refused to stop fueling Nazi and Fascist airplanes in Brazil until the United States put enemy plane companies on a blacklist.

Standard Oil's Farish never denied he shipped oil to a Japanese navy which made possible the attack on Pearl Harbor and Japan's ability to resist the Anglo-American Navies today. He excused himself by saying that Standard Oil was "an international concern."

Standard Oil supplied Franco during the Spanish Fascist uprising. Standard Oil supplied Franco-Spain after 1939, National Maritime Union men giving testimony that oil went to Germany and Italy, for use against France and Britain.

Technically Standard Oil was not committing treason then because the United States was not at war. This will be interesting news to the men on Bataan and the men in the United States Navy.

U. S. Cartridge Co. The facts about U. S. Cartridge were unearthed by the *St. Louis Star-Times,* one of the few brave crusading papers left in our country. (The Associated Press did not pick this story up and send it to its 1,200 subscribers, as it did the *Akron Beacon-Journal* Guadalcanal lie.)

Julius Klein and Ralph O'Leary, of the *Star-Times,* submitted their findings to the Office of Censorship, Washington, which made no objection to publication. The story is copyright. It says in part:

"Evidence indicating that thousands of defective cartridges manufactured at the St. Louis Ordnance Plant passed through plant inspection as good ammunition and might, unless stopped short of the war fronts, imperil the lives of United States fighters, has been obtained by the *Star-Times* through an independent investigation. . . .

"The *Star-Times* has learned that picked agents of the F.B.I. for weeks have been making a sweeping investigation into complaints they too have received that defective shells are being passed through company inspection at the ammunition works.

"This plant, one of the largest small-arms ammunition factories in the world, is operated for the government by the U. S. Cartridge Co., subsidiary of the Western Cartridge Company of East Alton, Illinois. . . .

"Evidence in possession of the *Star-Times* includes sworn statements by members of the U. S. Cartridge Co.'s inspection staff in the ordnance plant charging various types of imperfections in the cartridges produced there. The plant manufactures .50-caliber cartridges for machine guns and .30-caliber shells for rifles and machine guns. . . . The charges of faulty ammunition in each instance involve company inspection and production and are not made against government inspection.

"Five company employees have given affidavits to the *Star-Times* charging manufacture of defective ammunition. . . ."

It is not necessary here to explain the defects and the methods by which cartridges liable to explode within the rifle were passed. What is important is this: that the Department of Justice has taken up the case after an attempt to whitewash the corporation was made, according to a broadcast by Drew Pearson. Important also is this fact: no less than twelve persons, working men and women in the plant and inspectors who risked losing their jobs and livelihood, voluntarily came to the *Star-Times* office and signed sworn affidavits.

This is one of the thousands of proofs that the working men and women of our country place true patriotism above everything else, whereas many of our biggest corporations have been proven by United States investigations to place profits above patriotism.

U. S. Steel, Bethlehem Steel, etc. The main element needed for war is steel. A book could be written giving the documentary evidence of the sabotage of our war by our steel corporations. In case the reader does not have access to non-commercial newspapers, here are a few headlines indicating the nature of the story:

"SABOTAGE OF WAR PROGRAM CHARGED TO STEEL MAGNATES

"More Interested in Keeping Monopoly Than With Beating Axis, Senator O'Mahoney Declares"

—*Labor,* July 7, 1942.

"TRUMAN ACCUSES STEEL COMPANIES OF 'SABOTAGE'

"Senator Black Charges That Big Corporations Hamstring Production"

PM, June 6, 1942.

"STEEL SHORTAGE SCANDAL INDICATED AS COMPANIES FIGHT EXPANSION"

——*Federated Press,* October 17, 1941.

"BLAME FOR STEEL SHORTAGE PLACED ON TRUST DOORSTEP"

—*Labor,* June 30, 1942.

"BIG STEEL CONCERNS REFUSE TO FILL UNCLE SAM'S ORDERS"

—*Labor,* April 28, 1942.

Under the above heading the report is:

"It has become clear as the noonday sun that the vicious attack which has been made on the nation's workers in recent weeks was actually a red herring designed to divert attention from treasonable sabotage of the nation's war program by Big Business, which is being exposed by Congressional committees and defense agencies.

"Proof of that statement may reasonably be drawn from sensational and unbelievably shocking disclosures of a cold-blooded betrayal of national welfare by men whose only flag is the dollar sign. . . . One of the most shameful chapters in our history.

"1. The Carnegie-Illinois Steel Corporation, subsidiary of U. S. Steel, and the Jones & Laughlin Steel Company were charged by the War Production Board with having refused to fill government armament orders while diverting iron and steel to favorite civilian customers for non-essential purposes. The result is that shipbuilding and other war construction have been held up.

"2. The President directed the Navy to take over three plants of the Brewster Aero Company, accused of sabotaging the aviation program. . . .

"3. The United States faces a shortage of critical war materials because many outstanding industrial concerns have contracts with German monopolists restricting production here. . . ."

General Electric. Senator Bone's Patents Investigation Committee heard testimony April 16, 1942, that until Pearl Harbor the General Electric Co. observed an agreement with the Krupp Co. of Essen, Germany, under which the Nazi trust was permitted to limit American use of a vital element in arms production. The man who admitted this was Dr. Zay Jeffries, head of W.P.B. metallurgy committee, chairman of General Electric's subsidiary, Carboloy Co. The vital element is known as Pantena, or carboloy, or cemented tungsten carbide, which is almost as hard as diamonds and used for machine tools.

Aluminum Corporation (Mellon-Davis-Duke families). "If America loses the war it can thank the Aluminum Corporation of America."—Secretary of Interior Ickes, June 26, 1941. By its cartel agreement with I. G. Farben, controlled by Hitler, Alcoa sabotaged the aluminum program of the U. S. air force. The Truman Committee heard testimony that Alcoa's representative, A. H. Bunker, $1-a-year head of the aluminum section of O.P.M., prevented work on our $600,000,000 aluminum expansion program. Congressman Pierce of Oregon said in May, 1941: "To date, 137 days or 37½% of a year's production has been wasted in the effort to protect Alcoa's monopolistic position. . . . This delay, translated into planes, means 10,000 fighters or 1,665 bombers."

This, of course, is the answer to the boys on Guadalcanal and in Tunisia, and not absenteeism, the 48-hour week, or wage increases to meet the cost of living.

Automobile Industry

The big three of the auto industry, General Motors, Chrysler and Ford, refused to convert to war production, refused to extend plants, refused to give up civilian production, insisted on government cash and business as usual, thus delaying war production of tanks, guns and planes, while labor offered excellent war plans.

The pro-auto magazine, *United States News,* which carries big ads and boosts corporations, nevertheless admitted: "Today, 20% of U. S. effort is devoted to defense, 80% to meeting civilian demands. . . . Next year: armaments . . . will average 30% . . . leaving 70% for civilian demands."—Dec. 12, 1941.

United Automobile Workers Union President Thomas testified before the Tolan Committee that "of 1,577 machine tools in thirty-four Detroit plants, 337 are idle . . . not working more than 35% of capacity"; he urged coordination of unused equipment "... producing arms to frustrate Nazi designs for world domination." This was forty-seven days before Pearl Harbor. Autoworkers Secretary Addes on December 22 reported 64% machine tool idleness, "a crime against civilization and democracy in this critical hour." Very naturally Charles Coughlin's *Social Justice,* following the Nazi line, demanded that "the metropolitan dailies which have profited most from the automobile advertising dollar should campaign against this curtailment of production of American motor cars." (July 28, 1941.) Any shortage of guns and tanks is due to General Motors, Ford and Chrysler delay, not the autoworkers.

Ford. Delay in constructing Willow Run was due to management (and mismanagement), not labor. One of the major scandals was old man Henry Ford's decision to keep adequate workers' housing away from Willow Run—he plans to tear down the place when the emergency is over and return the land to his dearly beloved squirrels. The newspaper announcements, that the assembly line for bombers at Willow Run was in full operation and planes were being turned out so many per day, were all fakes. It was not until mid-1943 that the Willow Run works began operating efficiently.

Tank Failure. Mismanagement was blamed by the C.I.O. United Autoworkers for the failure, up to May, 1943, of the General Motors Tank Arsenal at Los Angeles to produce any finished tanks, although many men worked at their jobs. The union was forced to file a brief against General Motors with the War Production Board; it disclosed, incidentally, that when

Lieut.-Gen. Knudsen (former head of General Motors) made an official inspection of the Tank Arsenal, General Motors officials put on a fake show—the old Potemkin village trick. They had the men install and remove the same tank treads fifty-seven times, likewise the motors, giving Knudsen the impression that fifty-seven tanks were being produced, instead of one.

On April 21 "Time Views the News" (WQXR, New York), admitted the fact, known in Army circles, that one of our major failures was the much-advertised tank known as the M-7.

Production had been stopped, the news commentator announced, but he did not name the company making the M-7.

It was General Motors.

General Motors ads saying that the M-7 was a wonderful tank and was chasing the Japanese and the Italians and the Germans to perdition were still running in the newspapers when the War Department ordered them abandoned as being no good whatever.

As for the Army and Navy "E" pennants, the fact is that many of them are part of a racket, as *Space & Time,* advertising newsletter, first disclosed. Big advertising men in Washington arrange to award the Army and Navy pennants to war manufacturers who place advertisements in the right newspapers via the right advertising agents.

The Buick local of the C.I.O. believes the "E" pennant should be given for 100% cooperation between management and labor. General Motors, however, refused to recognize the Labor-Management Committee at the Buick plant, refused to permit the union a voice in deciding the merits of suggestions which labor supplies for increasing production, refused to comply with the W.L.B. order for maintenance of membership, refused to obey the law and pay women the same rates as men for the same work and, finally, refused to utilize fully for winning the war the machinery and manpower labor offered. Local 599 of the United Automobile Workers, Flint, Michigan, therefore refused to participate in the "E" pennant award ceremonies; they called them a fraud.

One of the great lies of this war and part of the newspaper campaign to smear labor—while defending the corporations which produced defective war materials and robbed the nation. The Guadalcanal story was a fake; it originated in the Akron Beacon-Journal, was spread throughout the country by the Hearst press, and others.

Treason in the Ships

When the history of what America did to rid the world of Fascism is written, one of the truly great pages will be that devoted to the maritime unions.

At the date of this writing they have given 4,500 lives to carrying the munitions of war across the Atlantic and Pacific to our own men, to Britain, China and Russia. They have suffered many wounded, and their list of torpedoed survivors is 12,000.

In proportion to the small number of men in this service the casualty list of the unions is many times as high as that in any service, not excepting aviation, tanks, or submarines.

On the other hand the shipowners and in several instances the ship construction companies and the ship lessees have committed crimes of profiteering tantamount to treason in wartime.

"An orgy of profiteering that staggers imagination" is how the *I.L.W.U. Dispatcher* reports the official revelations of war profiteering by the shipowners, made before the Congressional Merchant Marine subcommittee. James V. Hayes, general counsel, gave proof to the subcommittee that profits from a single trip of some vessels involved were enough to pay the entire book value of the ships many times over.

Eighty-one privately owned merchant ships made ninety trips to the Red Sea receiving charter hire of $21,364,880, it was testified. Profit was many times the cost price of these eighty-one ships. The American Export Line sent six ships on six trips. Profit was announced at $1,572,144; cost of ships was $232,350.

Two American Foreign Steamship Corp. ships worth $895,974 made a profit of $481,128 on two trips. Two American President Line, Ltd., ships worth $307,828 made $814,242 profit on three trips. Ten Luckenback ships valued at $1,426,857 made $8,879,729 on twelve trips. And so on.

Another report showed $26,874,176 profit on ninety trips. American Merchant Marine Institute lawyer J. J. Burns protested that the figures did not include overhead and depreciation of about $2,500,000, but that wouldn't change profiteering figures much.

Every labor union leader in America except John L. Lewis has plans to speed up victory. President Murray of the C.I.O., President Harry Bridges of the International Longshoremen's and Warehousemen's Union, President Joe Curran of the Maritime Union have presented the government complete detailed plans for helping victory. Says Bridges:

"If this war is to be won before millions of American and allied lives are wasted there has to be an integrated plan for shipping and a single, authoritative agency to administer it. The proper cargo has to be on the dock and properly sorted when a ship arrives. The required manpower has to be on hand and at the right place. The required number of seamen have to be ready to sail. The ship has to be dispatched to a port that can accommodate discharge of its cargo without delay. Provision has to be made for the skilled manpower to unload it at the foreign port. These things and a thousand others that need to be dovetailed require blueprinting of the highest order.

"Blueprinting isn't being done. Ships carry sand ballast to Africa and bring ballast back. Ships shop for low-fee piers. Ships wait at piers while somebody digs through red tape to find the heavy cargo that goes in first. Ships wait while prying agencies investigate seamen. Ships wait while longshore labor is being wasted at other piers.

"And *ships carry booze and bananas,* birdseed and artificial flowers while munitions pile up in warehouses. This space isn't long enough to begin a list of the delays and waste.

"In peace time the shipowners have an incentive for meeting schedules. It is the way they hold their business. Today they have no incentive. The government guarantees them a profit and they suffer no penalty for failing to deliver the goods on time. Naturally, they favor their old customers and that is how toothpicks and wine get crowded into shipping space so vitally needed for war supplies.

"The big failure of the War Shipping Administration to date has been its lack of a centralized plan. It hasn't called in labor or permitted labor to participate in its policies. In fact, it has no policy to speak of.

"The time has come for a plan to make the whole shipping industry operate as one integrated unit, regardless of the sacrifice it may demand of labor and the owners."

CHAPTER VI

THE SUPPRESSED TOBACCO STORY

FEW persons are aware that the two largest advertisers in the country are the manufacturers of the most expensive and the least expensive products, namely automobiles and cigarets. It is, therefore, natural that the press which protected the automobile industry during the first three years of war scandals should give the same protection to one of the most harmful of all industries, the tobacco manufacturers. The story of tobacco is told here to illustrate its power in dictating to the press, and also to satisfy the request of thousands who were unable to obtain the special issue (and 10,000 additional reprints) of the *In Fact* story. The entire report of Dr. Raymond Pearl is included in the Appendix.

"War is booming the Tobacco Business," say recent press reports; no less than 20,000,000,000 (twenty billion) cigarets are being made and smoked a month. Press and radio urge you to remember the fighters against Fascism by sending them tobacco.

But the American press and radio—at least 99% of each—have suppressed the facts, scientifically established, that the more tobacco a person uses the earlier he dies. Tobacco impairs the health of all users, moderate and heavy. But the tobacco companies spend fortunes—four (Camels, Lucky Strikes, Chesterfields and Old Golds) spend $50,000,000 annually—to keep the American public in ignorance.

The story is sensational. It must be said here that the term sensational is generally used against a newspaper to characterize it as yellow, biased, unfair, given to overplaying news. But sensational news can also be news really worth playing up, such as, for example, the discovery of the electric light, or the American landing in Sicily. These were sensational news items which no paper need be ashamed for headlining, whereas the Hearst press and the *New York Daily News,* which played up the Errol Flynn rape case for almost as much space as the Rommel defeat in Africa, were illustrating the sensationalism of yellow journalism.

Certainly the first scientific, documented report from the head of the biology department of Johns Hopkins University listing tobacco as first in impairing life, as causing users, of whom there are tens of millions in America alone, to die earlier than non-users, was a first-class story, a big story, and in a scientific way a sensational story, and worth the front page of any paper not corrupted by cigaret advertising. But to this day the story is suppressed by 99% of our commercial newspaper and magazine press, and if used at all in the other 1% (which is doubtful) it is buried or played down so effectively that not one-tenth of 1% of America's newspaper readers have ever heard of it.

And here is the evidence of the venality of the press as regards tobacco—an industry which pays the press much more than $50,000,000 a year.

In February, 1938, Dr. Raymond Pearl, then head biologist at Johns Hopkins University, gave the New York Academy of Medicine the scientific results of a study of the life histories of some 7,000 Johns Hopkins cases which, for newspapers, should have constituted a story "to scare the life out of tobacco manufacturers and make the tobacco users' flesh creep," as *Time* commented.

In brief, Dr. Pearl discovered that smoking shortens life. Between the ages of 30 and 60, 61% more heavy smokers die than non-smokers. A human being's span of life is impaired in direct proportion to the amount of tobacco he uses, but the impairment among even light smokers is "measurable and significant."

The Associated Press, United Press and special correspondents of New York papers heard Dr. Pearl tell the story. But a paragraph or two buried under less important matter, in one or two papers, was all that the great free press of America cared to make known to its readers, the consumers of 200,000,000,000 cigarets a year.

When the Town Meeting of the Air announced a debate, "Do We Have a Free Press?" January 16, 1939, the present writer sent to Secretary of the Interior Ickes documentary evidence proving quite the opposite. In the debate Mr. Ickes easily bested Frank Gannett, chain newspaper owner. During the question period someone asked for examples of news suppression and Mr. Ickes mentioned a few casually, adding, "I understand that at Johns Hopkins University there is a very sensational finding resulting from a study of the effect of cigaret smoking that has not appeared, so far as I know, in any newspaper in the United States. I wonder if that is because the tobacco companies are such large advertisers."

The statement was correct. Research had proved that although the A.P., U.P. and I.N.S. had sent the story to every paper in America, although New York science reporters were present and Science Service had sent an advance account to numerous big papers, 98% of the big city press, the press which takes the cigaret advertising, suppressed the story.

But because Mr. Ickes had said "in any newspaper" that same press threw a journalistic bombshell. It attacked and smeared Mr. Ickes, it lied outright and printed half-lies which are harder to nail, it distorted and faked the news, published untrue editorials and generally presented to America the spectacle of as corrupt a press as that usually charged to fascist nations.

The tobacco story, to be exact, appeared in some country papers, and one or two big city papers. Here is what happened in the great free press metropolis of New York:

Herald Tribune, totally suppressed.
Sun, totally suppressed.
News, totally suppressed.
Mirror, totally suppressed.
Post, totally suppressed.
Journal-American, totally suppressed.

World-Telegram carried a few lines.

Times carried a few lines.

The *World-Telegram* and the *Times* carried a three-fourth and half column story respectively, dealing first with the effect on long life of hard work and alcohol, then, at the end of the story, tobacco. This is all the *Times* had to say, and that at the bottom of the first column on page 19:

"Professor Pearl also presented the 'first life tables ever constituted' to show relation between tobacco and longevity. The tables showed, he said, 'that smoking is associated with a definite impairment of longevity.'

"This impairment, he added, is proportional to the habitual amount of tobacco usage in smoking, being great for the heavy smokers and less for moderate smokers. But even in the case of the moderate smoker, he said, the impairment in longevity is 'sufficient to be measurable and significant.'"

The tables had been seen by the press. The leading authority in America, if not in the world, had made a great discovery and presented the first scientific study in a controversial matter in which some 50,000,000 Americans consuming billions of cigarets were interested, and 75% of the New York press suppressed the story, 25% half-suppressed it, 100% of the press manhandled it.

The Federated Press, serving the labor press (which gets precious little cigaret advertising) reported that the *Herald Tribune* not only suppressed the tobacco story but claimed it never saw it. The F.P. said: "Wilbur Forrest, executive editor (said) his paper had been scooped on the tobacco story. Asked how an Associated Press member could be scooped on an A.P. story, he explained that the *Herald Tribune* does not get the A.P. local service. This excuse was punctured by A.P. executives, who insisted that the story went not only to the *Herald Tribune* but also to other New York papers that failed to print a line."

A large part of the controversy hinged on Dr. Pearl. In preparing the evidence, the present writer wrote Dr. Pearl, who replied:

"I may say that the newspaper coverage on my statement regarding the association between tobacco smoking and longevity was very widespread. Without taking the trouble to count them, for which I have not the time to spare, I should say that the point was amply and promptly reported in no less than 250 daily and weekly newspapers in this country."

Inasmuch as a search at the New York Public Library revealed that no San Francisco, Los Angeles, Boston, Chicago, Philadelphia, Detroit, Pittsburgh, Cleveland, Cincinnati newspaper, or, in fact, any big newspaper besides the *Washington Post,* had covered the story, Dr. Pearl was asked to name two or three newspapers, outside of country dailies and country weeklies (which are not subsidized by tobacco advertising), which ran his story. He refused to answer.

There are 200 big daily papers in America, some 1,700 smaller dailies and many thousand weeklies. Apparently Dr. Pearl had 249 country paper clippings plus the *Washington Post.* Science Service, asked to look through its files, found only the *Washington Post* story and the two buried references in New York.

But no sooner had Ickes mentioned Dr. Pearl than the A.P. rushed out a column story which the *Times* headlined: "Contradicts Ickes on Tobacco Story—Johns Hopkins Biologist Says Report . . . Was Widely Published.—'No Press Suppression.'"

Six cigaret companies grossed $200,000,000 in 1937 (SEC report). A combined profit after all charges of $83,000,000 that year was reported by the Census of American Listed Corporations (April 5, 1939).

The major companies' advertising bill a year on four brands is:

Company	*Best Known Brand*	1937	1939
Reynolds	Camels	$15,422,744	$9,296,470
Liggett & Myers	Chesterfield	14,822,120	8,926,148
Lorillard	Old Gold	9,714,286	1,722,563
Amer. Tobacco	Lucky Strike	7,441,554	5,002,056

The newspapers, *Editor & Publisher, Saturday Evening Post,* all say that advertising has nothing to do with editorial policy. The facts are:

1. The cigaret companies spend more than $50,000,000 a year.
2. News inimical to tobacco is not published.
3. Ninety-nine per cent of the American press suppresses government fraud orders against advertisers.

The tobacco advertisers share with peacetime automobile advertisers first place in spending money in newspapers and magazines. This is without doubt the reason the press suppressed the story. The press is therefore part of a system spreading actual poison throughout America. As for the poison of reaction (Fascism) the evidence is just as thoroughly documented.

Conclusion

VICTORY OVER FASCISM

If we take the "one world" view, the global view—regardless of the brilliant sneers of rattlebrained lady Congressmen who are too far removed from the men and women who are working and fighting for the Century of the Common Man to do more than make newspaper remarks—then we see that Fascism is being beaten back on every front and that the year of victory is near.

If we take the national view, the panorama is not so brilliant: at the moment of writing the Congress has reached one of its lowest levels of intelligence and honesty. The men elected with the money of the DuPonts, the Pews, the Mellon-Aluminum family and the other leaders of the NAM, have noted the reactionary trend in politics and dared openly to vote a dozen bills against the welfare of the majority and for the benefit of their paymasters. They passed the so-called 75% Ruml Income Tax bill, they killed the President's $67,200 salary limitation order (falsely called a $25,000 limitation by the press), they killed grade labeling, although a great part of the success of the maintenance of prices depended on it, they killed planning boards and the youth administration and they finally passed the Smith-Connally Anti-Labor bill which more than any other measure of the time approached typical Hitlerite and Mussolinian Fascism.

The Duce said, years ago, that two forces were striving for

world mastery, Fascism and Democracy; it is "Either We or They." The answer is now being given on every battlefield on the five continents, the seven seas, and all the air over them. It is the Duce's "They" who will win, it is "We," the democracies.

Thus the greatest drive and the greatest war in history which has been paid for by men and organizations owning a vast part of the world's wealth and covetous of all of it, will come to an end with the destruction of the world's special interests. A world ends for Privilege, the great day dawns for the peoples of the earth.

Unless our own State Department fascisti and the reactionaries in American political life, in business, and in the armed forces interfere, the outlook is brilliant for the restoration of all the old freedoms to European peoples and the additional freedoms from fear and from want—the economic freedoms which can be won for the democratic Many with no harm to anyone but the fascist Few.

All the enemies of the people of the world are united behind the Fascist International. When that is broken we will have come the main part of the way to a practical reality which previously had been regarded as a dream of idealists. Of course this will be possible only if Fascism (reaction) does not exist in disguise and wrapped in new flags and sheltered by wealth and power and accepted by peoples accustomed to being betrayed by rulers and the propaganda organs of these rulers, the world's corrupted press.

Fascism is Reaction. When we destroy international Fascism we must at the same time destroy national Fascism, we must replace the reactionary forces at home with truly democratic forces which will represent all of us.

Victory over foreign Fascism is certain. All of us will share in that. The American soldiers, sailors, airmen, marines will have fought in a war which will never be regretted. The thousands who gave their lives, notably the seamen of the Atlantic and Pacific, will have made a sacrifice equally as great as that of armed men, and even in greater proportions. And those of us who did anything at all to fight and destroy Fascism will reap a reward of satisfaction as well.

We, however, will also inherit the job left unfinished on the battlefield: it is we, the civilians, and the soldiers who will again become civilians, who will have to continue to fight native Fascism for many years. We will do this in the elections, in Congress, in the labor unions, in the press, in the churches, in the schools—everywhere. Otherwise we will stupidly have dropped the victory won in Africa, in Italy, in Germany and in Japan.

And since that victory will go down in history as the greatest to benefit mankind in all recorded time, it must cheer all of us on to fight the remaining enemies of a free people at home.

Appendices

APPENDIX 1: WHAT IS FASCISM?

MUSSOLINI: "Fascism, which did not fear to call itself reactionary when many liberals of today were prone before the triumphant beast [Democracy], has not today any impediment against declaring itself illiberal and anti-liberal. . . . Fascism knows no idol, worships no faith; it has once passed, and, if needful, will turn to pass again over the more or less decomposed body of the Goddess of Liberty." (Gerarchia, March, 1923.)

PALME DUTT: "The fascist system is a system of direct dictatorship, ideologically masked by the 'national idea.' . . . It is a system that resorts to a popular form of social demagogy (anti-Semitism, occasional sorties against usurer's capital and gestures of impatience with the parliamentary 'yelling shop') in order to utilize the discontent of the petit-bourgeois, the intellectual and other strata of society; and to corruption through the building up of a compact and well-paid hierarchy of fascist units, a party apparatus and a bureaucracy. At the same time, Fascism strives to permeate the working class by recruiting the most backward strata of the workers to its ranks, by playing upon their discontent, by taking advantage of the inaction of Social-Democracy, etc. . . ."

"The combination of social demagogy, corruption and active White terror, in conjunction with extreme imperialist aggression in the sphere of foreign politics, are the characteristic features of Fascism. In periods of acute crisis for the bourgeoisie, Fascism resorts to anti-capitalistic phraseology, but, after it has established itself at the helm of state, it casts aside its anti-capitalist rattle, and discloses itself as a terrorist dictatorship of big capital."

"Fascism is the open terrorist dictatorship of the most reactionary, most chauvinist and most imperialist elements of finance capital."—13th Plenum of Executive Committee of the Communist International, Moscow, 1933.

RAYMOND GRAM SWING: "Fascism is a reorganization of society to maintain unequal distribution of economic power and a substitution of barbaric values for individualist civilization."—"Forerunners of American Fascism."

HEYWOOD BROUN: "I am quite ready to admit that the word Fascism has been used very loosely. Sometimes we call a man a Fascist simply because we dislike him, for one reason or another. And so I'll try to be pretty literal in outlining some of the evidence which I see as the actual danger of Fascism in America. First of all, we need a definition. Fascism is a dictatorship from the extreme Right, or to put it a little more closely into our local idiom, a government which is run by a small group of large industrialists and financial lords. Of course, if you want to go back into recent history, the influence of big business has always been present in our federal government. But there have been some checks on its control. I am going to ask latitude to insist that we might have Fascism even though we maintained the pretense of democratic machinery. The mere presence of a Supreme Court, a House of Representatives, a Senate and a President would not be sufficient protection against the utter centralization of power in the hands of a few men who might hold no office at all. Even in the case of Hitler, many shrewd observers feel that he is no more than a front man and that his power is derived from the large munitions and steel barons of Germany . . . Now one of the first steps which Fascism must take in any land in order to capture power is to disrupt and destroy the labor movement. . . . I think it is not unfair to say that any business man in America, or public leader, who goes out to break unions, is laying foundations for Fascism." (May, 1936.)

APPENDIX 2: WHO OWNS AMERICA?

THE Temporary National Economic Committee, headed by Senator O'Mahoney of Wyoming, in its Monograph 29 ("The Distribution of Ownership in the 200 Non-Financial Corporations"), supplemented by Monograph 26 ("Economic Power and Political Pressures"), shows clearly that a handful of men and companies (Big Business, the Big Money, the NAM) own, control, boss and rule America in a manner which approaches the rule of Germany, Italy, and other fascist countries by similar elements.

Monograph 29, page 116, shows that of the 200 ruling families of America there are thirteen which top them all. Here is the official table:

TABLE 6

Identified stockholdings in 200 largest non-financial corporations of thirteen family-interest groups with holdings of over $50,000,000.

Family	*Total common and preferred stock*	*Corporations in which main holdings are*
1. Ford	$624,975,000	Ford Motor Co.
2. du Pont	573,690,000	du Pont de Nemours; U. S. Rubber.
3. Rockefeller	396,583,000	S.O. of N.J., Indiana, Calif.; Soc-Vac.
4. Mellon	390,943,000	Gulf Oil; Aluminum Co.; Koppers.
5. McCormick	111,102,000	International Harvester.
6. Hartford	105,702,000	Atlantic & Pacific Tea Co.
7. Harkness	104,891,000	S.O. of N.J., Indiana, Calif.; Soc-Vac.
8. Duke	89,459,000	Duke Power, Alum., Liggett & Myers.
9. Pew	75,628,000	Sun Oil Co. [Sun Shipbuilding].
10. Pitcairn	65,576,000	Pittsburgh Plate Glass Co.
11. Clark	57,215,000	Singer Mfg. Co.
12. Reynolds	54,766,000	R. J. Reynolds Tobacco Co.
13. Kress	50,044,000	S. H. Kress & Co.

Includes only holdings of family members and family-endowed foundations in stock of 200 largest non-financial corporations insofar as they were identified among twenty largest record shareholdings. Values represent in most cases market values at December 31, 1937; otherwise (particularly for Ford) book values.

In other words, this vast accumulation of wealth (which means vast power) does not represent the totality. The Ford family fortune is estimated at two billion dollars, which is four times the amount of stock held in their own corporation. The same multiple probably applies to the other twelve.

APPENDIX 3: WHO OWNS GERMANY?

At the start of the second World War the 25 most important landowners in Germany were:

GERMANY'S BIGGEST LANDOWNERS

Kaiser Wilhelm II's family	97,000 hectares
Prince of Pless	50,000 hectares
Prince of Hohenlohe	48,500 hectares
Prince of Hohenzollern-Siegmaringen	46,000 hectares
Prince of Solms-Baruth	38,700 hectares
Ernst von Stolberg-Wernigerode	36,700 hectares
Duke of Ratibor and Prince Hohenlohe-Schilling-fuerst	31,100 hectares*
Duke of Anhalt-Dessau	29,300 hectares
Count Thiele-Winkler	28,000 hectares*
Duke of Ahrenberg-Nordikirchen	27,800 hectares
Count Schaffgotsch	26,800 hectares*
Leopold Prince of Prussia	25,000 hectares
Count von Bruehl	22,900 hectares
Count Fink von Finkenstein	21,000 hectares
Prince Frederick Henry of Prussia	17,100 hectares
Duke Albrecht of Wurttemberg	16,100 hectares
Prince Schaumburg-Lippe	15,700 hectares
Family of Field Marshal von Kleist	15,200 hectares
Prince Henkell von Donnersmarck	15,000 hectares*
Grand Duke of Oldenburg	13,800 hectares
Prince Richard Sayn-Wittgenstein	12,000 hectares
Duke of Saxe-Coburg-Gotha	10,400 hectares
Hereditary Prince Josias of Waldeck	10,000 hectares
Prince Philipp of Hesse	7,000 hectares

One hectare equals 2.47 acres.

CAPITAL OF JOINT STOCK COMPANIES

With capital under 100,000 marks	No.	Cptl. in mill.	With capital 100,000—500,000 marks	No.	Cptl. in mill.
End of 1931	2720	98.6	End of 1931	3340	762.3
End of 1936	1445	62.1	End of 1936	2418	579.1
End of 1939	526	21.6	End of 1939	1687	402.4
End of 1940	447	18.3	End of 1940	1681	400.7

PERCENTAGE OF THE TOTAL CAPITAL

End of 1936	8.3	0.3%	End of 1936	33.6	3.0%
End of 1940	8.3	0.1%	End of 1940	31.1	1.9%

CAPITAL OF LIMITED LIABILITY COMPANIES

	Capital Under 20,000 m.		Cptl. 20,000-100,000 m.		Cptl. 100,000 - 500,000 m.	
	No.	Capital in mill.	No.	Capital in mill.	No.	Capital in millions
End of 1936	8875	53.0	23179	699.0	5563	1060.9
End of 1939	4027	24.6	13846	436.2	4114	795.1
End of 1940	3661	23.0	13346	424.8	4266	824.8

PERCENTAGE OF TOTAL CAPITAL

End of 1936	22.6	1.0	59.1	13.8	14.2	20.9
End of 1940	16.0	0.4	58.3	8.2	14.2	16.0

* NOTE — The Silesian magnates knew what they were doing when they greeted with enthusiasm Hitler's war against Poland. By the partitioning of Upper Silesia in 1921 Count Thiele-Winkler had lost 15,900 hectares, the princes and counts of Donnersmarck 37,000 hectares, the Prince of Hohenlohe-Ingelfingen, 18,700 hectares, the Count of Ballestrem, 4,900 hectares, and the Duke of Ratibor 2,600 hectares to Poland. In 1940 all their property on Polish soil was again restored to them.

(Reprinted from Albert Norden's *The Thugs of Europe,* with permission.)

APPENDIX 4: NAM: AMERICAN FASCISM

(Digest of Senate Report No. 6, part 3, 76th Congress, 1st session.)

"A subcommittee of the Senate Committee on Education and Labor, Senator Robert M. La Follette Jr., Wisc., Chairman. . . .

"The committee found that the purchasing and storing of 'arsenals' of firearms and tear- and sickening-gas weapons is a common practice of large employers of labor who refuse to bargain collectively with legitimate labor unions and that there exists a large business of supplying gas weapons to industry. . . . During the years 1933 through June, 1937, $1,255,392.55 worth of tear and sickening gas was purchased by employers and law-enforcement agencies, 'chiefly during or in anticipation of strikes.' The committee noted that:

> " '. . . all of the largest individual purchasers are corporations and that their totals far surpass those of large law-enforcement purchasers. In fact, the largest purchaser of gas equipment in the country, the Republic Steel Corp., bought four times as much as the largest law-enforcement purchaser.' "

The largest industrial purchasers of gas munitions were found to be:

Republic Steel Corp., $79,712.42 (Girdler; Vice-President and director of the NAM).

U. S. Steel, $62,208.12 (Contributed $41,450 to NAM in four years).

Bethlehem Steel, $36,173.69 (Contributed $29,250 to NAM in four years).

Youngstown Sheet & Tube, $28,385.39 (Contributor to NAM).

General Motors, $24,626.78 (Contributed $66,000 to NAM).

Anthracite Institute, $17,457.

Goodyear, $16,912 (Contributor to NAM and Associated Industries).

National Steel, $12,085 (of Weirton; E. T. Weir of the NAM, president).

Auto-Light, $11,351 (Contributed $4,800 to NAM in four years).

Goodrich, $7,740 (Contributed $2,600 to NAM in four years).

Pennsylvania Railroad, $7,466 (Contributed $10,000 to NAM in four years).

Chrysler, $7,000 (Contributed $35,400 to NAM in four years).

Thompson Products, $6,867 (F. C. Crawford, president of the NAM).

Seattle Chamber of Commerce, $5,873.

Waterfront Employers Union, San Francisco, $5,512.

Columbian Enameling, Terre Haute, $5,482.

Spang Chalfant, Ambridge, Pa., $5,281 (Contributed $5,750 to NAM in four years).

APPENDIX 5: ROSTER OF THE SIXTH COLUMN PRESS

Town	*Paper*	*Owner*	*Circulation*
ALBANY	TRIBUNE	SCRIPPS - HOWARD	14,000
ALBUQUERQUE	TIMES-UNION	HEARST	44,000
BIRMINGHAM	POST	SCRIPPS - HOWARD	75,000
BOSTON	RECORD	HEARST	326,000
BOSTON	AMERICAN	HEARST	157,000
BOSTON	ADVERTISER	HEARST	530,000
BALTIMORE	NEWS-POST	HEARST	190,000
BALTIMORE	AMERICAN	HEARST	225,000
CHICAGO	TRIBUNE	McCORMICK	1,000,000
CHICAGO	HERALD-AMERICAN	HEARST	466,000
CINCINNATI	POST	HOWARD	150,000
CLEVELAND	PRESS	HOWARD	240,000
COLUMBUS	CITIZEN	HOWARD	73,000
DETROIT	TIMES	HEARST	320,000
DENVER	ROCKY MT. NEWS	HOWARD	44,000
EL PASO	HERALD-POST	HOWARD	23,000
EVANSVILLE	PRESS	HOWARD	32,000
FORT WORTH	PRESS	HOWARD	39,000
HOUSTON	PRESS	HOWARD	71,000
INDIANAPOLIS	TIMES	HOWARD	92,000
LOS ANGELES	EXAMINER	HEARST	221,000
LOS ANGELES	HERALD-EXPRESS	HEARST	243,000
KENTUCKY	POST	HOWARD	
KNOXVILLE	NEWS-SENTINEL	HOWARD	60,000
MEMPHIS	PRESS-SCIMITAR	HOWARD	96,000
MEMPHIS	COMMERCIAL APPEAL	HOWARD	125,000
MILWAUKEE	NEWS-SENTINEL	HEARST	125,000
NEW YORK	DAILY NEWS	PATTERSON, J. M.	2,000,000
		(Sunday)	3,700,000
NEW YORK	MIRROR	HEARST	800,000
NEW YORK	JOURNAL-AMERICAN	HEARST	604,000
NEW YORK	WORLD-TELEGRAM	HOWARD	400,000
OAKLAND	POST-ENQUIRER	HEARST	48,000
PITTSBURGH	SUN-TELEGRAPH	HEARST	163,000
PITTSBURGH	PRESS	HOWARD	228,000
SAN FRANCISCO	CALL-BULLETIN	HEARST	106,000
SAN FRANCISCO	NEWS	HOWARD	100,000
SAN FRANCISCO	EXAMINER	HEARST	165,000
SAN ANTONIO	LIGHT	HEARST	53,000
SEATTLE	POST-INTELLIGENCER	HEARST	100,000
WASHINGTON	TIMES-HERALD	PATTERSON, ELEANOR	209,000
WASHINGTON	NEWS	HOWARD	85,000

APPENDIX 6: TOBACCO SMOKING AND LONGEVITY

By Dr. Raymond Pearl, *Johns Hopkins University*

In the customary way of life man has long been habituated to the routine usage of various substances and materials that are not physiologically necessary to his continued existence. Tea, coffee, alcohol, tobacco, opium and the betel nut are statistically among the more conspicuous examples of such materials. If all six are included together as a group it is probably safe to say that well over 90 per cent of all adult human beings habitually make use of one or more of the component materials included in the group. All of them contain substances of considerable pharmacologic potency if exhibited in appropriate dosage. Widespread and long-continued experience, however, has shown that the moderate usage of any of these materials, if measurably deleterious at all, is not so immediately or strikingly harmful physiologically as to weigh seriously against the pleasures felt to be derived from indulgence, in the opinion of vast numbers of human beings. The situation so created is an extremely complex one behavioristically, and not a simple physiological matter, as it is sometimes a little naively thought to be. Purely hedonistic elements in behavior, which are present in lower animals as well as in man, have a real importance. Indeed they frequently override, in their motivational aspects, reason as well as purely reflex physiological inhibiting factors. There are undoubtedly great numbers of human beings who would continue the habitual use of a particular material they liked, even though it were absolutely and beyond any question or argument proved to be somewhat deleterious to them. Most of them would rationalize this behavior by the balancing type of argument—that the keen pleasure outweighed the relatively (in their view) smaller harm.

The student of longevity is not primarily interested in the behavioristic aspects of the situation under discussion. His concern is to appraise quantitatively, with the greatest attainable accuracy, the effect of each of these habitual usages upon the duration of life. This problem is necessarily statistical in its nature, for in the ordinary way of usage the effect upon longevity of any of the materials mentioned is not sufficiently strong or immediate to be disentangled in the individual from the effects of other and more powerful factors that are involved, such as infections, for example. An approximate evaluation of the statistical effect of these minor and secondary factors influencing longevity can, however, be reached by the application of actuarial methods (life table construction) to groups of individuals. For the maximum effectiveness of this methodology in the premises, the groups to be compared should be each as heterogeneous or random as possible in their compositions relative to all other characteristics *except* the one of degree of habitual usage of the particular material under discussion, and as homogeneous as possible relative to that. We shall then have a dispersed and counterbalancing effect within each group of all such factors as economic and social status, occupational and racial differences, etc., the plus variants relative to each such factor offsetting more or less evenly the minus variants; while there will be a concentrated, unidirectional and statistically cumulative effect, if any, of the habitual usage factor under test, since all components of a group will be alike in respect of it.

The purpose of this paper is to report a part of the results of an investigation of the influence of tobacco upon human longevity, planned and carried out along the lines indicated above. The material was drawn from the Family History Records of this laboratory. It is composed of data collected at first hand and *ad hoc.* The accuracy of the data as to the relative degree of habitual usage of tobacco and as to the ages of the living at risk, and of the dead at death can be guaranteed. The figures presented here deal only with white males, and concern only the usage of tobacco by smoking. The material falls into three categories, as follows: *non-users* of tobacco, of whom there were 2,094; *moderate smokers,* of whom there were 2,814; and *heavy smokers,* of whom there were 1,905. In other words, the results presented here are based upon the observation of 6,813 men in total. These men were an unselected lot except as to their tobacco habits. That is to say, they were taken at random, and then all sorted into categories relative to tobacco usage.

Complete life tables have been constructed for the three groups defined above relative to tobacco usage by smoking. The tables start at age 30 and continue to the end of the life span, by yearly intervals. Here only a condensation of the tables can be presented. This is done in Table 1, where the death rate (1000 q_x) and survivorship (l_x) function are given by five-year intervals.

TABLE 1

THE DEATH RATE (1,000 q_x) AND SURVIVORSHIP (l^x) FUNCTIONS, AT FIVE-YEAR INTERVALS, STARTING AT AGE 30, OF (a) NON-USERS OF TOBACCO; (b) MODERATE SMOKERS WHO DID NOT CHEW TOBACCO OR TAKE SNUFF; (c) HEAVY SMOKERS WHO DID NOT CHEW TOBACCO OR TAKE SNUFF.
WHITE MALES.

Age	Non-users		Moderate smokers		Heavy smokers	
	1,000 q_x	l^x	1,000 q_x	l^x	1,000 q_x	l^x
30	8.18	100,000	7.86	100,000	16.89	100,000
35	8.78	95,883	9.63	95,804	21.27	90,943
40	10.01	91,546	11.89	90,883	23.91	81,191
45	12.04	86,730	14.80	85,129	25.69	71,665
50	15.16	81,160	18.61	78,436	27.49	62,699
55	19.82	74,538	23.67	70,712	30.09	54,277
60	26.73	66,564	30.49	61,911	34.29	46,226
65	36.88	57,018	39.83	52,082	41.20	38,328
70	51.69	45,919	52.84	41,431	52.72	30,393
75	73.02	33,767	71.28	30,455	72.33	22,338
80	103.22	21,737	97.95	19,945	100.44	14,494
85	142.78	11,597	136.50	10,987	139.48	7,865
90	197.49	4,753	190.23	4,686	193.68	3,292
95	273.2	1,320	265.1	1,366	268.9	938

However envisaged, the net conclusion is clear. In this sizable material the smoking of tobacco was statistically associated with an impairment of life duration, and the amount of degree of this impairment increased as the habitual amount of smoking increased. Here, just as is usually the case in our experience in studies of this sort, the differences between the usage groups in specific mortality rates, as indicated by q_x, practically disappear from about age 70 on. This is presumably an expression of the residual effect of the heavily selective character of the mortality in the earlier years in the groups damaged by the agent (in this case tobacco). On this view those individuals in the damaged groups who survive to 70 or thereabouts are such tough and resistant specimens that thereafter tobacco does them no further measurable harm as a group.

(This material originally appeared in *Science,* March 4, 1938, Vol. 87, No. 2253, pages 216-217.)

INDEX

The Book

"This book names the most powerful forces in Europe which organized the Fascist and Nazi parties and movement, the powerful American forces which own, control and subsidize native Fascism, and the spokesmen, radio orators, writers and other agents of reaction in America."

The Author

"'The real inside news, the kind newspapers frequently get but dare not print' … Mr. Seldes delighted in uncovering stories that had been overlooked by others, exposing corruption and challenging the practices of leading newspapers." — *New York Times*.

"George Seldes, the inventor of modern investigative reporting, led the sort of swashbuckling life that Hollywood might have scripted for a foreign correspondent and rebel reporter. He interviewed Lenin, Trotsky, Freud, Einstein, and Hitler. He filed dispatches from behind the lines during World War I and covered the Spanish Civil War with his wife, Helen. He was booted out of the Soviet Union in 1923 and fled Italy two years later fearing for his life, after implicating Benito Mussolini in a murder. Ernest Hemingway, Ezra Pound, and Sinclair Lewis were among his drinking buddies.

"Yet the glamour of journalistic success never blinded him to serious shortcomings in the American press." — Jay Walljasper, *Utne Reader*.

Seldes was Berlin, Rome, Dublin, Moscow and Baghdad correspondent for the Chicago Tribune from 1919 to 1929, but finally quit the mainstream media over censorship of his reports. He became an independent journalist, getting the true story out in his first two books, *You Can't Print That!* and *Can These Things Be!* In 1940 he started *In Fact*, a weekly newsletter of investigative reporting and criticism of the press, with a top circulation of 176,000. He uncovered big stories like major corporations trading with the enemy, and the link between smoking and cancer — which was hushed up for another 20 years, by mainstream media hooked on cigarette ads. *In Fact* was shut down in 1950 by an FBI witch hunt against subscribers.

In 1988 a film about the life of George Seldes, named *Tell the Truth and Run!* after one of his book titles, was nominated for an Oscar.

2016 BOOK LIST

ProgRESSive Independent Media.
ProgressivePress.com

Six by Webster Griffin Tarpley

9/11 Synthetic Terror: Made in USA — by a network of moles, patsies, killers, corrupt politicians and media. The 9/11 bible. "Strongest of the 770+ books I have reviewed" – R. Steele. 5th ed., 569 pp., $19.95 $14.

George Bush: The Unauthorized Biography Vivid X-ray of the oligarchy dominating U.S. politics, with a full narrative of GWHB's links to Iran-Contra, Watergate, and a long list of war crimes. 700 pp, $19.95.

Barack H. Obama: the Unauthorized Biography The abject corruption of a Wall Street lackey, with a richly detailed profile of the finance oligarchy. 595 pp, $19.95.

Obama – The Postmodern Coup: Making of a Manchurian Candidate. The Obama puppet's advisors are radical reactionaries. 320 pages of astute political insights. $15.95.

Surviving the Cataclysm**, **Your Guide through the Greatest Financial Crisis in Human History. The financiers who plunder our nation. Coping with crisis. 668 pp, $25.

Just Too Weird**: **Bishop Romney and the Mormon Putsch against America. Stranger than fiction. 284 pp., $14.95.

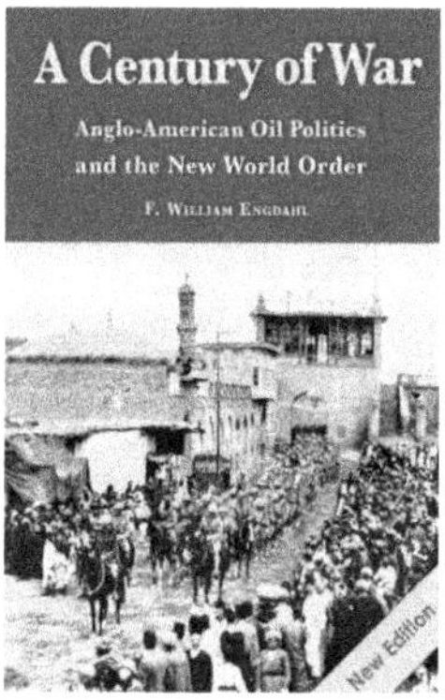

Two by Henry Makow

Illuminati: Cult that Hijacked the World tackles taboos like Zionism, British Empire, Holocaust. How bankers took over governments and the world. They run it all: wars, schools, media. 249 pp, $19.95.

Illuminati 2: Deception & Seduction, more hidden history. 285 pp. $19.95.

Five by F. Wm. Engdahl

A Century of War: Anglo-American Oil Politics and the New World Order. Classic exposé: the empire controls the oil to control the world. 352 pp, $25.

Full Spectrum Dominance: Totalitarian Democracy in the New World Order. They are out for total control: land, sea, air, space, outer space, cyberspace, media, money, movements. 258 pp, $23.95.

Gods of Money: Wall Street and the Death of the American Century. The banksters stop at nothing: setting world wars, nuking cities, keeping our world in chaos and corruption. 390 pp. $24.95.

Seeds of Destruction: The Hidden Agenda of Genetic Manipulation. A corporate gang is out to control the world by patenting our food. 340 pp, $25.95.

Target China: How Washington and Wall Street Plan to Cage the Asian Dragon. The secret war on many fronts to cripple China. 256 pp, $24.95.

Four by Michel Chossudovsky

Towards a World War III Scenario: The Dangers of Nuclear War. A first-strike nuclear attack on Iran. 103 pp, $15.95.

The Global Economic Crisis: The Great Depression of the XXI Century, by a dozen experts. 416 pp, $25.95.

The Globalization of Poverty and the New World Order. Corporatism feeds on poverty, pollution, apartheid, racism, sexism, and ethnic strife. 401 pp, $27.95.

The Globalization of War: America's Long War against Humanity. *A tour de force of the war fronts.* 240 pp, $22.95.

History

Two by George Seldes: *1,000 Americans Who Rule the USA* (1947, 324 pp, $18.95) and ***Facts and Fascism*** (1943, 292 pp., $15.95) by the great dissident. Plutocrats keep the media in lockstep, and finance fascism.

Two by Prof. Donald Gibson. *Battling Wall Street: The Kennedy Presidency*. JFK: a martyr who strove mightily for social and economic justice. 208 pp, $14.95.

The Kennedy Assassination Cover-Up. The moneyed elite killed JFK. 375 pp, $19.95.

Global Predator: US Wars for Empire. The atrocities committed by US armed forces over two centuries. Also by Stewart H. Ross: ***Propaganda for War: How the US was Conditioned to Fight the Great War*** — to make the world safe for the banksters. 350 pp and $18.95 each.

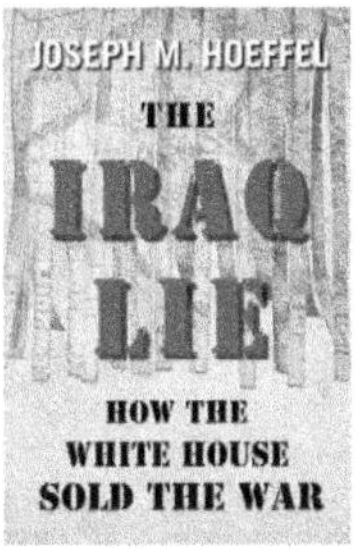

The Iraq Lie: How the White House Sold the War, by Rep. Jos. M. Hoeffel. Bush Lied about WMD – and took us to war. $14.95.

The Nazi Hydra in America: Suppressed History of a Century. US plutocrats launched Hitler. "Shocking... deserves to be widely read." – Howard Zinn. 700 pp, $19.95 **$12**.

Sunk: The Story of the Japanese Submarine Fleet, 1941-1945. The bravery of doomed men in a lost cause, against impossible odds. 300 pp, $15.95.

Terrorism and the Illuminati: A 3000-Year History. Who controls "Islamic" terrorists? 332 pp, $16.95.

Psychology

The Rape of the Mind. Tools for self-defense against torture or social pressure in open and closed societies. Classic by Dr. Joost Meerloo. 320 pp, $16.95.

The Telescreen: An Empirical Study of the Destruction of Consciousness, by Prof. Jeffrey Grupp. Fake reality steals our souls. 199 pp, $14.95.

Conspiracy, NWO

Corporatism: the Secret Government of the New World Order by Prof. Jeffrey Grupp. Corporations control all world resources. The NWO is the "prison planet" that Hitler aimed for. 408 pp, $16.95.

Descent into Slavery by Des Griffin. How the banksters took over America and the world. 310 pp, $16.

Dope Inc.: Britain's Opium War against the United States. 320 pp, $12.95.

How the World Really Works by A.B. Jones. Crash course in conspiracy offers digests of 11 classics like *Tragedy and Hope, Creature from Jekyll Island.* 336 pp, $15.

Killing us Softly: the Global Depopulation Policy. Both the How and the Why, by Kevin Galalae, 146 pp. $15.95.

The Money Power: Empire of the City* and *Pawns in the Game. The illuminist Three World Wars conspiracy – two geopolitics classics in one volume. 320 pp., $16.95.

Conspiracy: False Flag Operations

Conspiracies, Conspiracy Theories and the Secrets of 9/11, German best-seller explores conspiracy in history, before tackling 9/11. 274 pp, $14.95.

Gladio, NATO's Dagger at the Heart of Europe: The Pentagon-Mafia-Nazi Terror Axis. The blood-red thread of NATO terror, from 1945 to the present. 487 pp, $24.95.

JFK-911: 50 Years of Deep State. An Israeli strategy behind the JFK and 9/11 murders. 238 pp, $15.95.

Subverting Syria. Syrian "rebels" are US-backed provocateurs. 115 pp, $10.00.

Terror on the Tube: Behind the Veil of 7/7, an Investigation. Exonerates the patsies, proves the false flag. 322 pp, $17.77.

Truth Jihad: My Epic Struggle Against the 9/11 Big Lie, by the irrepressible Kevin Barrett. 224 pp, $9.95.

Coming Soon: *ISIS IS US; Prisoner's Diary; Subjugating the Middle East; The NWO in Action*

E-Books:

9/11 Synthetic Terror; Barack Obama Unauth. Biography; Gladio; Iraq Lie; ISIS IS US, JFK-911; Just Too Weird; Fall of the Arab Spring; Killing us Softly; Nazi Hydra; Rape of the Mind; Subverting Syria; Surviving the Cataclysm; Target: China

~ **PROGRESSIVEPRESS.COM** ~

info@progressivepress.com

Media Mail orders: $3.50 for first item, 50¢ per additional item. Priority mail up to 3.5 lbs, $6.00. For Ebooks & International shipping, please see website.

PROGRESSIVE

CPSIA information can be obtained
at www.ICGtesting.com
Printed in the USA
FSHW02n1954060618
49138FS

9 781615 770434